Mixed Economies in Europe

Mixed Economies in Europe

An Evolutionary Perspective
on their Emergence, Transition and Regulation

Edited by

Wolfgang Blaas

Associate Professor of Economics
Technical University
Vienna, Austria

John Foster

Professor of Economics
University of Queensland
Australia

Edward Elgar

Published by
Edward Elgar Publishing Limited
Gower House
Croft Road
Aldershot
Hants GU11 3HR
England

Edward Elgar Publishing Company
Old Post Road
Brookfield
Vermont 05036
USA

A CIP catalogue record for this book is available from the British Library

Library of Congress Cataloging-in-Publication Data
Mixed economies in Europe/edited by Wolfgang Blaas, John Foster
    p. cm.
   1. Mixed economy—Europe. 2. Europe—Economic conditions.
I. Blaas, Wolfgang. II. Foster, John, 1940– .
HC240.M654 1992
338.94—dc20
                                                           92–25820
                                                                 CIP

ISBN 1 85278 728 7

Printed in Great Britain at the University Press, Cambridge

Contents

Figures

Tables

Contributors

Dr Kurt Bayer is Senior Economist at the Austrian Institute for Economic Research, Vienna, Austria

Wolfgang Blaas is Associate Professor of Economics at the Technical University Vienna, currently on leave at the Austrian Academy of Sciences, Vienna, Austria

Len Doyal is Senior Lecturer in Medical Ethics, Royal London Hospital Medical College, London, UK

John Foster is Professor of Economics at the University of Queensland, Brisbane, Australia

Ian Gough is Senior Lecturer at the Department of Social Policy, University of Manchester, Manchester, UK

Paolo Guerrieri is Professor at the Faculty of Economics of the University of Naples, Italy

Jerzy Hausner is Associate Professor of Economics at the Cracow Academy of Economics, Cracow, Poland

Geoffrey M. Hodgson is Reader in Economics at the Department of Economics and Government, Newcastle upon Tyne Polytechnic, Newcastle, UK

Professor Kazimierz Laski is Professor Emeritus of the University of Linz, Austria and currently Research Director of The Vienna Institute for Comparative Economic Studies, Vienna, Austria

Dr Maria Lissowska is Researcher at the Warsaw School of Economics, Poland

Klaus Nielsen is Associate Professor at the Institute of Economics and Planning of the Roskilde Universitetscenter, Denmark

Bart Nooteboom is Professor of Industrial Organization at the Faculty of Management and Organization of the University of Groningen, The Netherlands

Wim Swaan is Assistant Researcher, University of Amsterdam and the Tinbergen Institute, Netherlands

Dr Andrew Tylecote is Senior Lecturer at Sheffield University Management School, UK

Bart Verspagen is Research Fellow at MERIT, the Maastricht Economic Research Institute on Innovation and Technology, University of Limburg, Maastricht, The Netherlands

Andrzej Wojtyna is Associate Professor at the Academy of Economics in Cracow and at the Institute of Economics, Polish Academy of Sciences, Warsaw, Poland. He is also Head of the Department of Macroeconomics at the Academy of Economics in Cracow.

1. Introduction: Evolutionary Perspectives

John Foster and Wolfgang Blaas

ECONOMIC EVOLUTION AND THE EVOLUTION OF ECONOMICS

Since the Second World War, economics has, in its orthodox form, espoused an approach which is static, mechanical and time reversible in character. Classical physics has been its role model. In this orthodoxy, the mixed economy is viewed as one where the state engages in 'intervention' in a market economy. Thus, the state is not an entity which is a component part of the economic system but something external to it. Whether intervention is viewed as a good or a bad thing by orthodox economists depends upon whether the private sector is viewed as self-equilibrating or prone to significant periods out of equilibrium. 'Equilibrium' is the Walrasian notion of general competitive equilibrium, which began to supplant the Marshallian vision of a competitive market in the inter-war period, when ideological necessities were more pressing than Marshall's goal of making economics a science.

This tendency was most marked in the United States where institutional economics had been the most influential school up to the Second World War. In Europe, a much more diverse set of economic approaches prospered in the post-war period, despite the reimportation of refined neoclassical thinking and methods from the United States. European traditions in economics were shaken – the defeat of the English in the intellectual battle of the Cambridges being the most dramatic example – but not eliminated. Today, we are witnessing a resurgence of these older traditions and adaptation of them to understand the dynamics of European economies in the late twentieth century. The broad banner of institutional and evolutionary economics has come to embrace this resurgence and development. The era of critique seems to have passed. The static approach of neoclassicism and the social dynamic approach of Marxism are no longer subject to much criticism – as they were in the 1980s – they are simply ignored or seriously qualified. The reconstruction of economics has begun.

The catalyst which has sparked off such rapid growth of interest in institutional and evolutionary economics was not primarily powerful critique, necessary as this must be in any transition from one paradigm to another, but the pace of economic change itself and the dramatic alteration in the ideological climate, following the end of the so-called Cold War. Events in both Eastern and Western Europe in the late 1980s simply could not be understood from a neoclassical perspective. The 'quick-fix' neoclassical economists, on their whistle-stop tours of eastern Europe, offered policy prescriptions which would have been laughable had the consequences not been so sad for the unwitting governments which tried to follow them. In Western Europe, attempts, again guided by neoclassical economics, to enact economic reform also proved to be ineffectual and distorting. The failure of Chicago-inspired Thatcherism in the UK offers the most dramatic example.

The static vision of the unproductive and interfering state, as an entity which exists outside the productive and self-correcting market economy, has presented a fundamental difficulty in neoclassical discussions of both existing mixed economies and of those coming into being in Eastern Europe. In this volume, the integrative, stabilizing and facilitating dimensions of the state in the economy are juxtaposed against the rent-seeking features of governments, focused upon by neoclassical economists and public choice theorists. By adopting such an approach, the excesses of the state, alluded to by the latter, but rarely quantified through detailed historical study, can be assessed side by side with the benefits of state involvement in the economic system. In history, political forces can yield governments which are perceived as benign and some that are perceived as malignant. Institutional and evolutionary economists have no fixed views on the general theoretical merit or demerit of state involvement in the economy. As with all institutions in an evolving economy, sometimes the state will be a force which generates inertia and at other times and in other places it will facilitate creative development of the economic system.

THE NEW ECONOMIC EVOLUTIONISM IN EUROPE

In this volume contributors do not merely document the history of mixed economies and speculate as to their future, but attempt to deal with the functioning, formation and interaction of mixed economies through the application of theoretical principles which attempt to address socioeconomic structural change. This is done in various ways, from the linguistic approach of philosophical discourse to the mathematical approach of evolutionary modelling. The future is discussed in terms of where a particular economy is now and how, in a pragmatic way, the state can design new institutional arrangements which are consistent and meet perceived needs, given the realities of evolutionary processes. Idealizations, and related theoretical abstractions, are not shunned but viewed as aspirational in character, not equilibria to which a system will, inevitably, tend. Steady states are not viewed as sacrosanct fixed points, but special cases determined by the precise historical dynamics of systems which exhibit degrees of irreversibility and openness.

Evolutionary economics does not yet have a unified set of theoretical principles. This is, of course, criticized by neoclassical economists but some institutional economists counter that evolutionary economics must remain heterodox in its approach if it is to have maximum applicability in the empirical domain. In Europe, there has been a clear tendency towards more general agreement as to what constitutes a theory of evolutionary dynamics in institutional structure. Hodgson and Screpanti (1991) have discussed this tendency and it is evident in the contributions in this volume. Furthermore, some divergence from American institutionalism seems to be occurring in Europe in the sense that American institutionalists tend to see evolution in cultural terms, drawing upon anthropology, whereas European evolutionary economists (for example, Foster, 1987 and Clark and Juma, 1987 tend to look towards biological analogies and metaphors to gain an understanding of evolutionary processes). Correspondingly, there seem to be much closer links between institutionalist and neo-Schumpeterian approaches than is typical in the United States.

The type of biological analogy or metaphor which seems to be favoured amongst more theoretically inclined European evolutionary economists (for example, Dopfer, 1991) is that of 'self-organization' of 'dissipative structures', originally an approach to reaction kinetics in chemistry pioneered by Ilya Prigogine. This has given rise to some unexpected dialogues in Europe between members of otherwise antagonistic schools of economic thought. Austrian economists, such as Witt (1991), see parallels between the notion of 'spontaneous order' and self-organization. Faber and Proops (1990) even attempt to reconcile Austrian capital theory and ostensibly post-Keynesian, Schumpeterian and institutionalist ideas, through the use of dynamic theoretical constructs, emphasizing irreversibility and evolution.

However, it would be fair to say that the self-organization approach has not yet gained widespread approval amongst European evolutionary economists. Many feel that reliance upon formal analogies and metaphors drawn from the natural sciences was debilitating in the past and that a specifically socioeconomic approach to evolutionary dynamics must be developed in the future. It is worth summarizing, in broad terms, the analytical themes which seem to receive widespread approval and to relate them to the context of the evolution of mixed economies.

SOME EMERGING ANALYTICAL THEMES IN EUROPEAN EVOLUTIONARY ECONOMIC THOUGHT

Economies are viewed as evolving through time as complex systems of production and consumption. Their ability to maintain their efficiency and to be equitable depends, predominantly, on how individual energies are being channelled into collective performance. Economic behaviour is guided not only by prices, incomes and costs, as orthodox economists assert. It is embedded in social institutions which allow only a subset of individual decisions and actions to emerge as a result of 'rational choice'. In the real world, price-guided behaviour and institution-influenced behaviour mix to an extent which makes it difficult to conceptualize them separately. Furthermore, it has been convincingly argued by, for example, Matzner (1991), that the whole social context, including institutions and (policy) instruments, is not only relevant in the explanation of economic behaviour but also indispensable in understanding the functioning of markets.

As a consequence, the competitive position of a particular economy in global terms is strongly influenced by the prevailing sociopolitical context which guides economic decisions. Central to these decisions are the stocks and flows of knowledge and information which exist. These stocks and flows are so diverse that even the fastest computer could not store and process them. This is so because there is more to knowledge than codifiable information. Knowledge in the productive process is often tacit and uncodifiable, because it is inseparably intertwined with skills. Thus, the neoclassical notion of perfect knowledge or information is of little value. For the evolutionary economist, engaged in the analysis of macroeconomic performance, it is crucial to understand how knowledge – in its various forms – is created and used in society. A significant difference in performance is expected in economic development between countries, dependent upon the degree of accessibility of scientific and technical knowledge to its citizens.

This emphasis on the role of knowledge, and associated studies of invention, innovation and diffusion, is a hallmark of modern European evolutionary economics, particularly amongst those who operate within a neo-Schumpeterian framework of analysis (see Dosi *et al.*, 1988), receiving relatively more attention than culturally derived habits and conventions so central in American institutionalism. When confronted with a simple free-market solution, the European evolutionary economist tends to worry about the technical repercussions, since such a solution can lead to the sacrifice of research and development activities in favour of good short-run performance on the stock market. Evolutionary economists realize that futures markets in uninvented, uninnovated, undiffused products are highly incomplete or non-existent so they perceive a serious threat to economic development from short-termism. It follows that the evolutionary economist is concerned with the financial structure of an economy and how it facilitates long-term planning in enterprises.

THE EMERGENCE AND EVOLUTION OF EUROPEAN MIXED ECONOMIES

Because of her or his emphasis upon the institutional structure of an economy, the evolutionary economist sees it as a dangerous fallacy to believe that, by introducing 'the market' in a previously centrally planned economy, there will be an automatic tendency for convergence to the average performance of western mixed economies. Given the wide range of underdevelopment of entrepreneurial capacities and non-administrative managerial skills in East European countries, such an outcome is highly unlikely. Privatization and liberalization are likely to have very different effects in different countries. The same argument can be made in the different context of trade liberalization in West European economies. Convergence is unlikely to occur if the empirical findings in this volume and elsewhere are to be relied upon. This evidence tends to support the view that divergent economic performance within the European Community will continue if state intervention, either at the Community or national level, is not designed to correct for it.

This question, with regard to the causes and conditions of convergence and divergence of mixed economies, is an important one with social and political, as well as economic, implications. It is a question which is explored from several different perspectives in this volume. Growing divergence between East and West contributed to the fall of communism in Eastern Europe, so we know that divergence in the 'new' Europe has the potential to be a disintegrating force. As such, it is a problem which requires state initiatives, both within and across a growing number of national borders. As Amin and Dietrich (1991) emphasize, the extent to which West European states have recognized the existence of structural change in their economies has been varied but, on the whole, very limited. In a very real sense, the fate of the emergent mixed economies in Eastern Europe will depend upon there being a rise in evolutionary consciousness in the policies, both internal and external, of West European states.

It is hoped that this volume will help to raise this evolutionary consciousness, particularly amongst policymakers, exasperated by the incomprehensible formal analysis offered by the neoclassical economists who advise them. Of course, we all want simple and easy solutions to problems but these will not be found between these covers. What lie here are examples of a way of thinking; not demonstrations of technical cleverness and intellectual power but fragments of wisdom and genuine knowledge of the complex world in which we live.

The volume is divided into four parts. The first part deals with the theoretical justification of an institutional orientation in dealing with mixed economies. The second part makes the case, using evidence drawn from West and East European contexts, for careful state reregulation in tandem with attempts to deregulate and privatize. The third part juxtaposes the more general macroeconomic and political realities of transition with attempts to define, broadly, a new role for the state as a regulator and supporter of basic human needs. The fourth part moves to the international level to consider whether mixed economies have experienced divergence or convergence in economic performance in the recent past.

JUSTIFYING AN INSTITUTIONALIST APPROACH TO THE MIXED ECONOMY

In Chapter 2, Geoffrey Hodgson makes an institutionalist case for state intervention in the monetary system, partly to police the currency against debasement and partly to legitimize its value. He takes as his point of departure the proposition of Austrian economist, Carl Menger, that money, law and language may all evolve without state intervention. The associated position of Friedrich Hayek on the 'denationalization' of money is also discussed. Hodgson argues that the Mengerian proposition is flawed in the case of money because it neglects potential quality variation in the emerging monetary unit. In the face of path-dependence, also neglected in the Austrian argument, a single optimal currency may not emerge. For similar reasons, the Austrian proposition is also seen as flawed in the case of law, leaving only language as the case where state intervention seems unnecessary. Hodgson argues that the matter of potential quality variation necessitates some state intervention and regulation in most complex markets. Although the Austrian case, that novelty and heterogeneity are fundamental to market activity, is supported, path-dependent divergence is viewed as a process which undermines the market.

In Chapter 3, Bart Nooteboom takes up the one Austrian case left largely untouched by Hodgson – that of the evolution of language. Although there is sympathy for the Austrian incorporation of dynamicism and differentiation in economics, Austrian adherence to methodological individualism is challenged by a post-modern perspective, whereby the individual gains his or her identity from interaction with others. An interpretation of the linguistics of Ferdinand de Saussure, in the tradition of European post-modern philosophy, is employed to integrate economics sociology and the theory of knowledge. The result is an approach which transcends methodological individualism and methodological collectivism. The Saussurian relation between the social, regulatory dimension of language and the dimension of individual parlance is taken as a model for the economic relation between market, firm and innovation.

Nooteboom offers us a philosophical foundation for evolutionary economics which is drawn from a European tradition – he does not relate to or draw from American institutionalism at all. Instead, he evaluates the claims of a more recent American movement - new institutionalism. The emphasis of the latter on transactions and bounded rationality is praised, but the adherence to methodological individualism is criticized on the post-modern grounds that the transaction is meaningful only in an interactive sense. Support for this position is drawn from the very applied context of marketing. Although Nooteboom does not deal with it directly, the implications for the analysis of the mixed economy are clear. The state cannot be viewed as an external entity, only as a product of interaction and, therefore, as an integrated social structure.

PRIVATIZATION, DEREGULATION AND REREGULATION

Part Two of the volume begins with Kurt Bayer's chapter dealing with a case study of privatization in Austria where he applies the aforementioned transactions cost approach (TCA) of new institutionalism to evaluate the success of accompanying regulation by the state. He shows how, in specific cases of privatization/deregulation the TCA approach can be very useful. The main lesson is that such structural changes must not simply involve handing over power to established managers of state corporations. The TCA approach predicts that this will lead to inefficiencies, waste of scarce resources, maldistributions of value-added and a popular distrust of the functioning of the reform process. Bayer documents evidence that these outcomes have been common in Austrian experience, therefore much more carefully considered state regulation is necessary if privatization is to be a success.

In Chapter 5 Wim Swaan and Maria Lissowska echo Bayer's concerns about managerial behaviour in an East European context. Theoretical insights are drawn from the evolutionary literature on market economies, following the work of Richard Nelson and Sidney Winter, and the behavioural approach to centrally planned economies, following the work of János Kornai. The evidence presented suggests that the TCA emphasis on opportunism and rent-seeking is not the whole story – as Bart Nooteboom argues in Chapter 3, methodological individualism is a misleading basis for understanding economic behaviour, particularly in organizations which were previously run along collectivist lines. Simple ignorance and the need for learning are found to be crucially important. This, path-dependent, evolutionary situation, they argue, must be understood in the transition period, when regulations are being formulated and implemented.

Unfortunately, the slow, measured transition to a mixed economy has not been typical in Eastern Europe. Political expediency has necessitated hasty action focused on macroeconomic policy. Encouraged by neoclassical emissaries from the West, stabilization programmes have been introduced which give priority to the elimination of inflation and the associated devaluation of the currency. With such supposedly stable macroeconomic conditions in place, the hope was that transition to a mixed economy would be easier. In practice, recessionary conditions emerged which made the transition more difficult. In Part Three, we turn to questions about the interface of macroeconomic policy and political factors in such transitions.

THE POLITICAL ECONOMY OF MIXED ECONOMY EMERGENCE IN EUROPE

In Chapter 6 Kazimierz Laski presents the facts of stabilization in East European countries, with particular attention to Poland. Although he does not deny the difficulties caused by path dependencies from the communist past and the collapse of COMECON markets, Laski feels that economic strategies and policies, deliberately selected by governments, are also responsible for the present situation. Reiterating the point, made in Chapter 5, that systemic transformation must be gradual, he goes on to examine what type of macroeconomic stabilization policy was chosen and how this was related to political and ideological considerations. He concludes that stabilization in most East European countries has been based upon the quantity theory of money rather than the theory of effective demand. The latter is compatible with a systemic approach whereas the former is incomprehensible in an economy which does not approximate the market ideal. Laski examines the macroeconomic consequences of such a policy and explains, in straightforward Keynesian terms, why the potential for growth has been reduced rather than enhanced. He points to the ideological reasons for such a situation and appeals for greater acceptance of the centrality of policy initiatives by the state in the transition to a mixed economy.

In Chapter 7 Jerzy Hausner and Klaus Nielsen engage in political economy rather than macroeconomics, focusing upon the specific implementation problems and forms of social struggle which arise in what they refer to as the 'systemic vacuum' which exists in post-socialist countries. Because these are country specific, they study only one country, namely, Poland. The evolutionary dynamics at work in a systemic vacuum are presented in a general schematic form from which Poland is derived as a particular case. Here the link between democratization and the legitimacy of state involvement in the economy is dealt with much more explicitly than is usual in the analysis of economists. Learning is much more than a technical matter. As is emphasized by Nooteboom in Chapter 3, it involves familiarization with an entire set of political institutions.

Hausner and Nielsen also point out that we should not think of the systemic vacuum as something which emerged overnight, following the political revolutions in Eastern Europe. The evolutionary process of disintegration in the economic system had been in train many years beforehand. They go on to discuss the chaotic complexity which is manifest in Poland's systemic vacuum, emphasizing the urgency of effective action by the state in the transformation process. The danger in a systemic vacuum is that inaction will lead to a return to a command economy, presumably at the opposite end of the political spectrum to that which went before.

In Chapter 8, Andrzej Wojtyna attempts to define, in general terms, what the economic role of the modern state should be in the emergent mixed economies of Eastern Europe. He reviews the theory of the state as it is presented in the West and discovers a broad range of disagreement. In any event, the established literature is not orientated towards post-socialist transformation conditions. Using Poland as his case, Wojtyna steers a course between the 'meta-intervention' of Chapter 7 and the Kornai-influenced position in Chapter 5. This crystallizes into a check-list of obligations that a post-socialist state must shoulder if economic progress is to occur. Wojtyna believes, like Kornai, that the state has a basic obligation to look after the national wealth until a more suitable owner appears, irrespective of whether this results in slow progress. In Poland, it could be that the state has failed, already, to meet this obligation with serious repercussions for the credibility of the mixed economy and the democratic process which sustains it.

In Chapter 9 Len Doyal and Ian Gough take up the theme of Wojtyna in Chapter 8, namely, that the state must shoulder certain social obligations, both in the transition period and beyond. They provide a timely theory of individual need which is both substantive and procedural. This theory is operationalized to develop indicators of individual need satisfaction and socioeconomic performance. The material and procedural preconditions to optimize need satisfaction are then evaluated. The objective criteria offered could be applied to any economy, but are most attainable in a mixed economy. Western mixed economies are already locked into their respective social policies, but social policy is still on the agenda in the East and, because it was such an important element of policy in the socialist era, there is ample potential for the implementation of Doyal and Gough's approach.

EUROPEAN ECONOMIC CONVERGENCE OR DIVERGENCE?

Part Four is concerned with the tendency for mixed economies to converge or diverge from each other in their economic evolution. In Chapter 10, Paolo Guerrieri considers the possible effects of future east–west trade integration in the light of trade and technological performance in the EC and the former Council for Mutual Economic Assistance (CMEA) countries over the past two decades. The study takes the neo-Schumpeterian evolutionary perspective, increasingly influential in Europe. In the EC, a severe loss of competitiveness is identified in highly R&D-intensive sectors over the last decade. Within the EC there are growing patterns of divergence over the same period. In the CMEA countries, a severe deterioration in competitiveness is identified over the past two decades. Guerrieri does not see simple openness as a solution in Eastern Europe. Deep microeconomic reform, backed by western capital which, in turn, must be orchestrated by state strategies through the EC, are necessary to avoid serious short- and medium-term problems both within the EC and in Eastern Europe. Guerrieri's contribution emphasizes the longer-term evolutionary tendencies which have been at work and the unavoidable international repercussions of economic developments in Eastern Europe.

In Chapter 11 Andrew Tylecote adds a core–peripheral dimension to the question of European divergence. He notes that, with product innovation, stratification has increased over time with the core centred on western Germany and Switzerland and with three peripheries, one western and two eastern. He argues that the evidence suggests that divergences in innovation and income will continue to increase as integration increases in Europe. A combination of policies is proposed. Heavy taxes on transport are proposed to protect local and regional markets and, thus, local and regional networks. These would also be ecologically consistent and part of a broader eco-taxation package on exhaustible resources to encourage local repair/maintenance activity rather than manufacturing. Localization of ownership and control would be legislated. Communication between distant localities would be facilitated by a Euro-grid of optical fibre telecommunications. These, and other radical policy proposals, are intended to redress the European core–peripheral imbalance. Although the political difficulties in their implementation are obvious, it is equally clear that the EC will have to develop some kind of regional policy to cope with the divergency problem, if it is to be a sustainable trading and integrated production bloc in the longer term. Tylecote has raised issues which simply cannot be ignored by EC policymakers.

In the final chapter of Part Four, Bart Verspagen looks at the convergence/divergency question from an evolutionary modelling perspective, building on worldwide, rather than European, data. He adopts a neo-Schumpeterian/ post-Keynesian framework, to derive dynamic equations with two-way feedback between competitiveness and the evolution of trade performance. Technical change is represented as a cumulative process, allowing a self-reinforcing effect into the growth process. The objective is to allow, as much as possible, for the process of structural change while keeping the model formal. Verspagen begins by looking at actual historical data for OECD countries and concludes that convergence of growth rates is not a general tendency but only found in particular sub-groups of countries. The model which he develops is intended to derive divergency solutions from differences in technological level, learning rates, consumption patterns and the adjustment speed of consumption patterns. Simulation experiments are undertaken to show how divergence occurs and the manner in which 'Goodwin-like' adjustment paths of growth rates occur.

CONCLUDING REMARKS

It is appropriate that the volume concludes with Verspagen's contribution simply because he demonstrates the technical possibilities available to the macro-modeller, when many of the evolutionary processes discussed throughout this volume are incorporated into a dynamic model with formal properties. As Verspagen acknowledges, this is a pragmatic exercise, necessitating the retention of some equilibrium relations. However, by proceeding in this way, the power of evolutionary ideas can be impressed upon the formally trained neoclassical mind. It demonstrates that the new evolutionary way of thinking can be, in his or her terms, 'hard' as well as 'soft'. Hopefully, the neoclassical economist will come to see, from the work of those such as Verspagen, that such a dichotomization is invalid. Evolutionary modelling requires the careful construction of the 'stylized facts' of history, drawing on much institutional and historical material. Without these, the system's structural properties cannot be understood and the outcome of its historical dynamics cannot be assessed. Equally, once we have performed a dynamic modelling exercise, we need a wealth of understanding of the particular circumstances of an economy and its interface with the non-economic spheres before we can begin to design policies which are both feasible and evolutionary-consistent.

The great advantage of a modelling exercise is that it enables us to stand back a bit from, for example, what is going on in Eastern Europe, so that we may see, through the political flurry, some evolutionary economic tendencies which have been quite orderly in their dynamics and in evidence well before the demise of socialist regimes. Several contributors to this volume have expressed the view that, from their specialist perspectives, they believe that such longer-term tendencies exist. Modelling which provides support to such informal observations makes us appreciate that the politicians of the day often overstate their role in history. It also demonstrates that political intervention with enduring beneficial effects involves the uncharismatic business of developing regulations, institutions and constitutions and implementing them over long periods of time through the equally unappealing process of striking a consensus with political opponents.

It is hoped that this volume has emphasized both the multifaceted nature of evolutionary processes in mixed economies and some of the common elements in their dynamics. Divergence is not evidence against this communality but simply indicative of the diversity and uniqueness of the institutions and history of individual countries. Applied economists must be able to understand both the diverse institutional complexity and the common historical tendencies of particular economies if they are ever to attain a position where they can make a constructive contribution to the process of 'context-making' (Matzner and Streeck, 1991) in structurally changing economies.

If we go back in time to the European tradition in economics which existed a century ago we find that Alfred Marshall, one of the founding fathers of neoclassical economics, took it for granted that a competent economist would have an intimate understanding of the diversity and uniqueness of the economic system under consideration, as well as an appreciation of the general evolutionary character of all economies. Thus, a pragmatic approach was deemed necessary in the application of what Marshall regarded as very rudimentary economic theory to real-world economic problems. Most of Marshall's evolutionary wisdom seemed to be forgotten or ignored by neoclassical economists in the post-war era. However, there are signs (see Hahn, 1991) that the mainstream is coming to appreciate that economics is an evolutionary science, to use Thorstein Veblen's famous words. This volume represents a further attempt to persuade the economics profession at large that such science is both possible and fruitful.

REFERENCES

Amin, A. and M. Dietrich (1991), *Towards a New Europe?* Aldershot: Edward Elgar.
Clark, N. and C. Juma (1987), *Long-Run Economics: an Evolutionary Approach to Economic Growth*, London: Frances Pinter.
Dopfer, K. (1991), 'Towards a Theory of Economic Institutions; Synergy and Path-Dependency', *Journal of Economic Issues*, **25**, 535–50.
Dosi, G., C. Freeman and L. Soete (1988), *Technical Change and Economic Theory* London: Frances Pinter.

Faber, M. and J.L.R. Proops (1990), *Evolution, Time, Production and the Environment*, Berlin: Springer.

Foster, J. (1987), *Evolutionary Macroeconomics*, London: Unwin Hyman.

Hahn, F.H. (1991), 'The Next Hundred Years', *Economic Journal*, **404**, 47–51.

Hodgson, G.M. and E. Screpanti (1991), *Rethinking Economics: Markets, Technology and Economic Evolution*, Aldershot: Edward Elgar.

Matzner, E. (1991), '*Policies, Institutions and Employment Performance*', in E. Matzner and W. Streeck (1991).

Matzner, E. and W. Streeck (1991), *Beyond Keynesianism: the Socio-Economics of Production and Full Employment*, Aldershot: Edward Elgar.

Witt, U. (1991), 'Reflections on the Present State of Evolutionary Economic Theory', in G.M. Hodgson and E. Screpanti (1991), *Rethinking Economics: Markets, Technology and Economic Evolution*, Aldershot: Edward Elgar.

PART ONE

Justifying an Institutionalist Approach to the
Mixed Economy

2. Commodity Variation and the Evolution of Money: A Place for the State?

Geoffrey M. Hodgson[1]

In a famous theoretical argument, the Austrian economist Carl Menger suggested that money, law and language may all evolve without state intervention. Subsequent theorists, such as Friedrich Hayek, have used this type of argument to endorse the policy of the 'denationalization' of money, in which private agents, not the state, are responsible for the issue of different and competing monetary units.

In this chapter it is argued that there is a gap in the Mengerian argument: a neglect of potential quality variation in the emerging monetary unit. It is shown here that once this is recognized the spontaneous process of evolution of the monetary unit may break down, requiring the intervention of the state, or other overarching authority such as a central bank, to maintain the currency unit. Attention to this factor suggests a possible case for state intervention in the monetary system, partly to police the currency against debasement, and to legitimize its value.

Furthermore, the argument suggests why law is not an entirely spontaneous institution and may require state sanction as well. In contrast, the argument shows why such state intervention is not generally necessary in the case of language.

Finally, the matter of potential quality variation suggests why some state intervention and regulation is necessary in most complex markets: at the minimum to maintain a commodity taxonomy and to ensure standards. Consequently, the Thatcherite vision of a European 'common market' without a European central authority is simply misconceived.

MONEY AS AN 'ORGANIC' INSTITUTION

Menger (1892, 1963, 1981) viewed money as a paradigmatic 'organic' social institution, alongside language or common law. By 'organic' he did not mean natural or biological, nor even the quality of being structurally inter-connected with the environment. For Menger, an 'organic' social institution is one which, although the product of human action, is not the product of human design.

In particular, money is seen to arise out of the combination and interaction of individual decisions, although no one may have intended the outcome. Accordingly, this view differs from the 'state theory of money' or 'monetary nominalism' of the institutionalist Georg Knapp (1924), which has roots in the works of Aristotle and has later been endorsed by some monetarists.[2] In opposition to the latter viewpoint, for Menger and the Austrian School the emergence and continuance of a monetary system of exchange does not necessarily require the legislation and backing of the state.

Menger (1963, p. 153) accepts that 'history actually offers us examples that certain wares have been declared money by law'. But these declarations are often seen to be 'the acknowledgement of an item which had already become money'. Although cases of the emergence of money by agreement or legislation are important, Menger argues that: 'the origin of money can truly be brought to our full understanding only by our learning to understand the *social* institution discussed here as the unintended result, as the unplanned outcome of specifically *individual* efforts of members of society' (Menger, 1963, p. 155).

An account of the supposed evolutionary process through which money could emerge is found in his Principles:

> As *each* economizing individual becomes increasingly more aware of his eco-nomic interest, he is led by this *interest, without any agreement, without legisla-tive compulsion,* and *even without regard to the public interest,* to give his com-modities in exchange for other, more saleable, commodities, even if he does not need them for any immediate consumption purpose. With economic progress, therefore, we can everywhere observe the phenomenon of a certain number of goods, especially those that are most easily saleable at a given time and place, becoming, under the influence of *custom,* acceptable to everyone in trade, and thus capable of being given in exchange for any other commodity. (Menger, 1981, p. 260)

Clearly, a trader may hold a stock of a commodity for reasons other than the purpose of direct personal consumption. In this case, and in a market economy, the commodity may be held with a view to future trade. However, com-modities will differ in their saleability. Some commodities will be widely accepted in exchange, others less so. A commodity that is seen to be accepted in exchange will have its saleability enhanced as individuals act on the basis of such a perception.

Hence the process begins on the basis of subjective evaluations, and becomes progressively reinforced through action and the perception of this action by other individuals. Furthermore, as Menger suggests, specific commodities may become more acceptable in exchange through the establishment or influence of custom:

> nothing may have favored the genesis of money as much as the receiving of eminently marketable goods for all other goods, which had been practiced for quite a long time on the part of the most perspicacious and ablest economic subjects for their own economic advantage. Thus practice and custom have certainly contributed not a little to making the temporarily most marketable wares the ones which are received in exchange for their wares not only by many economic individuals, but ultimately by all. (Menger, 1963, p. 155)

Money thus emerges as a result of some kind of evolutionary process. Apart from the attribute of being 'most marketable', which is a culmination and consequence of individual perceptions and choices, Menger (1963, p. 154) suggests that the good that emerges as money may be 'the most easily transported, the most durable, the most easily divisible'. Consequently, over time, a single commodity or group of commodities will emerge as money.[3]

EVOLUTION AND THE INVISIBLE HAND

As Gerald O'Driscoll and Mario Rizzo (1985, p. 192) remark, Menger's theory of money 'is reminiscent of Adam Smith's invisible hand reasoning'. Indeed, there is a direct lineage in the approach to evolutionary theory from Smith through to the Austrian School. Smithian evolutionary theory has a number of features, including: first, an emphasis on the spontaneous and unintended emergence of a social order, an 'invisible hand'; second, a process of evolution which normally reaches a harmonious steady state, rather than being continuously disrupted and undermined; and third, a disposition towards a non-interventionist policy based on the belief that such complex evolutionary processes cannot be readily out-designed, nor easily improved upon.

Menger goes further than Smith, however, in examining this process in more detail. For example, he shows how the initial emergence of a convention, or social institution such as money, may be largely accidental. Subsequent to its tentative emergence in a given locality, it becomes better established through a process of continuous feedback. The initial and local emergence of a convention is thus progressively reinforced by the positive feedback of perceptions and actions in accord with the convention.

Clearly, money is 'selected' here, in a sense. But it would be wrong to conclude that it is analogous to natural selection. What is 'selected' is the convention, or potential monetary unit, itself. However, as argued below, this is not the selection of what is analogous to the 'genetic' elements driving the system.

However, although the convention or monetary unit has durable qualities, there are still further reasons why its character is not at all like the gene in modern biology. Such a unit survives not because its genetically programmed qualities are well adapted in a given environmental context. The monetary unit is wanted because it is wanted; the convention is followed because it is followed. Such reciprocating causation means that cause becomes effect just as effect becomes cause.[4]

The Mengerian evolutionary process is Smithian in character, in that it posits the end state at which a given type of money (Menger) or the social order (Smith) has become widely accepted, established and thereby stabilized. For both Darwin and Lamarck, however, there was no such end-point to an evolutionary process.

For this reason, the Mengerian evolution of money certainly looks like ontogeny rather than phylogeny. The distinction between ontogeny and phylogeny is borrowed from biology. Ontogeny involves the development of a particular organism from a set of given and unchanging genes. In contrast, phylogeny is the complete evolution of a population, including changes in its composition and that of the gene-pool. These terms are applied for the purposes of analogy, not to imply that human behaviour is necessarily determined by the genes.

Clearly, the object of evolutionary analysis is an emerging monetary unit and the focus is on the cumulative reinforcement of a given unit. The 'genetic material' is the individuals with their given preferences and goals. Importantly, this 'genetic material' does not change during the emergence of money. There is not necessarily even a process of evolutionary selection between rival monetary units, nor is there a consideration of the changes in individual goals or preferences. The medium of exchange is 'selected', but through cumulative reinforcement, and not necessarily through the sifting and winnowing of competing alternatives. It involves the 'selection' of a path of ontogenetic development, as a plant responds to external stimuli by growing one way rather than another. It is not the full 'natural selection' observed in phylogeny. Indeed, we are confined to ontogeny.[5]

PATH-DEPENDENCY

Robert Jones's analysis of the Mengerian model raises some important issues. First, Jones (1976, p. 775) suggests that 'a very common good would emerge as a first commodity money'. Consequently, commonness or salience is more important than physical characteristics. However, local salience may vary from market to market. For this reason, and because of the existence of 'transaction costs', a single money commodity may not emerge. Indeed 'there may be several stable equilibrium levels of monetization of trade. Even for a single given distribution of ultimate exchanges, direct barter, full monetization, and intermediate mixes may all be locally stable situations' (Jones, 1976, p. 773).

Given that there is not a single, determinate equilibrium outcome, the evolution of the monetary unit is a case of path-dependency. Under certain plausible assumptions, not only is a mix of money and barter possible, but also mixes of different monetary units. Indeed, the selection process may also depend on a combination of accidents or initial perceptions. As long as the commodity is reasonably durable and not too cumbersome then it can serve as a medium of exchange. In this case the initial 'accidents' leading to the emergence of one rather than another commodity determine whether money is to be coins, cows or cowrie shells. This path-dependency undermines the sanctity of any *de facto* evolutionary outcome.[6]

This undermines Menger's (1963, p. 155) belief that the evolutionary selection process tends to favour and replicate the outcomes of actions 'of the most perspicacious and ablest economic subjects'. With strong path-dependency, the initial salience of an inferior outcome may lead to a result in which the outcomes of actions of less perspicacious and less able agents are favoured. This is one of the many cases where evolutionary outcomes are not necessarily the most efficient in such respects.

THE 'LEGAL RESTRICTIONS' DEBATE

The debate over whether it is possible to remove the state largely or entirely from involvement in the monetary system has simmered on in recent years, with most contributions favouring various proposals for the 'denationalization' of money.[7]

However, attempts to point to historical precedents for such a system of 'free banking' in modern times, particularly in Scotland up to 1848 and in New York State from 1836 to 1863, are not entirely convincing (Checkland, 1975; King, 1983; White, 1984a). In the Scottish case only note issue, not coinage, was unregulated. The notes were denominated in pounds sterling and thus had the backing of the English state across the border. In the New York case private banknotes had to be denominated in dollars, and dollars in turn were backed by a gold standard. The state authority printed and registered the notes, and the banks were required to hold specie reserves against circulating notes. The failure of the 'free banking' theorists to point to a convincing precedent raises serious questions about the viability of their proposal.

In his attempt to show that 'legal restriction' is not necessary for the emergence of an accepted medium of exchange, Karl Wärneryd (1989, 1990) shows that the selection of money depends not on the characteristics or efficiency of the commodity in question. Indeed, a type of unit that bears a higher rate of interest may not be selected. Wärneryd shows that the evolutionary selection of money has attributes of the kind of 'coordination game' discussed by Edna Ullmann-Margalit (1977). Once a unit begins to emerge, it establishes a 'convention' with strong 'network externalities'. Like other such conventions, such as language, or driving on the same side of the road, the network externality effect is that we are impelled to use or do something because it is used or done by others.

However, whilst Wärneryd supports the proposition that state intervention is not necessary for emergence of money, we are entitled to draw the conclusion from his analysis that the legal establishment of money by the state may sometimes be necessary to establish a more satisfactory outcome, or to maintain a given outcome in the face of disturbance or threat. State activity is not necessarily the best way of doing this, but at least such eventualities and their potential solutions should be considered.

THE PROBLEM OF QUALITY VARIATION

In Menger's theory, the emerging monetary unit is homogeneous and invariant. Although not all persons may recognize (say) gold as the emerging monetary substance, Menger assumes that they all know 24-carat gold when they see it. But even gold can be melted down and alloyed with inferior metals. As in modern biology, there is no single, pure, typological item. In contrast, Menger's analysis is a case of 'typological thinking'. There is a pre-existing variety in the set of commodity types. But within each type the possibility of quality variation is not considered.

Such 'typological essentialism' is an essentially Platonic idea in which entities are regarded as identifiable in terms of a few distinct characteristics which represent their essential qualities. This differs from the notion of 'population thinking' in which variety and diversity are all-important (Mayr, 1982, pp. 45–7). In typological thinking, species are regarded as identifiable in terms of a few distinct characteristics which represent their essence. Accordingly, all variations around the ideal type are regarded as accidental aberrations. By contrast, in population thinking, species are described in terms of a distribution of characteristics. Whereas in typological thinking variation is a classificatory nuisance, in Darwinian evolution the idea of variation encapsulated in population thinking is of paramount interest because it is upon variety that selection operates.

With potential quality variation, the purity and value of the emerging monetary unit may be in doubt. Some actors may notice the high frequency of the trade in a particular commodity, but in contrast to their associates, regard the commodity in question as unreliable and thereby avoid it as a medium of exchange. Such information problems, arising from potential quality variation, could subvert the evolution of the monetary unit. Despite the noted emphasis of the Austrian School on subjectivity and divergences of perceptions, this problem of information and knowledge is ignored in Menger's theory.

It is not suggested that Menger generally ignores problems of information and uncertainty; it is well established that he was one of the first major economists to give them precedence. However, the particular problem of quality variation is sidestepped by his implicit assumption that the emerging monetary substance is invariant, and recognizable by all agents. Despite the obvious problem of the debasement of coinage, the implications in terms of the Mengerian story of the emergence of money have not been fully explored.[8]

In general, it is normally assumed by economists that each commodity is homogeneous and well defined. One nineteenth-century exception is found in the work *On the Economy of Machinery and Manufactures* by Charles Babbage. Pointing to a widespread problem of potential adulteration and debasement of commodities, Babbage (1846, p. 134) argues that whilst in 'some cases the goodness of an article is evident on mere inspection', in others, like tea and flour, the commodity can be easily adulterated without ready detection.[9]

Furthermore, 'the difficulty and expense of verification are, in some instances, so great as to justify the deviation from well-established principles'. Babbage (1846, p. 135) thus suggests that it is necessary for the government to step in, 'to verify each sack of purchased flour, and to employ persons in devising methods of detecting the new modes of adulteration which might be continually resorted to'. In recognizing the possibility of adulteration and debasement, Babbage has put his finger on a possible reason for state intervention.[10] Such problems of quality variation and verification are neglected in Menger's theory of money.

Babbage's argument resembles the later and famous paper by George Akerlof (1970) in which he identifies the problem of information asymmetry in the exchange commodities of uncertain quality. Akerlof implies that the solution to this problem is some system of guarantees or 'quality arbitrage'. There is a related discussion of 'brand name capital' in the free banking literature. The argument is that there is some quality check through the market valuation of competing reputations.

But, to each single observer, 'reputation' is even more elusive, in quality terms, than the carat-value of gold. Whilst it is clear that the real-world market can help to evaluate the soundness and reputation of financial institutions, it is not convincingly demonstrated that this mechanism is generally reliable, or how the persistent and serious information problems can be overcome. There are cases of self-regulation by banks, but against this there are many cases of fraud and deception being uncovered by state authority. Without such central regulation, the problems of quality variation seem to be even further compounded.

Even if self-regulation was generally viable, cases where it has worked depend upon the initiative of a small number of strong, oligopolistic banking institutions, rather than a more competitive market. This seems to undermine the argument that money will emerge and become trusted and accepted without some such strong institutional verification. The issue is not clear-cut, but it is difficult to see how the reputation of quality-ensuring authorities could be sustained without some overarching regulatory authority: either the state or a group of strong private institutions.

Philip Mirowski (1990, 1991) makes a relevant and related point when he argues that money is 'a socially constructed institution'. However, 'precisely because it is socially instituted, its invariance cannot be predicated on any "natural" ground, and must continually be shored up and reconstituted by further social institutions, such as accountants and banks and governments' (Mirowski, 1990, p. 712). In other words, the 'value' of money is continually under threat from many devices and stratagems, from coin-clipping to the modern expansion of debt.

In sum, with the emergence of a monetary unit when perceived potential quality variation is a problem, a kind of Gresham's Law[11] may be in operation, when the evolution of any 'good' universal equivalent is continually undermined by the perceived problem of the 'bad'. Given this informational and cognitive problem, the emergence of a monetary unit may be much assisted by strong institutions committed to policing its quality and protecting it from debasement. The further legitimation of a given monetary unit by the state, and its endowment with symbolic significance and grandeur, is also advantageous in facilitating its emergence and stability.

Whilst each individual trader has an incentive to trade in the inferior and debased unit, only large institutions, encompassing the common interest in a sound currency, have an incentive to maintain its value and deter forgery and debasement. Clearly the state is a strong candidate to take on this role.

Of course, the disadvantage in the modern era of paper money is that governments may be tempted to print more cash and allow banks to over-expand their credit. This is a problem of which we are often reminded, and one which motivates the proponents of the 'denationalization' of money. It may or may not be possible to devise institutional safeguards. If it is not, then the state may generally devalue the currency by fuelling inflation, despite validating the monetary equivalent in individual transactions.

However, debasement by inflation is not the same phenomenon as debasement by (say) forgery or coin-clipping. The state can still act to guarantee the equivalence of every single unit of money whilst acting to undermine its general and common value. Forgery introduces a bad unit alongside the good, whilst inflation simultaneously undermines the general exchange value of all monetary units. Forgery or debasement creates a problem for current exchanges, even if their sustained effects may also be inflationary. Inflation primarily affects the holding of money, inter-temporal choices, and long-term contracts. These are different problems, and the state may play a role which is less positive in one rather than the other. The case for a monetary system based on the state must consider both the merits and demerits, and not assume that the state plays an unambiguously negative (or wholly positive) role.

Furthermore, the point being made here is that the Mengerian story of the supposedly spontaneous emergence of money is faulty, and strong encompassing institutions such as the state or central banks are essential to the creation and survival of a viable monetary unit, even if the state (or central bank) may bring associated problems.

MONEY, LAW AND LANGUAGE: SOME KEY DIFFERENCES

It is argued above that with potential quality variation individual agents have an obvious incentive to use a less costly or poor-quality version of the medium of exchange in preferment to the good. Similar incentives to debase social norms exist in the case of many laws. Laws restricting behaviour, and where there are perceived advantages to transgression, are the ones that require the most policing. Hence people frequently evade tax payments or break speed limits. Without some policing activity the law itself is likely to be debased or 'brought into disrepute'.

In the case of a few other laws, however, people have a direct incentive to conform. For example, there are obvious incentives to drive on the same side of the road as others and to stop at traffic lights. Although infringements will occur, these laws are largely self-policing.

Language also can be self-regulating, because individuals have an incentive to make their words clear. Although meaning – the signified – may be ambiguous, the coding itself – the signifier – must be unmistakable. In communication we are impelled to use words and sounds in a way that conforms as closely as possible to the perceived norm. Language is another example of a convention of standard which exhibits 'lock-in' (Arthur, 1988, 1989, 1990) due to the fact that once it becomes widely used then others have an incentive to do the same. In a similar manner, there are technological conventions, from railway gauges to computer software, which reproduce themselves because of 'network externalities' (Katz and Shapiro, 1985, 1986) and widespread use.

With language, our inbuilt drives to imitate are used to the full, and we have no incentive to bar their operation. Although languages do change through time, there are incentives to conform to and thus reinforce the linguistic norms in the given region or context. Linguistic norms are thus almost wholly self-policing, unlike currency values and most laws.[12] The argument for the intervention of the state is thus much stronger in the case of law and money than in the case of language.[13]

MARKETS AND QUALITY VARIATION

Notably, the argument about potential quality variation applies to most exchangeables, as well as money. Babbage's argument applied to all commodities where quality variation may exist and is not immediately and fully discernible by the purchaser. He suggests that the state has an important role in establishing and policing standards, using the means of regular inspection and even direct intervention in production. Accordingly, if the state is to regulate production and trade in this way, then it must act as a taxonomist, establishing definitions of each type of commodity so that particular rules in each case may apply. This is another important reason, to add to others I have discussed elsewhere (Hodgson, 1988, pp. 172–94), why modern markets are not aggregates of atomistic traders but institutions in their own right. Such an institution, furthermore, is necessarily supported by networks of other institutions, including the state.

This argument was made by Karl Polanyi (1944) in his classic work on the development of industrial capitalism in Britain. He argues that not only was the state necessary to establish *laissez-faire*, once a relatively 'free' market system had been established, as in Britain in the first half of the nineteenth century, the very operation of the supposedly 'self-regulating' system required continuous meddling and monitoring by the state:

> The road to the free market was opened and kept open by an enormous increase in continuous, centrally organized and controlled interventionism. To make Adam Smith's 'simple and natural liberty' compatible with the needs of a human society was a most complicated affair. ... [T]he introduction of free markets, far from doing away with the need for control, regulation and intervention, enormously increased their range. Administrators had to be constantly on the watch

to ensure the free workings of the system. Thus even those who wished most ardently to free the state from all unnecessary duties, and whose whole philosophy demanded the restriction of state activities, could not but entrust the self-same state with new powers, organs, and instruments required for the establishment of laissez-faire. (Polanyi, 1944, pp. 140–1).

Polanyi thus rebuts libertarian protestations against state intervention in the market. For him, this is as 'natural' – or otherwise – as the earlier creation of the comprehensive market. He showed that the creation of the 'free' market necessitated continuous and extensive state intervention to make the market 'work'.

THE CASE OF THE EUROPEAN COMMUNITY

The process of completion of the internal market of the European Community up to 1992 provides an important illustrative case. Polanyi's argument counters the belief – held by Mrs Thatcher and other neo-liberals – that such an integrated market is possible without corresponding federation or integration at the political level, and the genesis of a European state. It is forcefully implied that extended and integrated markets require a corresponding extension of the supervisory and regulatory apparatus, at a minimum to establish and maintain standards and to ensure contract compliance.[14]

This process, outlined in the EC White Paper of 1985 and subsequent reports, is not confined simply to the removal of tariffs, customs and other physical barriers to trade. Even with the addition of the measures to liberalize labour and financial markets, much more is involved. The 1985 White Paper declared at the start that 'barriers created by different national product regulations and standards ... fundamentally frustrate the creation of a common market for industrial products' (Commission of the European Communities, 1985, p. 17). Accordingly, much of the legislation was directed at the problem of creating standards which could be imposed with the force of Community law.

Inspection of the relevant EC documents will show that a similar number of legislative measures is involved in the process of commodity standardization and harmonization as on the removal of physical barriers themselves (Commission of the European Communities, 1986–91). Furthermore, the legislation on standardization and harmonization is very likely to increase through time, not only with the march of technical progress and diversification but also with the discovery of the need for new controls. In contrast, the removal of physical barriers between nation states is a one-off rather than an ongoing process.

In sum, the creation of a European Common Market requires both state legislation and state activity on a Community scale. Several hundred rules and regulations are involved in the Single European Act. Although the primary moves have been made by treaty and by individual approval of the member nations, it becomes increasingly obvious that a single European state authority is required to deal with the ongoing and ever more complex problems. The European Common Market cannot be consolidated without a common state apparatus within Europe, even if significant legislative powers on other matters remain with the constituent nation states.

CONCLUSION

In conclusion, Menger's explanation of the emergence of money does not provide us with a complete evolutionary perspective, of a phylogenetic kind, nor explain all the things that have to be explained. It would be mistaken, therefore, to use it as an exclusive guide to monetary theory and policy.

The main problem with Menger's theory is that, given potential quality variation, the spontaneous process of evolution of the monetary unit may break down, possibly requiring the intervention of the state or central bank to maintain the currency unit. In sum, there are good reasons to assume that money will be – to use Menger's terminology – a 'pragmatic' rather than a purely 'organic' institution.

Furthermore, the argument in this chapter suggests why law is not an entirely spontaneous institution and may require state sanction as well. In contrast, it is shown why state intervention is not generally necessary in the case of language.

Finally, the key matter of potential quality variation of commodities suggests why some state intervention and regulation is necessary in most complex markets: at the minimum to maintain a commodity taxonomy and to ensure standards. This is exemplified in attempts to create a 'common market' in Europe. Once the problem of quality variation is considered, and the associated need for state regulation, it is clear that Mrs Thatcher's vision of a European 'common market' without a European state authority is not viable. Modern, complex markets are of necessity mixtures of private contracts and central authority.

NOTES

1. The author is grateful for the supportive facilities of the Swedish Collegium for Advanced Studies in the Social Sciences in writing this essay, and to Mary Farmer, Sean

Hargreaves Heap, Tony Lawson, Tracy Mott, Ian Steedman and Adrian Winnett for discussions.

2. Timothy Congdon (1981) explicitly endorses Knapp's view. However, in contrast to Congdon and other supporters of the state monopoly of money such as Milton Friedman, Knapp rejects the quantity theory of money as an explanation of the price level. Knapp sees it as being determined by 'real' phenomena such as the level of wages, which 'constituted a first step towards the later theories of Keynes and his school' (Schefold, 1987, p. 54). For a comparative discussion of 'monetary nominalism' see Frankel (1977).

3. It is notable that the Mengerian account of the emergence of money is repeated by Ludwig von Mises (1980, pp. 42–6) and others of the later Austrian School.

4. For a more extensive discussion of the concept of causality in Menger's 'invisible hand' explanation of money see Mäki (1991), and for a more general discussion of 'invisible hand explanations' see Ullmann-Margalit (1978).

5. Note, for instance, Viktor Vanberg's (1989, p. 340) useful summary of the steps involved in Menger's theory of the emergence of money. Significantly, Vanberg writes of the 'discovery' of the monetary unit, rather than of its selection from a set of competitive rival units.

6. It is not implied here that Menger believed that markets reached optimal outcomes. In addition, Menger was not as opposed to state intervention as some later members of the Austrian School (Prisching, 1989; Vanberg, 1986, p. 99). As in the case of Smith, Menger's *laissez-faire* dispositions are qualified.

7. See, for instance, Black (1970), Dowd (1989), Fama (1980), Glasner (1989), Goodhart (1987), Hayek (1976), Hoover (1988), Selgin (1988), Wärneryd (1989, 1990), White (1986, 1987), Wray (1990), Yeager (1987, 1989). It should be noted, however, that Menger's theory is not always used to bolster non-interventionism. It is sometimes used as part of a critique of some specific proposals to limit the role of the state in the monetary system. Observe, for instance, the criticisms of the Greenfield and Yeager (1983, 1986) 'cashless competitive payments system' by Mott (1989), Selgin and White (1987) and White (1984b, 1989). Selgin, White and Mott all make some appeal to Menger's conception of money to rebut the Greenfield–Yeager idea that the government should define the unit of value but should be forbidden to issue money itself. However, Yeager (1989) disputes the relevance, but not the validity, of the Mengerian story in this context.

8. In his discussion of coinage debasement, von Mises (1980, p. 79) writes that: 'Not every kind of money has been accepted at sight, but only those with a good reputation for weight and fitness'.The question, then, is how such fitness is maintained?

9. Babbage's concept of quality variation is related to his concept of the division of labour. The idea of the division of labour in the works of Mandeville and Smith does not proceed from the assumption of the initial diversity of talent or skill. It assumes that such variations arise from learning in the process of production itself. Variety is thus a result of the division of labour, not its starting point. In contrast, for Babbage (1846, pp. 175–6), prior variations in skill are the economic foundation upon which the division of labour is built.

10. Alec Nove (1980, 1983) has also emphasized the problem of quality variation in his discussion of the limits and possibilities of socialist planning. However, in noting that 'a kilowatt-hour is a kilowatt-hour is a kilowatt-hour' he argues that commodities such as electricity which are least susceptible to such variation are the best candidates for planned production by the state. Unlike Babbage, therefore, Nove thus suggests that state intervention is less appropriate in cases of variable quality. What Nove ignores, however, is the problem of quality verification that is highlighted by Babbage. Consideration of all the relevant issues in the cases where there is significant potential quality variation suggests a market solution, but one which is highly regulated by the state.

11. Strictly, this is not the exact law associated with Sir Thomas Gresham (*c.* 1519–1579), which is taken to apply to the case where 'by legal enactment a government assigns the same nominal value to two or more forms of circulatory medium whose intrinsic values

differ' (Harris, 1987, p. 565). Understandably, agents prefer to make payments with the less costly or inferior form, and 'bad money drives out good'. This argument relates to the existence of a single state authority sanctioning and assigning invariant value to a debaseable currency unit. (Hayek's (1967, pp. 318–20) brief discussion of Gresham's Law is regrettably vague on this point.) In contrast, the idea discussed in the present chapter is of perceived differences arising within a class of commodities of the same perceived type. The taxonomic designation of the group of commodities, e.g. various degrees and types of impure gold, could arise from common perception and language, rather than by the assignation of the state.

12.   We may hypothesize that changes in language occur through something analogous to the 'genetic drift': the accumulation of small and possibly random changes in one general direction over time. Interestingly, as in biology, such 'genetic drift' is a source of change other than through evolutionary selection.

13.   However, there may even be a case for some institutional regulation of language, as in France, and spelling reforms, as in the Netherlands. There is no reason to presume that self-regulating linguistic evolution always leads to satisfactory outcomes.

14.   For Polanyi, furthermore, extended markets depend upon the symbolic and practical support of a unified currency and integrated banking system. And finally, in a democratic system subject to sustained pressure from trade unions and enlightened employers, the extension of market is likely, in response, to stimulate general measures to protect working conditions and to safeguard employees.

REFERENCES

Akerlof, G.A. (1970), 'The Market for "Lemons": Quality Uncertainty and the Market Mechanism', *Quarterly Journal of Economics*, **84**, (3), August, 488–500. Reprinted in G.A. Akerlof (1984), *An Economic Theorist's Book of Tales*, Cambridge: Cambridge University Press.

Arthur, W.B. (1988), 'Self-Reinforcing Mechanisms in Economics', in P.W. Anderson, K.J. Arrow, and D. Pines (eds), *The Economy as an Evolving Complex System* , Reading, MA: Addison-Wesley, pp. 9–31.

Arthur, W.B. (1989), 'Competing Technologies, Increasing Returns, and Lock-in by Historical Events', *Economic Journal*, **99**, (1), March, 116–31.

Arthur, W.B. (1990), 'Positive Feedbacks in the Economy', *Scientific American*, **262**, (2), February, 80–85.

Babbage, C. (1846), *On the Economy of Machinery and Manufactures*, 4th edn, London: John Murray.

Black, F. (1970), 'Banking and Interest Rates in a World Without Money: The Effects of Uncontrolled Banking', *Journal of Bank Research*, **1**, pp. 9–20.

Checkland, S. G. (1975), *Scottish Banking: A History 1695–1793*, Glasgow: Collins.

Commission of the European Communities (1985), *Completing the Internal Market: White Paper from the Commission to the European Council*, COM(85)310 final, 14 June, Brussels: CEC.

Commission of the European Communities (1986–91), *Report of the Commission to the Council and the European Parliament Concerning the Implementation of the White Paper on the Completion of the European Market*, nos 1–6, Brussels: CEC.

Congdon, T. (1981), 'Is the Provision of a Sound Currency a Necessary Function of the State?', *National Westminister Bank Quarterly Review*, August, 2–21.

Dowd, K. (1989), *The State and the Monetary System*, Hemel Hempstead: Philip Allan.

Eatwell, J., M. Milgate and P. Newman (eds) (1987), *The New Palgrave Dictionary of Economics*, 4 vols, London: Macmillan.

Fama, E. (1980), 'Banking in the Theory of Finance', *Journal of Monetary Economics*, **6**, 39–57.

Frankel, S.H. (1977), *Money: Two Philosophies; The Conflict of Trust and Authority,* Oxford: Basil Blackwell.

Glasner, D. (1989), *Free Banking and Monetary Reform*, Cambridge: Cambridge University Press.

Goodhart, C.A.E. (1987), 'Why do Banks Need a Central Bank?', *Oxford Economic Papers*, **39**, (1), January, 75–89.

Greenfield, R.L. and L.B. Yeager (1983), 'A Laissez-Faire Approach to Monetary Stability', *Journal of Money, Credit and Banking*, **15**, (3), August, 302–15.

Greenfield, R.L. and L.B. Yeager (1986), 'Competitive Payments Systems: Comment', *American Economic Review*, **76**, 848–9.

Harris, C.A. (1987), 'Gresham's Law', in Eatwell, Milgate and Newman (Vol. II, p. 565).

Hayek, F.A. (1967), *Studies in Philosophy, Politics and Economics*, London: Routledge & Kegan Paul.

Hayek, F.A. (1976), *The Denationalisation of Money,* London: Institute of Economic Affairs.

Hayek, F.A. (1988), *The Fatal Conceit: The Errors of Socialism, Collected Works of F. A. Hayek*, Vol. I, London: Routledge.

Hodgson, G.M. (1988), *Economics and Institutions: A Manifesto for a Modern Institutional Economics*, Cambridge and Philadelphia: Polity Press and University of Pennsylvania Press.

Hoover, K.D. (1988), 'Money, Prices and Finance in the New Monetary Economics', *Oxford Economic Papers*, **40**, 150–67.

Jones, R.A. (1976), 'The Origin and Development of Media of Exchange', *Journal of Political Economy*, **84**, (4), pt 1, August, 757–75.

Katz, M. and C. Shapiro (1985), 'Network Externalities, Competition, and Compatibility', *American Economic Review*, **75**, (3), June, 424–40.

Katz, M. and C. Shapiro (1986), 'Technology Adoption in the Presence of Network Externalities', *Journal of Political Economy*, **94**, (4), August, 822–41.

King, R.G. (1983), 'On the Economics of Private Money', *Journal of Monetary Economics*, **12**, (1), pp. 127–58.

Knapp, G.F. (1924), *The State Theory of Money,* London: Macmillan.

Mäki, U. (1991), 'Practical Syllogism, Entrepreneurship, and the Invisible Hand', in D. Lavoie (ed.), *Economics and Hermeneutics*, London: Routledge, pp. 149–76.

Mayr, E. (1982), *The Growth of Biological Thought: Diversity, Evolution, and Inheritance,* Cambridge, MA: Harvard University Press.

Menger, C. (1892), 'On the Origins of Money', *Economic Journal*, **2**, (2), June, 239–55.

Menger, C. (1963), *Problems of Economics and Sociology*, trans. F.J. Nock from the German edition of 1883 with an introduction by Louis Schneider, Urbana, IL: University of Illinois Press.

Menger, C. (1981), *Principles of Economics*, ed. J. Dingwall trans. B.F. Hoselitz from the German edition of 1871, New York: New York University Press.

Mirowski, P. (1990), 'Learning the Meaning of the Dollar: Conservation Principles and the Social Theory of Value in Economic Theory', *Social Research*, **57**, (3), Fall, 689–797.

Mirowski, P. (1991), 'Postmodernism and the Social Theory of Value', *Journal of Post Keynesian Economics*, **13**, (4), Summer, 565–82.

Mises, L. von (1980), *The Theory of Money and Credit*, trans. H.E. Batson, Indianapolis: Liberty Classics.

Mott, T. (1989), 'A Post Keynesian Perspective on a "Cashless Competitive Payments System"', *Journal of Post Keynesian Economics*, **11**, (3), Spring, 360–69.

Nove, A. (1980), 'The Soviet Economy: Problems and Prospects', *New Left Review*, **119**, (January–February), 3–19.

Nove, A. (1983), *The Economics of Feasible Socialism*, London: Allen & Unwin.

O'Driscoll, Jr, G.P. and Rizzo, M.J. (1985), *The Economics of Time and Ignorance,* Oxford: Basil Blackwell.

Polanyi, K. (1944), *The Great Transformation,* New York: Rinehart.

Prisching, M. (1989), 'Evolution and Design of Social Institutions in Austrian Theory', *Journal of Economic Studies*, **16**, (2), 47–62.

Schefold, B. (1987), 'Knapp, Georg Friedrich', in Eatwell, Milgate and Newman (Vol. III, pp. 54–5).

Selgin, G.A. (1988), *The Theory of Free Banking,* Totawa, NJ: Rowman & Littlefield.

Selgin, G.A. and L.H. White (1987), 'The Evolution of a Free Banking System', *Economic Inquiry*, **25**, (3), July, 439–57.

Ullmann-Margalit, E. (1977), *The Emergence of Norms*, Oxford: Oxford University Press.

Ullmann-Margalit, E. (1978), 'Invisible Hand Explanations', *Synthese*, **39**, 263–91.

Vanberg, V. (1986), 'Spontaneous Market Order and Social Rules: A Critique of F.A. Hayek's Theory of Cultural Evolution', *Economics and Philosophy*, **2**, (June), 75–100.

Vanberg, V. (1989), 'Carl Menger's Evolutionary and John R. Commons' Collective Action Approach to Institutions: A Comparison', *Review of Political Economy*, **1**, (3), November, 334–60.

Wärneryd, K. (1989), 'Legal Restrictions and the Evolution of Media of Exchange', *Journal of Institutional and Theoretical Economics*, **145**, (4), December, 613–26.

Wärneryd, K. (1990), 'Legal Restrictions and Monetary Evolution', *Journal of Economic Behavior and Organization*, **13**, (1), March, 117–24.

White, L.H. (1984a), *Free Banking in Britain*, Cambridge: Cambridge University Press.

White, L.H. (1984b), 'Competitive Payments Systems and the Unit of Account', *American Economic Review*, **74**, 699–712.

White, L.H. (1986), 'Competitive Payment Systems: Reply', *American Economic Review*, **76**, 850–53.

White, L.H. (1987), 'Accounting for Non-Interest-Bearing Currency: A Critique of the Legal Restrictions Theory of Money', *Journal of Money, Credit and Banking*, **19**, (4), November, 448–56.

White, L.H. (1989), 'Alternative Perspectives on a Cashless Competitive Payments System', *Journal of Post Keynesian Economics*, **11**, (3), Spring, 378–84.

Wray, L.R. (1990), *Money and Credit in Capitalist Economies: The Endogeneous Money Approach*, Aldershot: Edward Elgar.

Yeager, L.B. (1987), 'Stable Money and Free-Market Currencies', in J. A. Dorn and A. J. Schwartz, (eds) (1987) *The Search for Stable Money,* Chicago: University of Chicago Press.

Yeager, L.B. (1989), 'A Competitive Payments System: Some Objections Considered', *Journal of Post Keynesian Economics*, **11**, (3), Spring, 370–77.

3. Agent, Context and Innovation: A Saussurian View of Markets

Bart Nooteboom

INTRODUCTION

The linguistics of Ferdinand de Saussure (1979), with later applications and extensions in contemporary 'postmodern' thought, yields ideas which help to obtain a better understanding of markets; in particular of the dynamism of markets and the interplay of firms and their environment on which this dynamism is based. In a practical context, this understanding is required to explain and to guide the increasing interactions of firms, in strategic alliances and networks of innovation.

The present theoretical perspective has something to offer to theories in which markets or transactions play a central role, such as 'industrial organization', marketing and 'transaction cost economics'. In industrial organization it serves to clarify the relation between 'structure' (of markets) and 'conduct' (of firms), which in contemporary theory are seen to interact. In marketing it provides a deeper insight in (but can also borrow from) the notion of exchange, which serves as the key concept in marketing theory[1] and is sometimes taken to constitute a symbiotic relationship between buyer and seller.[2] In transaction cost economics it indicates the need to extend attention from transactions based on given preferences and knowledge to the effects of transaction relations on preference and knowledge formation, in the determination of perceived opportunism that is a cause of transaction costs.

In the context of social science as a larger domain, what we are aiming at is answers to fundamental questions concerning the relation between individual and collectivity. In the context of meta-science, what we are contemplating is a departure from the methodological individualism and the concept of equilibrium of traditional economics; from the notion that economic agents have an identity, with given perceptions, interpretations and preferences, prior to exchange; from the idea that supply settles down to equal a given demand, on the basis of given, common knowledge and technology. However, we also reject the methodological collectivism that characterizes

33

some sociology. We do not accept that individual behaviour is fully determined by codes imposed from social conditions. What we want to explore
further is an interaction between individual and social environment, in which
individuals develop knowledge and preference from interaction, but in an
idiosyncrasy which turns around to affect and shift inter-subjective perceptions, interpretations and norms. In economics, that is entrepreneurship. But
this entrepreneurship, even in the starkest Schumpeterian sense of the inno-
vating hero who commits creative destruction, requires institutions to exist
and to perform its role.[3]

In other words, we are aiming at an integration of economics, sociology
and theory of knowledge. What sociology does to economics is to embed it:
in history and in society with its institutions and politics, which implies
attention to the normative dimension (Etzioni, 1988) and to learning. In
economic parlance: learning and preference formation are endogenized in a
wider theory. This does not deny the role of the individual as a source of
idiosyncratic ideas and action, but it does deny his of her autonomy. In
rejecting both the methodological individualism of (mainstream) economics
and the methodological collectivism of (some) sociology we need a theory
of meaning, learning and action that allows for the mutual interaction between
on the one hand collective meanings, perceptions, interpretations and norms
and on the other hand individual parlance, cognition and action. This theory
should leave scope for individual idiosyncrasy and invention, while surren-
dering autonomy. In our theoretical framework we preserve the essential
tension of dissensus (lack of consensus) and diversity that goes with the
entrepreneurship that fires the dynamics of society.

In the present chapter, we employ the linguistic philosophy of Ferdinand
de Saussure (1979) as a possible model for such a theory. According to
Saussure there is in language both an inter-subjective order ('langue') which
provides the commonality required to communicate, and the diversity of
individual, idiosyncratic usage ('parole'), which provides the dynamic of
meaning change. Similarly (and the parallel with language is not used just
by way of metaphor), the economy requires standards and norms for con-
ducting business, plus the idiosyncrasy of entrepreneurship. The Saussurian
view of language and markets is related to symbolic interactionism in sociology in that it recognizes that knowledge, meaning and identity are achieved
from interaction rather than only generating action. It is different in the
recognition of the ongoing creative destruction of inter-subjective order
through idiosyncratic parlance (Saussure: 'parole') in language and entrepreneurship in markets. In this respect it differs from Habermas's (1982,1984)
'theory of communicative action'. The similarity lies in the common basis of
symbolic interactionism (originated by G.H. Mead), but there is an important
difference between Habermas's assumption and goal of ultimate consensus

and the present acceptance (and goal) of individual idiosyncrasy and entrepreneurship as a perennial source of diversity and dissensus.

Graphically, what we attempt to achieve is illustrated in Figure 3.1. A theory of language, inspired by Saussure, is explored as a pivot around which an integration can be construed of economics, sociology and theory of knowledge.

Figure 3.1   The pivotal role of language

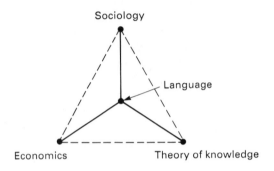

THE BASICS OF POSTMODERNISM

The basic ideas of postmodernism are that the individual does not have an autonomous consciousness, but needs communicative interaction with others to develop his or her own identity; that meanings are not given prior to communication but arise from it, and are context-dependent; that there is no universal and permanent but at best only a local and temporary unity of meaning and consensus on the rules of the game, which are continually broken and shifted in an ongoing process of differentiation and change.

The view of markets that postmodernism inspires is one of ongoing disequilibrium; of learning by doing and by interaction; of change of perception and technology; of inter-subjective difference; of product differentiation. In economics it links up with Austrian views, in its allowance for dynamism and differentiation, and in particular with Schumpeterian views, rather than the neoclassical orthodoxy. However, the notion that the individual gains his/her identity from interaction with others is contrary to the methodological individualism that is part also of Austrian economics. It is this feature in particular that brings in sociology.

The present chapter discusses the relevant ideas from postmodernism, and develops the resulting perspectives on markets in the fields of industrial organization, marketing and transaction cost economics. It focuses in particular on Saussure's theory of language, which constitutes one of the sources of postmodernism.

Elements of postmodernism are found in particular among contemporary French philosophers: Merleau-Ponty, Levinas, Lacan, Lévi-Strauss, Foucault, Derrida, Deleuze, Lyotard. These philosophers have drawn much inspiration from Nietzsche, Freud and Marx. Anglo-Saxon philosophers with important elements of postmodern thought are Quine, Rorty and Goodman, who are linked to American pragmatist philosophers (Peirce, James, Dewey). In Anglo-Saxon thought, however, there appear to be fewer extremes of the relativism that is characteristic of postmodern thought. In linguistics, there are important parallels between Saussure and Wittgenstein.[4]

In postmodernism the earlier, deeply rooted philosophy of the consciousness of the individual thinking subject is dropped, and communication and interaction between subjects is taken as the basis of philosophy. It represents a radical break with the philosophical tradition from Descartes, where 'consciousness was seen not only as the seat of thought, but also as the source of language and the quarry of truth'.[5] The seemingly self-evident reliability, impartiality and clarity of consciousness were undermined by the 'masters of suspicion', Freud, Marx, Nietzsche and Merleau-Ponty. Freud unmasked the hidden influence of the unconscious; Marx indicated the material backgrounds of motives, and thereby revealed the ideological nature of consciousness; Nietzsche exposed the role of instinct and the will to power; Merleau-Ponty indicated the roots of mind in the darkness of unconscious bodily functions. We have to deal with the 'treacherous wiles of consciousness'.[6] Since the time of the philosopher Kant, external reality has been eliminated as an anchor of truth: we cannot step outside our conceptual framework to grasp the world as it is in itself. Now the anchor of consciousness is cut as well. Truth in any form seems to escape our grasp. Philosophy breaks not only with Descartes, but also with Plato.

LANGUAGE

Communication rather than consciousness is taken as the basis of knowledge and hence philosophy of language occupies a central position. Postmodernism draws much from the philosophies of language of (the later) Wittgenstein (1976) and Saussure (1979). These two philosophers attack the view that words serve as names of objects or properties (meanings, concepts) which are given prior to language. Wittgenstein is more radical in this rejection than Saussure, who still grants that a word does stand for a concept, but denies that this concept somehow exists independently from the word.[7] They agree that language is not a set of relations between independently given words on the one hand and independently given concepts or features of the world on the other. 'To view language thus is both to isolate words from the linguistic systems to which they belong and, simultaneously, to isolate the language-user from the linguistic community' (Harris, 1988, p. 17). The meaning of a word is determined by its use, in the context of a 'language game' (Wittgenstein); it results from a collision between words in the field of communication (Saussure). Meaning is not something that is transferred as a previously existing entity, but something that arises and changes in the use of words and from that process forms thought. 'A word means what other words don't mean,' Saussure said.[8] Words arise and acquire meanings in discourse, and the meaning of a word is constituted by its relations to other words in sentences (syntagmatic relations) and to associations with other words (words that may substitute or complement it in similar sentences). According to Saussure the link between a word and the concept that it stands for is arbitrary in the sense that it is not based on any inherent, objective link of form or substance.[9] It is because of this arbitrariness that meaning is and can be inherently social rather than personal, and is subject to change. Meaning has no basis in essence and is purely conventional. There is no 'true' meaning outside of discourse. This is not to be regretted, but to be welcomed as a condition for inter-subjectivity, development and learning: if meanings constituted essences, it would be difficult to see how meanings could change or new meanings could arise in discourse.

Saussure understood language ('langage' in French) as consisting of a social order ('langue')[10] and individual usage ('parole'). *Langue* provides an existing ('synchronic' i.e. existing at a given point in time) inter-subjective order based on conventionally accepted relations and combinations of linguistic elements. *Parole* is a source of ('diachronic') change across time: deviant individual usage may catch on to be accepted as the conventional norm. We note that for this to be possible, the rules from *langue* are general but not universal in any imperative sense: there is a certain tolerance for heterodox language use. The 'logic' of language is not strict: there are no clear necessary and sufficient conditions for correct usage of a linguistic term. Rather, there are degrees of heterodoxy and acceptability. Sets of normality are fuzzy sets.[11] Like new product ideas in markets, most novel, idiosyncratic usage does not catch on. The meaning shift of a single linguistic element, if it is adopted from *parole*, causes reverberations through the coherent structure of *langue*. Also, there is no end to the change of meaning since there is no end to discourse. The use of language by individuals that emerges in living speech ('parole') conforms to the established inter-subjective order of language ('langue'), to a large extent, but also breaks it up. Commonality is partial, local and temporary, and is shot through with differences of perception, interpretation and expression between individuals. The saying dislocates the said. Individuals are formed by discourse but also shift it. There is a parallel between Saussure's concept of *parole* and Wittgenstein's notion of language as a 'form of life'. The notion of meaning as determined by relations within the total system of language is found also in Quine's (1951) notion of language as a 'seamless web'.[12]

INNOVATION AND DIFFERENTIATION

Saussure concentrated on the synchronic aspect of language (*langue*) and apart from mere mention hardly dealt with the diachronic aspect of meaning change in the interaction between *langue* and *parole*.[13] While building on the ideas of Saussure, French postmodernism shows a shift of interest from the consensus in *langue* to its disturbance in *parole*; to the diachronic aspect of the change of order, driven by a differentiation of meaning in individual usage.

In this interest in the destructive–creative role of *parole* we recognize the important influence in postmodernism of Nietzsche. The tension between fixity and flux is reminiscent of a similar opposition among pre-Socratic philosophers in ancient Greece. According to Parmenides all becoming, change and plurality is illusory, and behind them lies eternal being that can be grasped by thought. This is the thought behind Plato. On the other hand, for Heraclitus ('you never step in the same river twice') all is change and flux, and the conflict of opposites is essential for all existence. The crucial difference, however, is that the ancient opposition between fix and flux referred to views of the natural order, while the contemporary debate concerns meaning and man; knowledge and language. With this proviso one might say that postmodernism constitutes a shift from a Parmenidic to a Heraclitan view of things.

In spite of this shift to *parole*, however, the fundamentally social and interactive nature of meaning remains in the thought of most postmodernists. This is exhibited in the notion of 'otherness' ('altérité'), in the thought of Levinas (1987), for example. Interaction between people does not arise from an autonomous, prior identity; the identity of the subject is formed by interaction with the other. We need the other to become ourselves. Or in the words of Lyotard (1987, my translation): 'The self by itself is not much, but it is not isolated, it is taken up in a weaving of relations which is more complex and mobile than ever... it always finds itself in a nexus in communication circuits'. Without communicative interaction with others there is no nexus and hence no self. Identity is not a thing but a process (see in particular Derrida and Deleuze). But in opposition to this sociality there is the force of *parole* that disturbs the inter-subjective order. Interaction does not yield a common identity. In the words of Lyotard (1987, my translation): in the conduct of science

> the emphasis should henceforth fall on dissensus. Consensus forms a horizon that is never reached... there is always someone who disturbs the order of reason... consensus is a state, not the purpose of discourse... consensus is an obsolete, suspect value... if there is consensus on the rules which define each game and moves made within it, this consensus must be local, i.e. obtained by the present participants, and possibly subject to dissolution.

Differentiation and dissensus form a vital force. This Nietzschean element is particularly strong in Deleuze: traditional (i.e. 'modernistic') notions of identity, causality and lawfulness maim and constrict life which in itself is unbridled.

All postmodernists reject the notion of external, universal truths or cognitive entities that are external and yet immediately present to the mind, and accept the social, self-referential, coherence view of meaning and truth (in so far as one can still talk about truth). Some rebound radically from the order of language (langue) to the vitality and differentiation of *parole*. In the latter, dissensus, differentiation, diffuseness and ambiguity are not merely accepted but embraced. In postmodernism there are fundamental and irreducible tensions between community and differentiation, and between selfhood and otherness.

INDUSTRIAL ECONOMICS: THE DEMISE OF METHODOLOGICAL INDIVIDUALISM

Mainstream (neoclassical) economics is based on tenets of methodological individualism and rationalism that are untenable from the perspective of postmodernism.[14] Economic agents are assumed to have preferences prior to action in the market, which guide them to maximize utility on the basis of full relevant knowledge. Actions and outcomes are discussed with reference to states of equilibrium: between supply and demand; between exit and entry of firms in markets. These principles are carried over from microeconomics into theories and models of industrial organization. Industrial organization constitutes the study of the functioning of markets. It is a branch of economics that adresses the 'meso level' of markets and sectors, from the perspective of institutional conditions, market structure, conduct of firms and resulting performance. Traditionally, market structure was seen to determine conduct, but in later developments attention focused on the interaction of the two. Traditionally, the paradigm of competition is competition in price between suppliers of homogeneous goods (close substitutes), who have equal access to the same body of knowledge and technology. Product differentiation is added as a special case and is lagging in conceptual development.[15] More recent economic theories take into account bounded rationality, in the sense of the limited availability of information, as in transaction cost economics, to which we return later. Sometimes lack of information is accounted for in a highly paradoxical fashion by incorporating search costs in the maximization of utility. This is problematic, because, as recognized by Arrow (1971) how can one know the marginal cost and utility of information one does not have? Economic agents are seen as having knowledge (however limited) and preferences prior to and as the basis for action. The origin of knowledge and preferences, and hence learning, is not on the agenda of economics (partly for largely tacit ideological reasons: the autonomy of the individual is maintained as a principle of theory for fear that attention to knowledge and perception leads to their manipulation).

These principles of economics have been heavily criticized from sociological, psychological and philosophical perspectives. For recent criticism see for example Etzioni (1988) and Hodgson (1988). Etzioni (1988) objects that economics is under-socialized, in that it fails to acknowledge that individuality exists only in relation to others, and thereby presupposes society. Community is not an aggregate of individuals, as economists tend to assume, but a condition for individuality. Furthermore, neoclassical economic theory lacks the moral dimension. With the assumption that all relevant motives can be subsumed in a one-dimensional preference ordering, the tension between personal satisfaction and altruistic or community-oriented ethical/moral considerations is ignored. The machinery of economic theory and modelling can go strikingly far in reconstructing moral/ethical behaviour: thus churchgoing has been explained as the maximization of the present (discounted) value of eternal life,[16] and helping others to one's own detriment can be explained as attaching more utility to feeling virtuous than to serving one's material interests. But this may say more about the unfalsifiability of economic theory than about its explanatory force. Would it not be more straightforward and more fruitful to assume a tension between self-seeking and altruism?

Hodgson (1988) objects that the most fundamental problem of bounded rationality, neglected by most economists, is that alternative options are often not known prior to choice but emerge after a choice has been implemented.[17] Furthermore, economics is based on the primitive, indefensible epistemology that reality is perceived as it is, equally by all. From the perspective of Kantian epistemology, knowledge is contingent upon a conceptual framework, which (from a more Hegelian perspective) will shift in time, and may depend on context and background, whereby different agents do not necessarily share common perceptions and interpretations. The notion that a given body of common knowledge and technology is equally accessible to all is unacceptable.

Postmodernism radicalizes this criticism: it represents the antithesis of methodological individualism. Preferences do not exist prior to and independently of exchange, in the same way that meanings do not exist prior to and independently of communication. Knowledge does not precede action but is acquired in it. Products do not have utility prior to and apart from the market, but acquire it in interaction with other products (substitutes and complements) in the market. To paraphrase Saussure: a product is what other products are not. Product differentiation and differentiation of consumers constitute normality rather than exception. Production, usage and appreciation of products has an inter-subjective element, associated with received practice, fashion, convention and shared culture, as in *langue*, but also has an idiosyncratic element, as in *parole*. A firm is embedded in a constellation of firms and other institutions as a speaker is embedded in a speech community. These parallels between products and words, between utility and meaning, between speaker and economic agent are intended not just as metaphor but as a more literal similarity. As recognized long ago by Veblen, consumers express and distinguish themselves in consumption. Entrepreneurs do not try to make a given product most efficiently with a given technology, but to distinguish themselves with new products and technologies. Postmodernism provides the philosophical basis for Schumpeterian economics that is lacking in the works of Schumpeter himself.

Note that this criticism does not wipe out economics. If economics is under-socialized, one's view of society should not be over-socialized either, as Etzioni pointed out. The point is that individual and society presuppose each other, that causal relations run either way, and that there is an ongoing tension between them. The merit of postmodernism is that it further explores this tension without trying to eliminate it. This relation full of tension shows up in the relation between Saussure's *langue* and *parole*, which keep each other in suspense.

In industrial organization, the relation between *langue* and *parole* may provide a useful model for the relation between market structure and conduct. It may be useful to view market interaction as discourse; to compare the utility of products to the meaning of words. To explore this we now turn to the field of marketing.

MARKETING: FROM EXCHANGE TO INTERACTION

Broadly speaking, the development of marketing thought can be seen as a shift of attention from self (producer, product) to other (customer, customer benefits). It developed from a focus on the product (roughly in the period 1900–30), via a focus on sales (1930–50) to the so-called 'marketing concept' (from 1950).[18] This concept can be described as the notion that the desires and wants of customers are central and form the point of departure. A renewed interest in marketing theory arose in the early eighties (see in particular the 1983 volume of the *Journal of Marketing*). The theoretical re-flections were fairly fundamental, and even philosophical, at times. A number of people have been working on a common foundation for a general theory of marketing, and the central concept that has emerged is that of 'exchange' or 'transaction' (see, for example, Bagozzi, 1975, 1979. It may seem self-evident or trivial to say that marketing deals with exchange. But the concept of exchange is being developed beyond a one-sided influencing of one party by the other, as a 'technology of influence', towards a two-sided 'social process of interaction'. Despite its professed customer orientation the 'mar-keting concept' has retained a mentality of one-sided influence. This ap-pears, for example, in the key article 'A Generic Concept of Marketing' where Kotler (1972) laid the claim for a far-reaching extension of the domain of the marketing concept. The fourth axiom of this 'generic concept' was as follows: 'Marketing is the attempt to produce the desired response by cre-ating and offering values to the market.' Kotler was criticized for this, particularly since the concept was also applied to the 'selling' of government goals, as part of 'social marketing'. Tucker (1974, p. 32) put it this way: 'Generic marketing is defined as an overt attempt to change the behavior of someone else... the old marketing myopia of seeing the world from the channel captain's seat, continues. The organisation is the marketer and the "publics" are merely "buyers". This seems to have as its corollary the dictum that marketing theory need not consider the public except as marketing targets.' To be fair, one should note that Kotler did leave room for mutual influence (Kotler 1972, p. 49): 'Mutual marketing describes the case where two social units simultaneously seek a response from each other.' Neverthe-less, Tucker had a point in that 'mutual marketing' had to be added as a special case. Perhaps marketing should always be, or inherently is, mutual.

As indicated, it appears that this view of exchange as a two-sided (or many-sided) 'social process of interaction' was inspired to some extent at least by resistance to the broadening of the marketing concept to 'social marketing', where the 'technology of influence' is applied to the 'selling' of social measures or policies. The idea is that if the domain of marketing is broadened in this way, the marketing concept must also be developed into a two-sided process of influence. Then marketing should not only be available to producers but also to consumers.[19] The issue is perhaps particularly poignant in view of new technological opportunities provided by telematics (telecommunication plus computers). These opportunities can be used as a powerful instrument for one-sided control and regulation, enforcing the position of 'channel captains', but they can also be used for interaction and two-sided debate.[20]

The debate suggests that the opposition to the view of marketing as a process of one-sided influence stems from a humanistic sense of justice, democracy and human dignity: consumers should be able to influence producers (and government) to avoid manipulation. That certainly is a valid source of opposition. But it is important to note that in the present chapter two-sided influence is seen as the basis for marketing for *epistemological and linguistic* reasons. It is not only or even primarily a matter of justice, but of meaning, communication, identity and knowledge. One-sided influence in marketing is not so much sinister as unproductive, from the perspective of the producer. It applies not only to social marketing but to marketing in any form, in any area, since it applies to all human agency. Like words, products do not have a meaning or use value by themselves but obtain it only in use, in interaction with other (complementary or substitutive) products. If a producer shuts himself off from the influence from others he loses his marketing identity. It is by two- or many-sided influence, in a nexus of market relations, that one obtains the perception and understanding required to make sense in the market. This is the postmodern, or perhaps one should say the Wittgensteinian or Saussurian view of markets.

It is also important to note that this view does not imply naivety in the form of blindness to conflicts of interest. Indeed, in postmodern thought conflicts of view and interest are seen not only as inevitable but as forming a vital, constructive force. In this it differs sharply from the view of discourse as converging to consensus, in Habermas's (1982) *Theory of Communicative Action*. As indicated by Lyotard (1987, p. 28), postmodernism finds its ground not in the 'homology' of experts, but in the 'paralogy' of the discoverers. There is an essential, ongoing difference between agents which drives novelty. In terms of Saussure: while *langue* provides the inter-subjective basis for discourse, *parole* continually deviates from it and thereby shifts it. In markets, entrepreneurship blossoms in the attempt to be better, different and ahead of competitors. But to be successful in this one should be even less myopic in marketing than the traditional marketing concept proscribes. That concept should be carried to its conclusion of letting customers into the firm; of welcoming the complaining customer; of using the customer to specify one's product.

Postmodernism serves only to give a deeper philosophical basis, from epistemology and linguistics, for ideas that in marketing have already gained widespread recognition: in von Hippel's (1988) notion of the 'leading customer', for example.[21] In particular, Swedish network theory in marketing already goes a long way in incorporating these ideas and problems. For publications in English see Håkansson (1982, 1987), Johanson and Mattson (1985, 1987), Hellgren and Stjernberg (1987). The essential features of this network theory that distinguish it from previous approaches in marketing are as follows:

- a shift from dyadic relations (supplier–customer) to networks of multiple participants or stakeholders, with indirect as well as direct links.[22] This compares to the postmodern notion of a subject having an identity only by virtue of his or her position as a nexus in a communication network.
- a shift from incidental transactions based on present competences and preferences to investments in ongoing relations, with learning and mutual adaptation of competence and preference. This compares to the postmodern notion that meaning and understanding issue form rather than (only) produce discourse.

To further explore transactions in the context of buyer–seller relations we now turn to transaction cost theory.

TRANSACTION COST THEORY: FROM TRANSACTIONS TO RELATIONS

Transaction cost economics (TCE), as developed predominantly by Williamson (1975, 1985), has gained widespread attention among economists. It yields concepts and analyses which contribute to our understanding of the existence, size and form of organizations and other structures for the governance of transactions. The core of TCE is that as a result of opportunism and bounded rationality, transaction costs occur to the extent that assets required to conduct the transaction are specific to it (are 'sunk' in the transaction; have no or much less value outside of the transaction). In case of asset specificity, partners to the transaction become dependent on each other (are 'locked in'). In the typical case, the producer is locked in, after committing himself to an investment required to produce a specific product required by a specific customer, because if the transaction is discontinued he loses his investment. The user is likely to be locked in because outside of the transaction he cannot obtain a product that similarly satisfies his specific demands at the same cost. Transaction costs are not necessarily symmetric, however: the switching costs for one partner may be less than for the other. Opportunism, bounded rationality and transaction specificity of assets are all necessary conditions for the occurrence of transaction costs. In the absence of opportunism, one can leave contracts open and trust that unforeseen contingencies will be met in good faith, to mutual benefit. If rationality were unbounded one could foresee all contingencies and regulate them in a complete contract. If no assets are specific to the transaction, one can easily switch to an alternative transaction partner, and thus cannot become the victim of opportunism. Opportunistic partners may exploit events which were unforeseen, and hence not covered in the contract, or conditions of informatiom asymmetry, to gain advantage at the expense of the partner, who cannot costlessly switch to an alternative. When switching costs are high (investments are large and highly transaction specific), this is a reason to make rather than buy (opt for 'hierarchy' rather than market, in Williamson's parlance), or to search for schemes to reduce the risk.

As defined by Williamson (1985, p. 1): 'A transaction occurs when a good or service is transferred across a technologically separable interface.' A transaction is an event that occurs during a process of exchange, in which one can distinguish three stages: contact, contract and control. The stage of contact involves time and costs of search, to become aware of a need and of opportunities to satisfy it; to explore alternatives. The stage of contract involves the preparation of an agreement, in the form of an implicit or explicit contract plus possibly some 'governance scheme'[23] to reduce costs involved in risks of opportunism. The stage of control involves costs of monitoring events and performance, judging conformance to the agreement or opportunities to diverge from it, identifying and solving disagreements ('haggling'). The three stages are not independent: in the contact and contract stages ('ex ante') one will already anticipate on potential problems in the control stage ('ex post').

Note that whereas a transaction is an event (a point in time), transaction cost in the form of a possible loss of investment or a loss due to a want of supply is related to a process (a line in time). Loss occurs if the exchange process is discontinued; if a planned transaction does not occur, or only part of a number of planned transactions occurs, after investments that are specific to the transaction or series of transactions have been made. This may arise on the occasion of unforeseen events that occur during the process. Thus the problem of transaction costs is essentially related to the lapse of time: they occur because investment, production and delivery are not instantaneous and simultaneous with the making of the agreement to do business. But if we allow for lapse of time, we should allow for a feedback from the process of exchange to the perceptions, knowledge and preferences of the transaction partners, and resulting changes in attitudes (including proneness to opportunism). If there are costs of transaction, we should not think in terms of transactions as isolated events in time but in terms of transaction relations, with attendant dimensions of trust and 'atmosphere'. We note that Williamson's theory does not exclude these dimensions of the transaction relation, and that he did make allowance for the 'atmosphere' of contractual relations, but the notion is not developed and does not constitute a systematic part of the theory. What we want to emphasize here is that from the perspective of postmodernism interaction in an exchange relation affects the conditions, terms and perspectives of the relation. In fact, the main value of the transaction relation may not lie in the satisfaction of an already given demand derived from a given purpose on the basis of given technology, but in developing novel perspectives of purpose and technology. In terms of postmodernism: we may need the other to become ourselves; to realize our potential. And we need the other precisely because he or she is different in outlook; contributes his or her idiosyncratic *parole*.

In other words, in spite of its departure from standard economic theory in its assumption of bounded rationality and its recognition of the impossibility of 'complete contracts', TCE appears to adhere to the methodological individualism of neoclassical economics. By neglecting the dependence of meaning on interaction and the generation of perception, understanding and preference by interaction, TCE appears to neglect what may be the most crucial feature of transactions. This feature derives not from the isolated transaction but from the transaction relation in which it is embedded, and is more pronounced to the extent that the relation is prolonged.

Awareness of the importance of the transaction relation, and of durable relations, is more evident in marketing. See Sweeney (1972); Levitt (1983); Day and Wensley (1983); Houston and Gassenheimer (1987); Dwyer, Schurr and Oh (1987). In the words of Levitt (1983, p. 111): 'the sale merely consummates the courtship. Then the marriage begins. How good the marriage is depends on how well the relationship is managed by the seller.'

This perspective is of particular importance in present conditions, where firms have to concentrate more on their core activities and thereby need to make less and buy more; to contract out activities which are crucial to their products. Value chains of firms are becoming more interlaced in processes of design, development, engineering, planning, ordering/booking, quality control, invoicing, repair diagnosis and logistics. Information technology provides the means for such linkages, whereby intermediate forms of organization arise between market and 'hierarchy' (Williamson). A difficult search arises for a balance between commitment and keeping options open; between give and take; between co-operation and conflict; between influencing and being influenced; between consensus and dissensus. But it seldom is merely an issue of maximizing utility or minimizing costs at given perceptions and knowledge; with given preferences and options. It is often also concerned with developing novel perceptions, options or perspectives.

CONCLUSION

The preceding sections illustrate the relevance of postmodernism, and particularly Saussure's linguistics, to theories of markets. But one might ask what it adds to insights already available from sociology; in particular from theories of social exchange or social action: symbolic interactionism (G.H. Mead, for example) and ethnomethodology (Garfinkel, for example). There is a clear affinity. Perhaps one can say that postmodern philosophy provides a deepening of insight; a conceptual grasp on a more fundamental level, resulting from a culmination and breakdown of 300 years of philosophy since Descartes. Its application to theories of markets shows a reconceptualization, compared with traditional economics, that cuts quite deep: down into concepts or intuitions of knowledge, perception, truth, meaning, individuality, identity and society. The postmodern or Saussurian perspective gives insight not only into sociological necessity, but more deeply into the cognitive, epistemological, semantic, linguistic necessity of social interaction for the individual; not just for his or her functioning but for the very constitution of his or her identity.

Since language is not a vehicle of pre-existing concepts but structures thought, and language does not precede communication but is constituted by it, and communication is by definition interactive and inter-subjective, the knowledge of individuals and their identities are inherently social. Schematically:

sociality → communication → language → thought → identity →
consciousness

This represents a reversal of the order of older consciousness theories of knowledge and meaning.

Corresponding with this linguistic-cognitive imperative of the link from other to self there is a truth-theoretic imperative: if there is no basis for absolute, universal truth present to the mind from objective, external reality (based on elementary observational terms or statements, as in logical empiricism, or based on some Hegelian realization of absolute spirit), and truth can only be temporary and local, based on coherence in a 'seamless web' of knowledge, perception and language, then truth is inherently social, due to its dependence on coherence and language. Truth is of the same category of order as *langue* in Saussurian theory of language.

But there is more, which is perhaps more specific to postmodernism. The order of truth (in the coherence sense) and *langue* is general, but not strictly universal: there are no closed and clear necessary and sufficient conditions for correct usage of language or for truth judgements. In this sense the order is 'fuzzy'. It is this condition that allows for individuality and differentiation (in Saussurian language theory: *parole*, in Lyotard's parlance: 'paralogy'). This differentiation between individuals can go so far, yielding 'incommensurabilities' in discourse (cf. Lyotard), as to make communication problematic. Yet this is not to be deplored but to be greeted, because it is necessary for change; to provide leeway for *parole* to exercise its creative destruction. Or in other words: this warns us not to over-socialize socioeconomic science. There is still scope for an economic next to a sociological perspective, although in a form that is very different from neoclassical economics. While allowing for the creative destruction of entrepreneurship and innovation, it must accept a perspective of social interaction. It is not just that we 'need each other' in some vague or cosy sense, or out of moral obligation, but for deep reasons of epistemology and linguistics. Even if Etzioni were wrong, and we could do without the moral dimension, we would still need a self–other perspective for epistemological reasons.

To make allowance for the postmodern perspective on *parole*, we now need to correct our previous linear scheme running from other to self, to include the influence from self on other, by supplementing it with *parole* and bending the linear scheme into a circle, as illustrated in Figure 3.2.

Figure 3.2   The circle of self and other

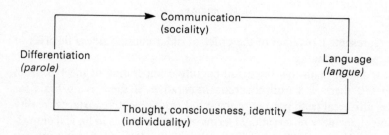

It is in this circular process that language, including claims of truth in the coherence sense, develops as a 'seamless web' (Quine), and continually transforms itself.

We have shown how the present perspective dismantles the methodological individidialism of neoclassical economics, and contributes to a better understanding of the interaction between economic agents and their environment in markets; between conduct and structure in industrial organization. Market structure is associated with Saussurian *langue*, and conduct with *parole*. In the same way that in language the differentiation of meaning is essential (in *parole*), product differentiation and innovation are essential in markets. They do not constitute a special case, an appendage to homogeneity, or a disturbance of an equilibrium that is the norm, but constitute the core of market activities. Thus the postmodern perspective provides depth to Schumpeterian theory in economics. We have shown how it links up, in marketing, with the development of exchange as the core concept of theory, with increasing emphasis on the two-sidedness of influence. In transaction cost economics it shifts the focus from the transaction to the relation in which transactions are embedded, with a feedback from the relation to the perceptions, knowledge, competences and perspectives of transaction partners. In each of these theoretical contexts the point is that identity is both constituted and constituting in the give and take of exchange. Thus we affirm the supposition that postmodern philosophy contributes to our insight in the working of markets, and provides a new perspective in which different theories concerning markets (industrial organization, marketing, transaction cost theory) are related; have a common core. In this perspective learning and change, in the interaction of agent and environment, are central, as opposed to traditional economic theory in which knowledge, technology and preferences are assumed to be given.

NOTES

1. See e.g. Bagozzi (1975, 1979, 1984) and Houston and Gassenheimer (1987).
2. See Adler (1966) and Varadarajan and Rajaratnam (1987), and Nooteboom (1992).
3. Elsewhere, in Nooteboom (1991), this is argued in more detail on the basis of the theory of transaction costs.
4. Cf. Harris (1988).
5. Vasterling (1987, p. 215); my translation from the Dutch.
6. Struyker Boudier (1987, p. 64); my translation.
7. Cf. Harris (1988), p. 14.
8. Saussure (1979), p. 162. The full and exact quote is as follows: 'instead of ideas given in advance, values emanating from the system. When one says that they correspond to concepts, one implicitly understands that these are purely differential, defined not positively by their content, but negatively by their relations with other terms of the system.

Their more exact characteristic is to be what the others are not' (my transalation; italics added).

9. It is not arbitrary in the sense that the connection between words and meaning can be changed at will. Clearly not by an individual, since meaning is conventional. But not usually by a conventional decision (by the plenum of some linguistic party, say) either, but more tacitly as the outcome of inter-subjective practice. To decide upon a change of meaning would require a possibly endless tracking through of the linguistic system to adjust meanings of other words related, directly or indirectly, by syntagmatic or associative linkage. This is impossible to plan and design, and is best left to the forces of discourse. Arbitrariness further does not equate randomness, and may allow for greater or lesser degrees of motivation for meaning–word combinations. Harris (1990) discusses the example of a word like 'nineteen', which is 'motivated', but not totally since it could have been 'teen-nine' as in French ('dix-neuf').

10. One might question what is meant in the present chapter by 'the social', 'social order' and 'sociality'. Camic (1989, p. 76) wrote: 'In the course of intellectual history, the concept of the social has been used to mean different things, among them relations, groups, institutions, patterns of change and more.' The meaning intended here and throughout this article is 'inter-subjective relations and their role in patterns of change'.

11. This notion of a fuzzy order in *langue*, to yield scope for *parole* and for language change, is not explicit in Wittgenstein or Saussure. Indeed, the parallels of games that they were fond of using to illustrate the working of language, in particular chess, suggest a fixity and rigour of order that is not characteristic of language. This is where the metaphor of games breaks down. Cf. Harris (1990).

12. Cf. Quine's famous statement, in Quine (1951): 'Total science is like a field of force whose boundary conditions are experience. A conflict with experience at the periphery occasions readjustments in the interior of the field. Truth values have to be redistributed over some of our statements. Re-evaluation of some statements entails re-evaluation of others, because of their logical interconnections.' See also his statement in Quine (1962) that our knowledge constitutes a seamless web, in which 'no statement, taken in isolation from its fellows, can admit of confirmation or infirmation [disconfirmation] at all', and 'our statements about the external world face the tribunal of sense experience not individually, but only as a corporate body'.

13. Saussure's diachronic studies were limited to phonetic change and its impact on grammar.

14. For an attempt to reconstruct the 'hard core' and the 'heuristics' of mainstream economics according to the 'methodology of scientific research programmes' of Lakatos (1970, 1978), see E.R. Weintraub (1988). This reconstruction sharply points up the assumptions concerning autonomy and rationality of economic agents.

15. For the progress that is being made, on the basis of Lancaster's notion of a multiple attribute space, for example, see up-to-date textbooks on industrial organization, such as for example Tirole (1989).

16. Arndt (1983).

17. This is related to Frank Knight's well-known distinction between risk and (fundamental) uncertainty.

18. Leeflang and Beukenkamp (1981), pp. 7–12.

19. Cf. Anderson (1983), p. 28.

20. Cf. Lyotard (1987), p. 169.

21. For case studies of co-operation in product development between producer and users, see also Biemans (1989).

22. Burt (1982) extends and formalizes the notion of influence without direct linkage with the concept of 'structural equivalence'.

23. We distinguish between governance 'structures' and 'schemes'. A governance structure, as treated in standard TCE, refers to the type of transaction and the parties involved: the market, a hierarchy, a bilateral or a trilateral structure. A governance scheme refers to a specific construct, in the form of agreements on content, procedures and rules, designed to govern a specific transaction.

REFERENCES

Adler, L. (1966), 'Symbiotic Marketing', *Harvard Business Review*, **44**, 59–71.

Anderson, P.F. (1983), 'Marketing, Scientific Progress, and Scientific Method', *Journal of Marketing*, **47**, 18–31.

Arndt, J. (1983), 'The Political Economy Paradigm: Foundation for Theory Building in Marketing', *Journal of Marketing*, **47**, 44-54.

Arrow, K.J. (1971), 'Economic Welfare and the Allocation of Resources for Invention', in D.M. Lamberton (ed.), *Economics of Information and Knowledge*, Harmondsworth: Penguin.

Bagozzi, R.P. (1975), 'Marketing as Exchange', *Journal of Marketing*, **39**, 32–9.

Bagozzi, R.P. (1979), 'Toward a Formal Theory of Marketing Exchanges', in O.C. Ferrell, S.W. Brown and C.W. Lamb (eds), *Conceptual and Theoretical Developments in Marketing*, Chicago: American Marketing Association.

Bagozzi, R.P. (1984), 'A Prospectus for Theory Construction in Marketing', *Journal of Marketing*, **48**, 11–29.

Biemans, W.G. (1989), 'Developing Innovations within Networks', PhD, University of Eindhoven, The Netherlands.

Burt, R. (1982), *Toward a Structural Theory of Action*, New York: Academic.

Camic, C. (1989), 'Structure after 50 Years: The Anatomy of a Charter', *American Journal of Sociology*, **95**, 38–107.

Day, G.S. and R. Wensley (1983), 'Marketing Theory with a Strategic Orientation', *Journal of Marketing*, **47**, 70–89.

Dwyer, F.R., P.H. Schurr and S. Oh (1987), 'Developing Buyer–Seller Relationships', *Journal of Marketing*, **51**, 11–27.

Etzioni, A. (1988), *The Moral Dimension: Toward a New Economics*, New York: The Free Press.

Habermas, J. (1982), *Theorie des kommunikativen Handelns, Teil I & II* [Theory of Communicative Action], Frankfurt: Suhrkamp.

Habermas, J. (1984), *Vorstudien und Ergänzungen zur Theorie des kommunikativen Handelns*, Frankfurt: Suhrkamp.

Håkansson, H. (ed.) (1982), *International Marketing and Purchasing of Industrial Goods – An Interaction Approach*, Chichester: Wiley.

Håkansson, H. (ed.) (1987), *Industrial Technological Development: A Network Approach*, London: Croom Helm.

Harris, R. (1988, 1990), *Language, Saussure and Wittgenstein*, London: Routledge.

Hellgren, B. and T. Stjernberg (1987), 'Networks: An Analytical Tool for Understanding Complex Decision Processes', *International Studies of Management and Organisation*, **17**, 88–102.

Hippel, E. von (1988), *The Sources of Invention*, Oxford: Oxford University Press.

Hodgson, G.M. (1988), *Economics and Institutions*, Cambridge; Polity Press.

Houston, F.S. and J.B. Gassenheimer (1987), 'Marketing and Exchange', *Journal of Marketing*, **47**, 3–18.

Johanson, J. and L.G. Mattson (1985), 'Marketing Investments and Market Investments in Industrial Networks', *International Journal of Research in Marketing*, **2**, 185–95.

Johanson, J. and L.G. Mattson (1987), *Interorganisational Relations in Industrial Systems – A Network Approach Compared with the Transaction Cost Approach*, Uppsala: University of Uppsala.

Kotler, P. (1972), 'A Generic Concept of Marketing', *Journal of Marketing*, **36**, 46–54.

Lakatos, I. (1970), 'Falsification and the Methodology of Scientific Research Programmes', in I. Lakatos and A. Musgrave (eds), *Criticism and the Growth of Knowledge*, Cambridge: Cambridge University Press.

Lakatos, I. (1978), *The Methodology of Scientific Research Programmes, Philosophical Papers Vols I & II*, ed. J. Worrall and G. Currie, Cambridge: Cambridge University Press.

Leeflang, P.S.H. and P.A. Beukenkamp (1981), *Probleemgebied Marketing* [Problem Area Marketing], Leiden: Stenfert Kroese.

Levinas, E. (1987), *Totalité et Infini* [Dutch translation], The Hague: Martinus Nijhoff.

Levitt, T. (1983), *The Marketing Imagination*, New York: The Free Press.

Lyotard, J.F. (1987), *La condition postmoderne* [Dutch translation], Kampen: Kok Agora.

Nooteboom, B. (1991), *Transaction Costs and the Role of Institutions*, working paper, School of Management and Organisation, Groningen University, Groningen, The Netherlands.

Nooteboom, B. (1992), 'Marketing, Reciprocity and Ethics', *Business Ethics*, A European Review, **1** (2), 110–16.

Quine, W.V.O. (1951), 'Two Dogmas of Empiricism', *Philosophical Review*, **60**, 20–43.

Quine, W.V.O. (1962), *From a Logical Point of View*, Cambridge, MA: Harvard University Press.

Saussure F. de (1979), *Cours de linguistique générale*, lectures given between 1906 and 1911 (first published in 1916), Paris: Payot.

Struyker Boudier (1987), 'Voorbij fenomenologie en structruralisme' [Beyond Phenomenology and Structuralism], in P.L. Assoun (ed.) *Hedendaagse Franse filosofen* [Contemporary French Philosophers], Assen/Maastricht: van Gorcum.

Sweeney, D.J. (1972), 'Marketing: Management Technology or Social Process?', *Journal of Marketing*, **36**, 3–10.

Tirole, J. (1989), *The Theory of Industrial Organization*, Cambridge MA: MIT Press.

Tucker, W.T. (1974), 'Future Directions in Marketing Theory', *Journal of Marketing*, **38**, 30–35.

Varadarajan, P. and D. Rajaratnam (1987), 'Symbiotic Marketing Revisited', *Journal of Marketing*, **50**, 7–17.

Vasterling, V. (1987), 'Jacques Derrida' [in Dutch], in P.L. Assoun (ed.), *Hedendaagse Franse filosofen* [Contemporary French Philosophers], Assen Maastricht: von Gorcum.

Weintraub, E.R. (1988), 'The Neo-Walrasian Program is Progressive', in N. de Marchi (ed.), *The Popperian Legacy in Economics*, Cambridge: Cambridge University Press.

Williamson, O.E. (1975), *Markets and Hierarchies: Analysis and Antitrust Implications*, New York: The Free Press.

Williamson, O.E. (1985), *The Economic Insitutions of Capitalism: Firms Markets, Relational Contracting*, New York: The Free Press.

Wittgenstein, L. (1976), *Philosophical Investigations* (first published 1953), Oxford: Basil Blackwell.

PART TWO

Privatization, Deregulation and Reregulation

4. Ownership and Control: Lessons for Privatization. A Case Study of the Austrian Industries Corporation

Kurt Bayer

This chapter investigates the problem of management control for corporations in transition from a nationalized to a private form of ownership. The theoretical framework applied is transaction cost analysis (TCA). Within the framework of TCA the proposition is developed that corporations require specific control mechanisms in order to monitor management. During the transition process of deregulating or of privatizing a nationalized corporation, special care must be taken to develop instruments to assure that corporations are not left solely at the discretion of management.

The case of deregulating the Austrian Industries Corporation (AIC) is used as an example of how not to deal with this question: the AIC was virtually handed over to management, after the rightful owner effectively eliminated himself from the control structure. If this happens in a country with an existing institutional and legal framework in place to deal with such a question, even more care must be taken during the privatization process in the new reform countries.

AN INSTITUTIONAL (TRANSACTION COST) FRAMEWORK TO CONTROL PROBLEMS

According to O. Williamson's pioneering arguments about contractual relations,[1] the owner–management relation of a firm can be viewed as a contract situation. Given the usual behavioural assumptions of bounded rationality and opportunism on the part of economic subjects, the question arises whether market ordering suffices as a control instrument to monitor management's performance, or whether specific 'private' ordering (special control instruments) must be devised in order to curb management's discretionary powers. Under the above assumption about economic agents' behaviour, management's information and operative advantages *vis-à-vis* controlling interests will lead

to managers being able to pursue their own preferences at the expense of
those of the owners.

There is little doubt that the relationship between a company owner and
management is (in Williamson's terms) 'asset specific' (see Williamson
1985, p. 305). While it may be argued that the individual small shareholder
may be indifferent about which companies he holds shares in (a k=0, asset-
unspecific relation; see Figure 4.1), because he can switch between different
assets, the totality of shareholders (or the single private or public shareholder)
or a specific corporation have additional interests. From a control point of
view the individual company owners can be seen as having a summary,
common interest in keeping the company in business (as a going concern).
This is even more true for a public owner, especially where private minority
owners do not exist. This interest can thus be interpreted as similar to an
'asset-specific' relationship (k>0).

If this is the case, the owner must make a decision whether to leave this
special relation unsecured (s=0), i.e. leave management control to the market,
or whether to devise special incentive mechanisms and control institutions,
in order to safeguard his interests (s>0).

Transaction cost reasoning helps solve this decision problem: if (actual or
potential) costs arise because of management being able to pursue its interests
in a relatively unfettered way,[2] special control instruments which incur

*Figure 4.1   Williamson's contract scheme extended to incorporate
            instrumental objectives*

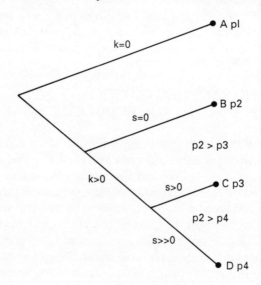

transaction costs can lead to lower total (product plus transaction) costs than market control. Such a collective (private) owner would locate at node C in Figure 4.1.

Neoclassical finance economics does not share this view. Among others, Henry Manne (1965) and Michael Jensen (e.g. 1988) have argued forcefully in favour of the strong control incentives exerted by the 'market for corporate control'. The latent threat that a badly run firm might be taken over, management replaced and 'new value' created would provide strong incentives for management to perform well in the eyes of the financial markets (and the owners). This argument has been contested widely. Criticism does not deny the existence of incentives exerted by a market for corporate control, but rather its effectiveness and the effects of an unregulated market for corporate control on the economy as a whole. Arguments applied to this critique refer to imperfections of the capital markets, the conditions of takeovers and their possible effects on the economy (see e.g. Ravenscraft and Scherer, 1987; Caves, 1989; Mueller, 1989; and Bayer, 1989 for a brief survey of the literature).

In reality, all corporations have some kind of 'private' ordering control system. These reach from the outside (non-executive) directors on the boards of Anglo-American-style corporations, to the board of supervisors in the two-tier German/Austrian companies, to the cross-share holdings and *noyaux durs* arrangements in French, Italian and Scandinavian companies, to the interlocking bank–industry directorates in Japanese firms. The specific market-private ordering mix differs widely from country to country and company to company, however.

In addition to these more formal control systems, a number of other restrictions work on managers, especially in publicly owned firms: e.g. political and institutional factors, sanctions available to politicians, the pressures of the market for managers (see Estrin and Perotin, 1991), and others.

If a public owner intends to pursue 'instrumental'[3] objectives by means of ownership rights in an industrial company under international competition (the only rational justification to maintain ownership in such companies, in contrast for example, to utility companies) in addition to those usually pursued by private owners, Williamson's simple contracting scheme should be extended by another node. If such a public owner decided to safeguard his specific interests in the company, he would locate at node D (Figure 4.1.) where total costs would be lower than at B (and possibly at C). This would mean that because of special interests to be safeguarded, special control institutions ($s>>0$) must be devised, which go beyond those of privately owned companies.[4] The assumption behind this reasoning is that otherwise, the owner (in this case the government, or society as a whole) would incur high costs in the form of a failure to achieve 'instrumental' objectives, in a number of macroeconomic and/or political areas. If these additional costs exceed the transaction costs incurred by setting up a specific monitoring mechanism, it would be rational to locate at D.

In order to achieve an optimal solution, the costs of setting up effective control instruments (transaction costs proper) must be compared to the costs arising to the company (and in the case of a nationalized firm also the costs to the national economy) from not instituting such instruments. Economically speaking, setting up additional control institutions will be advantageous only if total costs (sum of transaction plus production costs) are lower than the costs incurred in the absence of such an institution.

The argument of this section establishes quite clearly the need for special management control instruments in corporations, be they privately or publicly owned. Such instruments are necessary to assure the efficient functioning of corporations and their contribution to the well-being of the economy. This is not the place to discuss the desirability of 'instrumental' objectives being pursued by publicly owned companies. The case of the Austrian Industries Corporation, and much more so, the attempts in the Eastern European reform countries to privatize their nationalized conglomerates (or parts thereof) show that the mere size of these corporations alone warrants special attention to their fate. In the light of the above argument this would give a strong assumption for a rational owner to locate at node D. This would require special monitoring systems to be set up for managers, going even beyond the institutions known in the western countries.

CONTROL LOSS CAUSED BY AUSTRIAN INDUSTRIES' DEREGULATION

In the aftermath of the Second World War a large segment of the Austrian industrial sector was nationalized. The major part of the nationalized companies had been German property during the war. Most of coal and ore mining, the iron and steel industry, non-ferrous metals, petroleum and basic chemicals industries (around 70 firms altogether) were nationalized under the First Nationalization Act 1946. Austria's nationalized industries today are the single largest block of industries under public ownership in western industrial countries (relative to the size of the economy; see Hanisch, 1990). Today, the Austrian Industries Corporation[5] comprises around 13 per cent of manufacturing sales and employment and commodity exports, 19 per cent of manufacturing R&D expenditures and 20 per cent of investment.[6]

Since nationalization the organizational form of the AIC changed a number of times, as did the specific form of the execution of ownership rights. Party-political as well as functional considerations accounted for these changes.

The most recent change occurred in 1986, after Austrian industries had suffered severe losses in the market. The (politically) responsible government minister dismissed most of the top management, removed (formally) all party-political influence from the running of the corporation, and ordered to whole sector to be reorganized according to private-ownership criteria.[7]

The 1986 Austrian Industries Act subjugated the AIC to the rules of Austrian Corporation Act of 1965, removed all 'instrumental' (higher-order) objectives from the AIC's charter and gave the government minister the exclusive right to nominate the members of the supervisory board. Before then, this right had been split according to the relative representation in parliament among the two major parties. The subsequent 1987 Austrian Industries Finance Act decreed a 'last-time' capital influx (of around 30 billion Austrian Schillings, at the time more than US $2 billion), and removed all remaining control rights from parliament (see Riemer, 1990).

The AIC was organized in the form of a holding company with (at the time) six sectoral divisions (oil, chemicals, iron & steel, non-ferrous metals, electronics-electrical machinery, non-electrical machinery), with the holding company empowered to give directives to the divisions and receiving seats on their supervisory boards. The top executives of the divisions, together with the two top holding company executives form the board of an intermediate body controlling the divisions.

The 1986 Austrian Industries Act decreed that the (fourteen member) supervisory board of the Austrian Industries Holding Company be nominated by the Federal Minister for Public Enterprise and Transport with the exception of two members to be nominated by the Austrian Chamber of Labour. The only restriction to the minister's right to nomination is that one board member must be from the Ministry of Finance and one from his own ministry. The supervisory board is to be appointed by the relevant parliamentary committee. The AIC was exempted from the co-determination rules for Austrian corporations. Apart from this exemption and the specifics of the supervisory board nomination, the 1986 Act decrees that it is to be run like a private corporation.

Formally and on the surface the AIC today is just like any other Austrian corporation (with the exception that it is by far the largest). The events leading up to the 1986 Act, however, resulted in much more far-reaching steps. To appease the widespread public outrage expressed when information about serious financial losses, control loss, party-political and regional influence, mismanagement and corruption came to the fore in a very gradual fashion, the socialist-dominated government of the time set out to remove all party-political influence from the AIC. Since parliamentary elections were coming up in the fall of 1986, there was little time to seriously plan the restructuring of the AIC. Thus the 1986 Act was passed quickly, and the minister went so far into the direction of the promised 'de-politicization' of the company as to appoint mainly businessmen, lobbyists and bankers to its supervisory board. The provisions of the Austrian Corporate Act and this composition of the supervisory board make it impossible for the minister (as owner-representative) to exert legitimate ownership rights. In addition, the exemption from co-determination rules means that no employees' representatives are on the board, except the two nominated by the Austrian Chamber of Labour.[8]

According to Austrian corporate law, the supervisory board which is appointed by the General Assembly of shareholders has the task to supervise management and to participate in certain strategic decisions, such as approving major mergers and sell-offs (see Fehr and Van der Bellen, 1982). The board is to be guided primarily by the interests of the company, with secondary consideration for the interests of the shareholders, the employees and the general economy. Thus the board may disregard shareholders' interests (at the danger of not being reappointed next time) if it thinks they endanger the company.

The 1986 and 1987 Austrian Industries Acts, and even more strongly the actual practice of appointments to the board, have resulted in a self-emasculation of the rightful company owner.[9] This has reinforced the so-called 'management-monopoly' principle (the right to manage the company is reserved for management) in Austrian corporation law. In this way Austrian Industries' management has achieved an almost uncontrolled position of power in the company.

A twofold control-failure can be diagnosed for the AIC:

1. The present mode of appointing supervisory board members has caused the owner to be prevented from exercising his rightful ownership rights.[10] The owner cannot even act as a private owner would.
2. The removal of 'instrumental' company objectives from the AIC's charter in 1986 and parliamentary control rights in 1987 has in effect removed the reasons for public ownership. If public ownership is to make sense, it must be connected to specific, national economic political and social objectives (instrumental objectives) which the AIC is supposed to fulfil. Such objectives must be formulated and monitored by control instruments going beyond those necessary in private companies. Such objectives cannot be observed any longer; consequently no specific monitoring instruments exist. In addition no monitoring exists to assure that Austria's largest corporation is run so as to yield its largest benefit to the country. Mere (relative) size in itself would warrant special monitoring.

CONTROL SOLUTIONS FOR DEREGULATED OR PRIVATIZED CORPORATIONS

Power Distribution in Corporations across Countries

In western market economies corporate law and practice yield different control structures for corporations. In this brief survey the Anglo-American system and the German-Austrian system are confronted.

The comparison includes not only the principal–agent relationship, but also refers to the other 'players' in large corporations: these range from the employees, the capital markets (financing insitutions), regional and national economies to the political and social systems underlying economic activity. In order to keep the number of 'players' manageable, they are condensed into five groups, the owner(s), management, capital market, employees and the 'outside world'.

Table 4.1 shows typical power and influence constellations in an Anglo-American corporation (A), a German-Austrian corporation with widely dispersed ownership (B), one with a single or very dominant owner (C), a US leveraged buyout partnership (D) and – finally – just as a reference mark, an 'even' distribution of influence and power (E). These are not descriptions of real world corporations, but rather of 'typical' constellations. The table shows that employee and 'outside world' influence and control possibilities are weak in all types, that capital market influence is strong in the US/UK cases, but weak in the others and that management dominates in the US/UK corporate case and the German corporation with dispersed ownership and that the owners dominate in the German single-owner corporation and in the

Table 4.1   Power distribution in different types of corporations

	A	B	C	D	E
Management	1	1	3	3	2
Owner	2	2	1	1	2
Capital markets	1	3	3	1	2
Employees	–	3	3	3	2
Outsiders	3	2	2	3	2

1: dominant; 2: strong; 3: weak.
A: USA–UK
B: Germany – public corporation
C: Germany – owner corporation
D: LBO partnership
E: Even distribution

LBO partnership. In the last case the functions of the owner and the capital markets are combined.

If the control and power distribution of the AIC before and after deregulation is classified along the same lines, the pattern in Table 4.2 emerges. Now there exists a corporation with extreme management domination, where ownership interests are put in the hands of a board beyond the owner's control, capital market restrictions have increased and outside and employee representation has been weakened considerably. The gist of this comparison is that while deregulation has without doubt improved some of the factors leading up to the 1985 AI disaster (eliminating party-political influence in board and management appointments, restricting 'outside' intervention and inside intervention by non-business considerations, etc.) it has handed the fate of the AIC completely over to management.

Table 4.2   Control solutions, AIC

	Past	Now	Future
Management	3	1	2
Owner	1	3	2
Capital markets	0	3	2
Employees	1–2	3	2
Outsiders	1–2	3	2

1: dominant; 2: strong; 3: weak.

Control Issues in Austrian Corporate Law and in Reality

This short survey shows that control over the AIC lies predominantly in the hands of management. The top officers of the AIC are appointed by the supervisory board, which in turn is appointed by parliament, but nominated by the Federal Minister of Public Enterprise and Transport. Austrian corporate law requires the members of the supervisory board as well as the managers to primarily pursue the interests of 'the company'. They are legally liable for complying with this objective. Furthermore, corporation law puts management in a very strong position by awarding them a *monopoly right* to manage the firm. Thus, by law, Austrian corporations are typically management dominated.

Participatory and control rights of the supervisory board are restricted to expressly listed cases (Fehr and Van der Bellen 1982, p.130 ff.). The major right the board possesses is the power to appoint the top executives and to approve the annual financial statement. The supervisory board has no apparatus, the law permits only occasional consulting services and no permanent advisory body may be installed.[11] The owner, i.e. the General Assembly (in the case of the AIC, the minister) which appoints the board members to five-year terms may remove them only for grave reasons. In general, the majority owner appoints all board members, but there are some minority restrictions. For private companies, this need not represent a major problem, because it may rightly be assumed that the General Assembly of shareholders appoints members to the supervisory board who enjoy the trust of the owners.

An attempt to change the present composition of the board of the AIC, especially one which could be interpreted as showing personal or party-political preferences on the part of the minister in charge, would (in the absence of a thorough debate on the longer-term objectives of AIC) invariably arouse public opposition and loss of credibility for the minister's political party, since the present board was nominated under the heralded auspices of 'de-politicization' of the AIC.[12]

This situation strengthens the informational and power asymmetries in favour of management. In a number of cases AIC management (with the consent of the supervisory board) has taken decisions against the expressed will of the owner-representative (the minister), without any observable sanctions.[13] Such differences of opinion concerned certain sell-offs of major AIC operations, plus a number of other strategic decisions.

In addition to such (semi-)open differences between the owner-representative and the management, a number of problematic AIC management decisions could also be traced back to the lack of efficient control. Such decisions concern a number of reversals of major strategy elements for AIC core industries (e.g.: VÖEST-Alpine iron & steel works, reorganization of the AMAG aluminum division, mergers of chemical and oil operations, merger of machinery and electrical divisions). Such strategy reversals, and moreover the threat of control loss in strategic areas might in the medium run result in major costs to the company (see e.g. the recent clashes between AIC top management and its division holdings on the future of the company).[14]

Such cost elements of control failure include:

- costs to the company: direct costs of planning and strategy errors and reversals; indirect costs of reduced employee motivation; loss of goodwill to customers;
- costs to the economy: higher total costs, costs of loss subsidization by taxpayer; loss of export income; higher unemployment costs; higher costs of delayed action, etc.

In addition to these more economic considerations there is also a strong argument relating to democracy and concentration of power: If, as it is argued here, the Austrian Industries Corporation top management has practically unlimited control of one sixth to one fifth of Austrian industrial employment, investment, sales, exports and R&D potential, this can be seen as an unhealthy agglomeration of power. Furthermore, if the turnaround of AIC is completed in the near future and Austrian Industries Corporation starts to expand again, this unchecked power is likely to increase even more. Since there can be no guarantee that management's interests will always be in line with those of the owner, there is a potential danger that a costly and devastating power struggle might arise.[15] Even in the absence of such a strong scenario the non-existence of an effective system of checks and balances in this sensitive sector of Austrian industry and society could lead to high social costs.[16]

Control Alternatives for Deregulation and Privatization

Deregulation of the Austrian Industries Corporation can be used as a case study for the task of privatizing the large production conglomerates in Eastern European reform countries. The lesson to be learned is that the objective of deregulation and/or privatization must not lead to a neglect of the need for strong control elements essential for a smooth functioning of the deregulated/privatized corporations. Handing control over to management will lead to inefficiencies, waste of scarce resources, maldistributions of value added and – importantly – to a popular distrust in the functioning of the reform process.

In the case of the Austrian Industries Corporation the installation of an 'industry council' in between the owner and the supervisory board could help prevent further control loss (Bayer 1991). This industry council could be made up of five members (experts and representatives from stakeholder institutions) and appointed to (once renewable) six-year terms, should on the one hand advise the owner-representative with respect to 'instrumental' objectives and the effects of AIC on the Austrian economy, but also receive information and consulting rights *vis-à-vis* the management and monitor strategic development. A possible model for such a council is shown in Figure 4.2. Figure 4.3 shows how this body would fit into the existing net of institutions. In this way the individual functions to be fulfilled in a publicly owned industrial company would be taken care of by specialized institutions. The result would be a much more even distribution of power (interests) in the company, with the advantage that the Austrian Industries Corporation would function primarily to the advantage of its owners, and only secondarily to the benefit of its officers.[17]

Figure 4.2   Control model for Austrian Industries

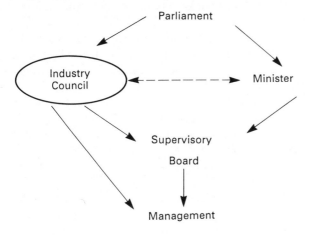

Figure 4.3   Locus of industry council

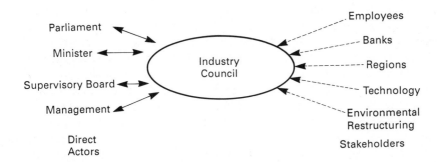

The advantage of such an industry council over strengthening the minister's direct control rights would be that the council would be a specialized agency exclusively concentrating on its monitoring task, while the minister has to fulfil a large number of other obligations and balance a large number of different interests. Further, the Council would be less liable to exert party-political influence and would also not be guided in its decision-making by legislative terms and election considerations. To this end, it would be advisable to appoint the Council member to six-year terms (the legislative period in Austria is four years), a period also better suited to strategic decision-making than a four-year period. In order to remove Council members' decisions from interest group influence, the members should be well-paid and have an appropriate staff. They should not have close ties to existing interest groups.

At this time such a solution does not conform to Austrian corporate law. For this reason a new legal framework for AIC needs to be devised (either a special statute, or a general statute for public enterprises), or AIC would have to be turned into a limited liability company (Gesellschaft mit beschränkter Haftung) in which a direct chain of command runs from the owner to the board to the manager (see Bayer, 1991, p. 51 ff).

Even if AIC is (partially) privatized in the future (there are plans to this effect), a new control structure will be needed, because it is hard to imagine that private investors will be content with leaving management in 'their' company unmonitored.

For the privatization of firms in Eastern European reform countries the need to establish clear and workable control structures is even more important, since the new/old managers in these firms possess even more information advantages *vis-à-vis* their owners than do those in the Western countries. In societies largely in flux, the opportunities to pursue managerial objectives at the expense of society are even larger than in the West.

As long as the state has ownership interests in these companies, clear statements and strategies as to which aims to pursue are necessary. Control bodies, e.g. in the ministries, or better, made up of non-governmental experts should be set up. A large number of proposals have by now been made, on how the transition process towards company reorganization and/or privatization could be organized (see e.g. Blanchard *et al.*, 1990). Many different forms of control mechanisms are discussed there. They often presuppose the existence of functioning capital markets as major monitoring devices. For quite a long time to come such capital markets will not exist in reform countries. Therefore private ordering mechanisms must be set up, in order to guide the transition process.

Whether or not priority should be given in these countries to solving the ownership question or the problems of restructuring,[18] the questions of management control are also likely to play a prominent role in these countries' future development.

NOTES

1. See e.g. Williamson (1985, 1989).
2. Of course, even without specific internal or external control or incentive mechanisms, even in the absence of a market for corporate control, management is not completely free to pursue its interests, since some degree of limitation is enforced by competition in the factor and commodity markets. Costs in this context arise from deviations from

profit maximization (profits forgone), or in a wider sense constitute the sum of those effects which arise from a principal–agent conflict, because management has control over the company.

3. By 'instrumental' objectives of a publicly owned firm are meant all those which the public owner intends to pursue in addition to purely profit-oriented ones. They include regional, structural, employment, technology, industrial policy, balance-of-payments and stability objectives (see e.g. the recent volume edited by Thiemeyer, 1990).

4. Estrin and Perotin paint the following picture of the control structure in publicly owned firms: 'The shareholder-management relationship of the firm monitored by the capital market is replaced in the public sector by a chain of principals and agents where the objectives are determined politically, to be conveyed by an institutionalised policy-making structure to management.' (Estrin and Perotin, 1991, p. 69).

5. The name, organization and governance structure of this conglomerate, which today comprises well over one hundred firms, changed several times. A recent count found ten different organizational forms during the past 45 years (Kepplinger, 1986).

6. During the peak years of the mid-1970s, these shares were between 20 per cent and 25 per cent.

7. In what follows, a 'private' company is owned by non-government institutions or persons, a 'public' firm owned by the public hand (at whichever level).

8. One of the two at present is the chairman of the federation of labour representatives of the AIC.

9. At this time the Austrian government still holds 100 per cent of the shares, but partial privatization is planned for 1992.

10. If the Minister of Public Enterprise were to remove the incumbent board members according to his legal rights, there would surely be a public outcry against 're-politicization'of the AIC.

11. The rationale behind this restriction is that supervisory board members are supposed to have enough expertise themselves.

12. For this reason, he is unlikely to advance such steps.

13. Such sanctions would also be illegal.

14. It need not be pointed out that all these decisions were taken by management with due approval by the supervisory board. So far no differences of opinion between the board and management have become public (see Fehr and Van der Bellen, 1982 on the 'real power' of the board *vis-à-vis* management).

15. In the inter-war period the Italian and German owners of industrial capital in Austria were already giving a helping hand to the rise of fascism in Austria (see März, 1986).

16. This does not mean that the two top executives of the Austrian Industries Corporation are not honourable men: there is not the slightest indication that they are not. But a sober analysis of their interests, in conjunction with the assumption of opportunism, will reveal the need of effective control mechanisms.

17. Additional checks on the balance of powers would be provided by commodity and financial markets. The present discussion abstracts from possible incentive schemes for managers.

18. The present chapter does not enter into the discussion of whether first to reorganize and then privatize. The author has strong preferences for solving reorganization questions ahead of the ownership question, but realizes the political importance of this issue.

REFERENCES

Bayer, K. (1989), *How Efficient is the Market for Corporate Control as an Incentive Mechanism?* (WIFO Working Papers 33), Vienna.

Bayer, K. (1991), *Zur optimalen Verfügungs- und Kontrollstruktur der Verstaatlichten Industrie*, Vienna.

Blanchard, O., R. Dornbusch, P. Krugman, R. Layard and L. Summers (1990), *Reform in Eastern Europe. Report of the WIDER World Economy Group*, Washington, DC.

Caves, R. (1989), 'Mergers, Takeovers and Economic Efficiency: Forsight vs. Hindsight', *International Journal of Industrial Organization*, **7** (1), 151–74.

Estrin, S. and V. Perotin (1991), 'Does Ownership always Matter?' *International Journal of Industrial Economics*, **9** (1), March, 55–72.

Fehr, E. and A. Van der Bellen (1982), 'Aufsichtsräte in öffentlichen Unternehmen', *Zeitschrift für öffentliche und gemeinwirtschaftliche Unternehmen*, **5**, 123–50.

Hanisch, W. (1990), 'Eigentümerrolle und wirtschaftspolitische Instrumentalisierung staatlich kontrollierter Industrieunternehmen', *Wirtschaft und Gesellschaft*, **2**, Vienna, 225–50.

Jensen, M. (1988), 'The Takeover Controversy: Analysis and Evidence', in Coffee, Lowenstein and Rose-Ackerman (eds), *Knights, Raiders and Targets*, Oxford, pp. 314–34.

Kepplinger, H. (1986), 'Bedeutung, Aufgaben und Probleme der verstaatlichten Industrie, *Wirschafts- und Socialpolitische Zeitschrift*, WISO, **9** (2), Linz, 2–38.

Manne, H. (1965), 'Mergers and the Market for Corporate Control', *Journal of Political Economy*, **73** (2), 110–26.

März, E. (1986), 'Eine Lanze für die Verstaatlichte!' in H. Kepplinger (ed.), *Ausbau statt Schrumpfung*, WISO, **9** (2), Linz, 17–26.

Mueller, D. (1989), 'Mergers, Causes, Effects and Policies', *International Journal of Industrial Organization*, **7** (1), 1–10.

Ravenscraft, D. and F. Scherer (1987), *Mergers, Sell-Offs and Economic Efficiency*, Washington DC: Brookings Institution.

Riemer, G. (1990), 'Die Bildung des ÖIAG-Konzerns', *Wirtschaftsrechtliche Blätter* **4**, Vienna, 1–54.

Thiemeyer, Th. (ed.) (1990), *Instrumentalfunktion öffentlicher Unternehmen*, Baden-Baden.

Williamson, O. (1985), *The Economic Institutions of Capitalism*, New York.

Williamson, O. (1989), 'Transaction Cost Economics', in R. Schmalensee and R.D.Willig (eds), *Handbook of Industrial Organization*, Vol. I, Amsterdam and New York: Elsevier.

5. Enterprise Behaviour in Hungary and Poland in the Transition to a Market Economy: Individual and Organizational Routines as a Barrier to Change

Wim Swaan and Maria Lissowska

1. INTRODUCTION

This study is concerned with enterprise behaviour in the transition from a centrally planned economy to a market economy. While there has been much attention to questions of economic policy and stabilization and the need of ownership changes in the previously centrally planned economies, there has been little analysis of the micro-level supply response to the disintegration of the old system on the one hand and to attempts at making a start with the transition to a market economy on the other hand (a notable exception is Murrell, 1990). The central argument of this chapter is that the initial supply response will have a strong negative impact on performance and the speed of the transition process, and that conventional policy instruments can influence this only weakly. At the level of the individual, human constraints put limitations on the speed of learning, whereas organizations tend to follow routines developed in the past, the continuation of which may aggravate the supply response in an unexpected way.

We will illustrate the argument with evidence from Hungary and Poland. These were among the first countries where the state socialist system disintegrated. Comparison of the two countries is particularly interesting in view of the entirely different policy choice they made in early stages of the transition: whereas Poland opted for a spectacular shock therapy, liberalization in Hungary was implemented step by step in about two years. Already under the system of central planning both countries had implemented substantial economic reforms: at the level of the enterprise compulsory planning instructions were abolished in Hungary in 1968 and in Poland in 1982, and replaced by a system of indirect bureaucratic control. A related paper provides an analysis of the impact of these reforms on enterprise behaviour and the process of economic learning (Swaan and Lissowska, 1992; see also Lissowska, 1990 and Swaan, 1991). This will prove to be useful as a frame of reference in the present analysis.

The structure of the chapter is as follows. In section 2 the main principles of our approach are set out. Section 3 briefly summarizes the process of disintegration of the old system and the policy choices made in Hungary and Poland in the period 1988–90. In section 4 we will see what factors related to the disintegration of the party-state bureaucracy may in the short run encourage a shift towards more market oriented routines and what factors rather delay this. Here we will also consider the possibilities and limitations of privatization as a policy instrument. In order to construct an analytical benchmark, in section 5 we will consider the impact of economic liberalization on behaviour under the assumption that enterprises continue to follow previously developed routines. In section 6 we will compare the available evidence on enterprise behaviour in the two countries with this benchmark of unchanged routines. In section 7 some implications are drawn as regards the process of marketization. First we raise the question how enterprises can afford to continue their previous inapt routines without facing troubles or without breaking down. Next we consider the implications for policy. Conclusions are drawn in section 8.

2. THE BEHAVIOURAL APPROACH TO INSTITUTIONAL CHANGE

The approach we take here extends the usual principle of methodological individualism in two important ways: first by taking account of the concrete history of particular individuals as a factor influencing their present behaviour, and secondly by acknowledging that behaviour of individuals is not autonomous, but embedded in formal and informal networks of social interaction. Whereas in stable environments it might be useful to abstract from these types of influence in the analysis of particular economic problems, it definitely leads to improper understanding, wrong predictions and ill-founded policy recommendations in times of thorough economic change. Our argument is not that conventional economic analysis cannot be applied at all to centrally planned economies in transition, but rather that it should be complemented with an explicit analysis of the particular history of the individuals and organizations in these countries.

A particularly useful assumption in analysing the supply response to systemic change is the notion that actors in all environments use to develop various procedures and routines as a guideline for their actions (see Simon,

1976, and in particular Nelson and Winter, 1982, pp. 14–19, 96–136). In view of their cognitive constraints, and to facilitate the process of searching, individuals and organizations deliberately limit the repertoire of actions to be considered. Frequently, this leads to a continuation of behaviour that under full knowledge and unbounded rationality would be sub-optimal (Heiner 1983). While in the end there might not be much difference with the assumption of full rationality, the process to that hypothetical final state might prove pivotal in understanding and predicting actually observed behaviour.

Accordingly, it is useful to distinguish two different types of influences on behaviour in the transition from a centrally planned economy to a market economy. On the one hand there is a structural impact to the extent that systemic change will lead agents to reconsider their repertoire of actions and adapt their routines. This impact will mainly make itself felt in the long run. It takes time for actors to consider actions outside their existing repertoire, and then to develop the skills to undertake these actions successfully. As we shall see, in the short and medium run there are even factors at work that discourage a change of routines. On the other hand there is the direct impact of economic liberalization, given particular behavioural routines as they developed in the past. Without the countervailing power of *ad hoc* bureaucratic interference, the continuation of routines developed under the old system may well have a negative impact on behaviour, outweighing for a time the positive impact of changing routines. The problem with enterprise behaviour under central planning was not its irrationality, but its *different* rationality, due to the different systemic environment (see for instance Kornai, 1980; Dembinski, 1991).

Our argument stands in the tradition of the behavioural view of institutional change, which goes back to the works of, *inter alios*, Menger, Hayek, Schumpeter, Kornai and Popper (Schotter, 1986, p.117–18; see also Ellman, forthcoming). This view sees institutions as the unintended outcome of human action, and is sceptical about the role of a benevolent social planner. Economic institutions and behaviour develop step by step in mutual interaction. In this chapter we will apply these considerations in particular to the process of privatization (section 4) and marketization (section 7). Readers who feel uncomfortable with the approach we take and would rather stick to the framework of individual maximization under unconstrained rationality are invited to read the chapter as an analysis of the various types of costs, for instance information costs, that agents in a previously centrally planned economy take into account when considering behavioural change.

3. THE DISINTEGRATION OF THE PARTY-STATE AND THE CHANGES IN ECONOMIC POLICY

Both in Hungary and in Poland the state socialist political system disintegrated very quickly during 1989. This was coupled with a change in economic policy and regulation and opened the way for the transition to a market economy. In both countries, constraints on the private sector and on capital imports were removed. This was coupled with a strict monetary policy and liberalization of prices, imports and trade in foreign exchange. In Poland these changes were implemented all at once in January 1990, as part of a stabilization programme, commonly known as the Polish shock therapy or the Balcerowicz programme. In Hungary liberalization was implemented step by step during 1988–90, partly parallel to the political disintegration of the party-state. Various radical measures, such as import and price liberalization and extended possibilities for the private sector were still prepared in the framework of the socialist party-state in 1988. Their implementation was started at the beginning of 1989. Monetary restrictions have been somewhat less severe in Hungary, which is related to the fact that inflation and shortages were more moderate than in Poland. Another difference is that by 1991 the domestic currency was still not formally convertible in Hungary, although the official and free market exchange rate hardly deviate from each other in practice. In both countries the privatization of existing state enterprises proceeds very slowly and appears to be full of practical problems.

4. THE DISINTEGRATION OF THE PARTY-STATE AND MANAGERIAL ROUTINES

In investigating the supply response to the disintegration of the party-state hierarchy and the related economic liberalization, let us first see to what extent the latter encourages a shift towards more market-oriented routines and to what extent it rather retards this. First we will formulate our argument in general terms, independent of the ownership form under which agents are working; then we will see to what extent privatization may be used as an instrument to enhance behavioural change.

Factors Retarding a Shift of Routines

In the short run there are basically two factors that are likely to delay the shift towards more market oriented routines. First of all, with circumstances changing from day to day, there is high *uncertainty* as to where the process of disintegration and transition will actually lead and at what speed. In 1990 the extent to which the old system was disintegrating still dominated over the establishment of a new system in Poland and Hungary. Note that the process of transition is not the outcome of a carefully planned programme, but that it follows from an unexpected disintegration of the old system. In addition to uncertainty there is *partial ignorance*: it is not just that people do not know which of the possible outcomes will eventually materialize, they may be completely unaware of some possible outcomes, or of the final effect of some of the developments they observe (on the distinction between uncertainty and ignorance see Loasby, 1976, in particular pp. 7–10). There is especially large ignorance among managers as to how to react effectively to changes in the environment.

As was emphasized by Heiner (1983, pp. 564–5) in his model of behavioural change, the decision to change a given repertoire of actions is not only dependent upon the potential gains of new types of actions (which have clearly increased in the new circumstances), but also on the degree of stability of the actor's environment. High instability in the environment leads to low reliability in selecting the right action at the right time and accordingly encourages actors to stick to their previously developed repertoire of actions. Heiner (1983, p. 562) speaks in this respect of a *C-D gap* between the agent's competence and the difficulty of the decision problem. In the context of centrally planned economies in transition we might add to this a *P-C gap* between the perception of the need for change and the capability and skilfulness to accomplish this: the awareness of the need for drastic change is no longer so rare – but most actors are ignorant of what to do or they are unable to implement it successfully. As we argue elsewhere in detail (Swaan and Lissowska, 1992), actors in a centrally planned economy suffer from strong cognitive constraints: they are not used to thinking in market concepts and are hardly exposed to examples which may function as a target for imitation. The disintegration of the old system even led to cognitive destruction: the knowledge of how to operate as a *homo sovieticus* or *homo systemicus* (Dembinski, 1991, pp. 47–9) has lost much of its value, whereas the knowledge of how to operate in a market economy has yet to be developed. Instead of focusing on input markets and the contradictory expectations of the various central organs, enterprises should now shift their attention to output markets. This *P-C gap* is a type of behavioural constraint which has no precedent in developed market economies, at least not in such a huge form and on such a massive scale.

The impact of environmental uncertainty on behaviour operates in a number of ways. As regards the composition of production and the investments to be made, there is uncertainty about the future development of relative prices and disposable income. This is reinforced by output and price shocks that arise as a result of the disintegration of the system. In addition, the possibility of overnight dismissal, due to changed property arrangements or anti-nomenklatura sentiments, may encourage incumbent management to be prudent in making strategic efforts. For actors at all levels, uncertainty is enhanced by the fact that the organizational equilibrium within which they were operating is disrupted by the disintegration of the hierarchy. As a consequence, the degree of trust and the quality of co-operation among the various actors at enterprise level is likely to suffer in the short run, in spite of the fact that political trust on a national level has clearly improved (see for instance Karpinska-Mizielinska, 1991, on the troublesome relations between directors and workers in post-socialist Polish enterprises; on the importance of trust in business organizations in general see Ouchi, 1981, and Aoki, 1990). Clearly, the organizational disruption caused by the disintegration of the system is in itself a positive development, as the current organization of firms appears to put a constraint on the development of market oriented behaviour (cf. Inzelt, 1988). The point we are making is that the new organizational equilibrium takes time to become established and that this has an impact on the speed of behavioural change. As the content and effectiveness of routines are closely related to the particular way a firm is organized (cf. Cyert and March, 1963; Nelson and Winter, 1982), the combined change of the institutional environment of the firm, its own organizational structure and the routines functioning within that structure will be both slower, and potentially more thorough than a change of routines within a stable organizational environment. Nonetheless, there clearly is a danger that the re-established external networks of the new business organizations, for instance their contacts with banks and with ministries, will be too much a continuation of the extensive networks of the party-state bureaucracy, with a similar negative impact on economic performance (see for instance Stark, 1990; Górniak and Jerschina, 1991; Crane, 1991).

Factors Enhancing a Shift in Routines

On the positive side, the disintegration of the party-state is easier to perceive than piecemeal changes within a system of bureaucratic control. Accordingly, it establishes a much clearer signal for managers that it is time to develop a more market-oriented attitude. In addition the potential rewards for successful behavioural change are clearly visible and much larger now. These rewards are especially high for entrants in the private sector, but some improvement may also be achieved within the state sector when regulation is tightened up properly, for instance by linking managerial remuneration more closely to market performance, and by shifting regulation from individual treatment by enterprise to general monetary and fiscal instruments. Previously, this type of regulatory shift was largely frustrated by the internal dynamics of the party-state bureaucracy, which was outside the direct control of the policymakers, and which led generic policy instruments mostly to degenerate into just another form of bureaucratic control (see for instance Laky, 1980; Kornai, 1986; Csanádi, 1987, 1989, 1990; Swaan, 1989, 1990).

The Impact of Previous Reforms on Economic Learning

The direct positive impact of the disintegration of the system is likely to be considerably stronger in countries where economic reforms had already put an end to orthodox systems of directive planning, such as Hungary and Poland (see also Crane, 1991). Although the reforms in themselves cannot be considered very successful, they paved the way to behavioural change after the disintegration of state socialism in two ways. Both of these effects are stronger in Hungary, where behavioural change in fact already started during the reforms, but they are also present in Poland (for details see Swaan and Lissowska, 1992).

First the reforms helped to create a small group of market-oriented enterprises that were constrained only by unproductive regulation and not so much by lack of economic competence. These firms may now push through, and quickly shift their frame of reference from a resource-constrained to a demand-constrained economy. For individual managers the barriers to exit disappear. In the old system these barriers were extremely high, both within the state sector and to the private sector, leading to low managerial mobility (cf. Laky, 1976). Managers who have won their spurs in a state firm may now easily find employment in a private firm or even find resources to found a firm by themselves, for instance by reorganizing (parts of) an existing state enterprise.

Secondly, through the reforms, managerial perception and cognition has been moulded in the direction of market concepts. Even the managers who previously behaved in a very passive manner, may after the disintegration of the old system appear to adapt themselves more quickly to market oriented behaviour than their colleagues in other countries, who were not exposed to economic reforms. We would especially point out the fact that the firms were already responsible themselves for the composition of production, implying that supply and demand were actually meeting, which in non-reformed countries still has to be established; and to the relatively developed domestic private sector in Hungary and Poland, which provided a source of learning by example for actors in the state sector; and to the shift towards financial concepts in bureaucratic bargaining and managerial thinking. The advantage of Hungary and Poland in this respect is of course relative: it will take managers considerable time to implement more market-oriented routines successfully. Properly speaking, the reforms rather mitigate the negative impact of behavioural habits inherited from the state socialist system.

The Potential Impact of Privatization on Managerial Routines

Our previous argument on why a shift towards market-oriented routines might be delayed actually applies not only to state firms, but also to agents in newly privatized firms. Clearly, under the circumstances we are talking about, a private firm would *in principle* in most cases be better suited to develop and implement new routines than a state firm would be, for instance by offering more appropriate incentives. In spite of this, the impact of privatization on performance is likely to be rather limited in the short run, as (potential) actors in the private sector face the same kinds of constraint as agents in the state sector: a lack of skills, uncertainty as to the direction and speed of change in the economy and underdeveloped or inappropriate organizational networks. These constraints are in fact also retarding the decision of individuals to leave the state sector and found or participate in a new private firm.

As was pointed out by Kornai (1990, pp. 50–57; 1991, pp. 3–15), successful privatization is a historical process, involving social and cultural developments of various kinds. Particularly important is the process of embourgeoisement, that is the development of an economically well endowed middle class. The countries of Eastern Europe have been badly lacking such a middle class in their history, first due to the unproductive domination by the nobility and later due to state socialism. Hunya (1991) makes the useful distinction between *surface privatization* by means of state measures, such as issuing vouchers or transferring property rights to new holding companies, and *deep privatization*, with institutional or personal owners who are able to exert effective control over their firms. Surface privatization might be an instrument to reach deep privatization at a later stage, but is in itself no guarantee of quick behavioural change. The barriers to effective privatization will be lower to the extent that previous reforms have already changed perception and cognition in the direction of market concepts. As an implicaton, the barriers are lower in Hungary than in Poland, and again lower in Poland than in other post-socialist countries. Privatization can be enhanced by proper policy measures, but effective or deep privatization would be rather a *result* of behavioural change than a technical policy instrument with which the new governments can influence managerial behaviour at will. In a similar fashion, it is impossible to create at one stroke the institutions which are indispensable to discipline enterprises in a market economy based on private ownership, such as financial markets, a banking system and an appropriate legal framework (see also Kowalik, 1991a, 1991b on these points). The actual functioning of these institutions ultimately depend upon the behaviour of people giving content to formal arrangements created by law; for example lawyers, judges, bankers and their staff. Here too people at all levels have to make themselves familiar with completely new routines. The common hope that quick privatization might break the links between the state and the enterprises and end bargaining over subsidies, underestimates the possibility that these networks simply continue independent of the policymakers' intentions and the formal institutional arrangements, as they did in the old system. As Stark (1990) says: 'If twenty years of experience with reforms demonstrated that markets are not possible without private ownership, the next decade of experiences with transformation in Hungary might yet demonstrate that private ownership is not sufficient to create thorough marketization.' In section 7 we will consider the limits to the speed of the marketization process in more detail.

5. THE IMPACT OF ECONOMIC LIBERALIZATION UNDER UNCHANGED ROUTINES

A priori considerations led us to assume that the impact of the disintegration of the system on the development of market-oriented routines will be fairly mixed in the short and possibly even in the medium run. In order to get a more precise view, let us as a first approximation single out one aspect, that of behavioural developments within existing state firms in manufacturing industry. This approach has both advantages and limitations. The advantage is that previous analysis of enterprise behaviour under reformed state socialism (Swaan and Lissowska, 1992) allows us to create a benchmark case of how state firms would react to economic liberalization under the assumption that they continue to follow previously developed routines. Comparison of this benchmark with actual behavioural developments may give an indication of the speed of structural change in behaviour. The limitation is that we will not be concerned with privatization in its various forms: the transformation of state firms into private firms, the exit of managers from the state sector into newly founded private firms and on behavioural developments within private firms. These questions are highly relevant to behavioural change during the transition process, but to exclude them from the present chapter is less serious than one might think. Although the number of private firms has been growing substantially in the first years of the transition in Hungary and Poland, most branches of manufacturing industry are still strongly dominated by the state sector in the period 1990–91. There has been a lot of restructuring of state firms into corporations, but with the exception of some acquisitions by foreign firms, these corporations ultimately continue to be owned by the state. In addition, as argued above, the future private sector in manufacturing industry has to be built largely on the managerial labour force of the existing state sector, which enhances the importance of understanding state enterprise behaviour in the first years of the transition. The privatization process in trade and services, and the spectacular, but nonetheless hesitant development of small-scale entrepreneurship in these sectors, has already gained wide attention elsewhere in the literature (see Laky, 1991; Stark, 1990, 1991; Hunya, 1991; Hare and Grosfeld, 1991).

In constructing our benchmark of state enterprise behaviour under unchanged routines, we will revert to two behavioural characteristics of the socialist firm. Neither of these was really affected by the reforms prior to the disintegration of state socialism:

1. the perverse short-run supply response to changes in price and output control, given a certain demand structure. This can be said to result from three sub-routines:
    (a) 'Do not dismiss resources, because what is superfluous today will be in short supply tomorrow';
    (b) 'React to relaxation of price control by raising prices';
    (c) 'React to relaxation of output control by lowering output'.

2. the weak response to exogenous shifts of the supply and demand curve, in particular to demand contraction. This is not so much a result of a particular routine, but rather implies the lack of routines that are normal in market economies:
    (a) 'There is no need to develop a market strategy' (compare Nelson and Winter, 1982, p. 133 on a market economy: 'the fundamental heuristic imperative for top management is: "Develop a strategy"');
    (b) 'There is no need to search for cost reductions, other than economizing on inputs in short supply' (cf. Burkett, 1986).

After having dealt with these two characteristics in detail we will investigate the multiplier effects and see what implications our argument has for the character of inflation in post-socialist countries. For clarification we will compare the assumed supply response of the firms with that of firms in a developed market economy faced with similar exogenous changes in their environment. Our argument will probably raise the question of how enterprises can afford to continue their previous inapt routines without facing trouble or without breaking down. This is indeed an important question, the answer to which greatly aids the understanding of the transition process, but treatment of it will be postponed to section 7.

The Perverse Short-run Supply Response

As a result of repeated bureaucratic bargaining and redistribution of excess resources the short-run supply curve of a socialist firm is downward sloping (cf. Kornai, 1985; Ellman, 1989, pp. 247–9). The enterprises have become effort minimizing monopolists subjected to continuous pressure by the authorities to satisfy demand on a higher output level and at lower prices. They tend to preserve shortages by choosing an output level below the level of demand as implied by the prices set or allowed by the authorities (see Figures 5.1 and 5.2).

Relaxation of the pressure of the authorities, or its complete disappearance, as in Poland in January 1990 and in Hungary gradually during 1989 and 1990, puts enterprises in the position of lowering supply while increasing prices, implying a reduction of productive efforts as reflected in the increased level of average costs. The perverse supply response is further reinforced by the fact that in the old system pressure to maintain a particular level of supply used to be coupled with allotment of various subsidies and resources, which will now either decrease or completely disappear.

As regards the habit of shortage-preserving supply behaviour, the disappearance of this depends in particular upon two things: first, the degree to which restrictions on the commodity convertibility of enterprise money are removed and a unitary currency is established (see also McKinnon, 1991, p. 119); secondly, the degree to which the disintegration of the networks of party and state organs puts an end to the 'balkanization' of regulation and taxation (see Szalai, 1991, on balkanized regulation and its impact). Both of these reduce the value of artificial, strategic shortages as a means of siphoning off extra resources and increase the value of money for sold products. When shortage-preserving supply behaviour eventually disappears, some equilibrium price will emerge (see Figure 5.3).

It is instructive to compare the expected response of a post-socialist, effort-minimizing firm with the textbook exposition of the impact of removing price controls on a profit-maximizing, competitive enterprise (Figure 5.4). In that exposition shortages are a consequence of keeping prices under their equilibrium level. Removal of price controls will lead to an expansion of output along the supply curve until equilibrium is reached at higher prices and higher output. In Figure 5.5 the supply response to price liberalization of an effort-minimizing monopolist (EMM) is compared with that of a profit-maximizing competitive enterprise (PMC). The effort-minimizing monopolist ends up with higher prices and lower output (point C), both in comparison with the situation before liberalization (point A) and with the supply response of the profit maximizing competitive enterprise (point B). Inexperience with the response of the market to price increases and uncertainty as regards input

Figure 5.1   *Supply and demand under indirect bureaucratic control (IBC)*

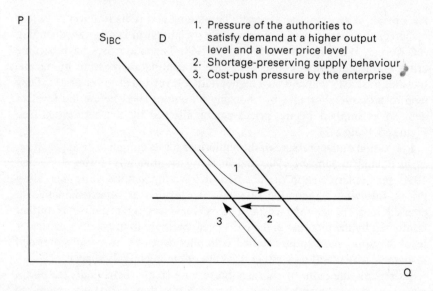

1. Pressure of the authorities to satisfy demand at a higher output level and a lower price level
2. Shortage-preserving supply behaviour
3. Cost-push pressure by the enterprise

Figure 5.2   *The supply response of a firm under indirect bureaucratic control (IBC) to relaxation or abolition of price controls*

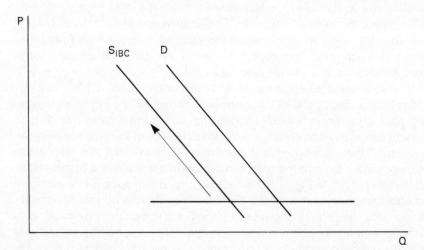

Figure 5.3   *The initial supply response of an effort-minimizing monopolist (EMM) to the process of transition from a bureaucratic economy to a market economy*

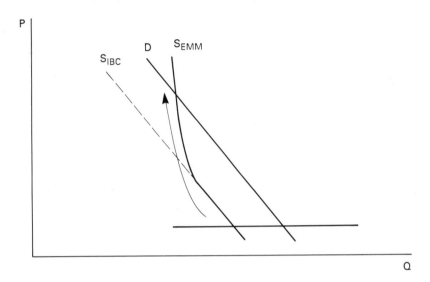

Figure 5.4   *The supply response of a profit-maximizing competitive enterprise (PMC) to price liberalization*

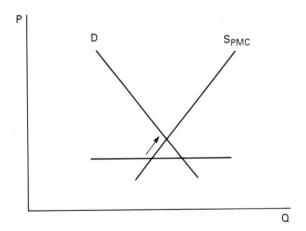

Figure 5.5   *The short-run supply response to price liberalization: the effort-minimizing monopolist (EMM) compared to the profit-maximizing competitive enterprise (PMC)*

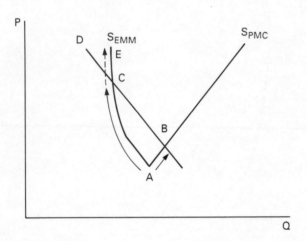

price developments may lead the post-socialist enterprises to increase their prices beyond the intersection with the demand curve (point E).

The Weak Ability to Absorb Cost Increases and Demand Shocks

Our discussion of Figures 5.1–5.5 concentrates on the movement *along* the supply curve as a response to the removal of price controls, given a certain demand structure. Economic liberalization will clearly also lead to a shift *of* the demand and supply curve of the firm. For most firms, both will shift to the left due to the increase of input prices and a reduction of subsidies (supply curve) and a decrease of real income of the population (demand curve), with a fall in output as a result. This is reinforced by multiplier effects (cf. Caselli and Pastrello, 1991).

In a developed market economy, such exogenous shocks (like the oil price shocks of the 1970s) not only *cause* a rearrangement of relative prices, they also lead to increased innovative efforts to counteract the fall of output. Process innovations and more efficient organization of existing technology reduce marginal unit costs and lead the supply curve of the firm to shift back to the right, whereas product improvement, changes in the product mix and entry into new markets make both the supply and demand curve of the firm move out to the right. Even if structural supply changes take a long time to be effectuated, and quantitative effects at first dominate over price effects, the fall in output is considerably dampened by short-run adaptation, such as accelerated implementation of existing innovation plans, minor product or process improvements, increased efforts to export to countries or regions not hit by the supply shock, and so on.

In previously centrally planned economies, like Hungary and Poland, this kind of supply response is likely to be much weaker, especially in the short and medium run. The degree to which firms can rely upon suitable existing innovation plans is much lower than in a market economy, and so is the degree to which their skills and routines are suitable for instantaneous adaptation to the changed circumstances. It should be noted that the way enterprises in the reformed system responded to falling demand differed considerably in Hungary and Poland. In Hungary an increasing number of firms were already concerned with shifting the demand curve for their products out to the right, even if the degree to which this happened was yet far from satisfactory. In Poland this was much less the case.

The Multiplier Effects of a Weak Supply Response

So far various aspects of the expected supply response of post-socialist enterprises to economic liberalization have been considered. It is useful to consider which of these will mainly have an impact in the short run, and which are likely to work in the long run as well.

The impact of the perverse supply curve on inflation and the fall of output will be especially strong in the short run as an immediate response to price liberalization and a reduction of subsidies. In the medium run the direct impact of a perverse supply response is likely to be much weaker, depending upon the degree to which liberalization puts an end to shortage-preserving supply behaviour and the degree to which expenditures are constrained by monetary policy – the less this succeeds, the more price liberalization will lead to continued price increases.

The weak ability to absorb cost increases and demand shocks, on the other hand, will make itself felt for a much longer period of time, as it requires extensive learning to improve on this. What is more, this behavioural shortcoming implies that the first-round effects of the perverse supply response will spill over to the next periods with multiplier effects larger, the higher managerial inabilities are. Consequently, not all of the fall in output arising after liberalizing a socialist economy can be considered a reduction of wasteful production: much of it results from the collapse of final demand and from weak managerial skills to adapt to changing circumstances (see also Ellman, forthcoming). Even if the decline of output in the state sector may be partly offset by growth of new firms in the private sector, the lack of economic competence in the economy as a whole will lead to a total fall in output (far) beyond the normal Keynesian multiplier effects in a market economy in depression. This aspect has not gained much attention in the literature. Winiecki (1990, pp. 781–3, 1991), for instance, acknowledges that the fall in output in Poland has been somewhat aggravated by policy mistakes, but basically welcomes it as a reduction of wasteful production.

Note also that weak managerial skills increase the vulnerability of the economy to external shocks, such as a loss in the terms of trade or a loss of export markets, as has been happening especially in trade with the Soviet Union.

The Character of Inflation

Another implication of the foregoing is that inflation in (post-)socialist countries is not of a purely monetary character. This behavioural, non-monetary component of inflation, which stands in close relation to the fall in output (cf. Figures 5.1–5.5), can best be named as *institutional-structural stagflation* (László Csapó in Tardos *et al.*, 1991, pp. 109–10, 193–5; see also Kolodko and McMahon, 1987; Balcerowicz, 1989; Bauer, 1990; and Kolodko *et al.*, 1991). The problem is *not* so much that enterprises are classical, rent-seeking monopolies as the conventional argument goes (see for instance Blanchard *et al.*, 1991, pp. 17–18). In view of the fact that the remuneration of managers in socialist enterprises is very low in absolute terms, even when including non-pecuniary benefits, it is somewhat odd to consider them as rent-seekers in the proper meaning of the word, as for instance Winiecki (1989) does. The problem rather is that they are leisure-seeking or effort minimizing monopolists with low managerial abilities. A normal rent-seeking monopolist in a developed economy would be concerned with expanding demand for its products and with pushing down unit costs in order to regain its rents, when faced with the type of shocks Polish and Hungarian enterprises have experienced. Post-socialist monopolists, however, are not interested or not able to absorb cost increases and sales reductions: they do not dispose of the required individual and organizational capabilities as a result of repeated leisure-seeking and persistent shortages on both input and output markets. The lower these capabilities are, and the less enterprises have been adapting the routines as they developed under orthodox central planning, the stronger the stagflationary pressure will be. Consequently, with output reductions in the state sector leading to lower tax income, and with enterprises possibly postponing tax payments, even committed stabilization policy is confronted with a structural budget deficit after some time (see for instance Winiecki,

1990, p. 783; McKinnon, 1991). Standard diagnoses of inflation in (post) socialist economies, independent of whether they are Keynesian or monetarist, tend to ignore these systemic and institutional aspects (cf. Dembinski and Morisset, 1990).

6. STATE ENTERPRISE BEHAVIOUR IN THE TRANSITION: THE AVAILABLE EVIDENCE

In the previous section we created a benchmark for how state firms would react to economic liberalization under the assumption that they continue to follow previously developed routines. Let us now confront this with actual behavioural developments, and see whether there is an indication of structural change, in the sense of a shift to market-oriented routines. It should be emphasized that the available evidence is necessarily limited and that no definitive claims can yet be made. This is partly because of the relatively short time that has passed, but especially because the chaotic nature of the disintegration process necessarily extends also to the quality of available information, which is scattered, unreliable and incomplete. We will confine ourselves here to the developments until the end of 1990.

Poland

The response of enterprises in Poland to the disintegration of the hierarchy and the shock therapy of the newly elected government was to adopt defensive recovery measures rather than active strategies (for overviews see Winiecki, 1990; Dabrowski *et al.*, 1991). Actually, the principal reaction of the firms to the stabilization programme was to implement huge price increases at the cost of falling output, in order to boost profits and to cover themselves against the uncertainty of input price increases (Dabrowski *et al.*, 1991, p. 19). They did not simultaneously determine prices and output in order to maximize profits as the textbook monopolist would do, but rather followed their traditional behavioural pattern of cost-plus pricing (Caselli and Pastrello, 1991, p. 65). Accordingly, various firms underestimated the fall of output, which led them to lower their prices from March to May (Boguszewski, 1991; Dabrowski *et al.*, 1991). The enterprises were very hesitant to dismiss employees, even when they were extremely superfluous in the period of deep recession. This made the fall in employment much lower than that in output. Enterprises preferred to squeeze wages or to send their workers on 'vacation', to avoid or postpone lay-offs as much as possible (Smuga, 1991a, & 1991b). This behaviour is both a new variation of labour hoarding and a means of protecting the workers as a response to pressure from the workers' councils. Clearly, this has dampened the depth of the recession (cf. Caselli and Pastrello, 1991).

The fall in output led some, but not all, firms to improve their sales performance through negotiating prices, anticipating the needs of buyers, creating or developing marketing and sales divisions, and selling directly to consumers on the streets (as the wholesale trade system proved to be extremely rigid and inefficient). In a sample of 50 firms, only 27 employed any new form of sales activities (Dabrowski *et al.*, 1991, pp. 20–23). Whereas small firms proved more flexible in adjustment to the home market, large firms with some experience in selling directly abroad were expanding their exports as a way of counterbalancing the fall of sales at home. Endeavours of this kind were successful in branches where no additional innovation was necessary to sell goods abroad, such as in food processing, textiles and clothing, machine parts, pulp and paper – but not in chemicals, electronics and machine tool industries (Dabrowski *et al.*, 1991).

Adjustment of the structure of production to market requirements, if considered at all, was mostly restricted to small changes in assortments or a change in the proportions of existing production. The introduction of completely new product lines, on the other hand, was initiated by only five firms out of a sample of 50, but none of these projects has yet been successfully completed (Dabrowski *et al.*, 1991, p. 22). On the whole, enterprises are still very reluctant to modernize their equipment and production. The extended economic crisis throughout the 1980s and the high decapitalization of equipment have led to a dramatic situation as regards capital stock. During 1990 this only deteriorated and investment in branches important to technological progress decreased. The uncertainty coupled with the disintegrating system, the recession and the expected shifts in the production structure of the economy made enterprises even less interested in technological innovation than before (Kotowicz, 1991a, 1991b).

During 1990 the differences in the possibilities and in initial endowments of Polish enterprises revealed themselves very clearly. There is a limited group of advanced producers disposing of modern technology, offering modern products, well established on the world markets. For them alleviation of shortages and of administrative obstacles was positive and they adjusted relatively easily to the more rigid financial environment. This is, however, a small minority. The majority of enterprises encountered a lack of skills and resources. Some of them were aware of possible actions, but found themselves unable to undertake them. Other companies even lack clear perception of the difficulties as well as the ability to imagine possible solutions.

It is interesting to note that the half-hearted changes and increased heterogeneity of market behaviour in the first year of the Polish stabilization programme are very similar to behavioural developments in Hungary from around the mid-eighties (see Swaan and Lissowska, 1992). The difference is mainly one of emphasis: in Poland in 1990 enterprises were more attentive to intensification of sales efforts given the product mix as it developed in the past, whereas in Hungary during the 1980s enterprises seem to have been somewhat more concerned with expanding and restructuring their range of activities. This is clearly related to the more developed marketing skills of Hungarian managers, but also reflects the different economic situations of the two countries: in Poland the fall of demand was relatively stronger and the scarcity and cost of capital relatively higher during 1990 than it was in Hungary throughout the 1980s (see for instance Kotowicz, 1991a, 1991b). Another similarity with Hungarian behaviour, both in the old system and in the transition, is the low sensitivity to cost increases of Polish enterprises during 1990. In spite of the strong demand contraction and continued increases in material costs and in wages, enterprises preferred to reduce output instead of looking for sources of increased efficiency. Only a few companies, for instance, were looking for cheaper suppliers abroad (Kolinska-Flakiewicz, 1991). The continued propensity of hoarding superfluous labour also points to weak cost sensitivity.

Hungary

In Hungary, economic liberalization was implemented gradually, albeit over a short period of time. Because of this and because of the fact that the process of behavioural change had already started some years before, we can note here mainly a continuation of previous practice, with behavioural change spreading at an accelerated pace. The type of behaviour that emerges can best be described as quasi-market-oriented. This has the following characteristics:

- Enterprises are somewhat more active on sales markets, both at home and on the world market.
- They are in general more interested in expanding or changing their range of activities than in enhancing the efficient utilization of existing capacity.
- Improved behaviour is mostly not the result of well developed market strategies, but rather arises *ad hoc* as a reply to changes in regulation or in the market environment.
- The changes are far from uniform: enterprises that completely fail to adapt, or even show a regression in behaviour, are no exception.

As this type of behaviour, as well as its limitations, has been discussed elsewhere in detail (Swaan and Lissowska, 1992), let us here just point out a few new developments.

By the end of 1989 the government initiated a strong decline of exports to the Soviet Union. This was part of a purposeful long-term strategy to divert trade to western markets, among other things as a result of the increased inability of the Soviet Union to comply with its commitments. Many (but not all) of the enterprises indeed succeeded in regaining a substantial part of their sales in western markets, which is quite surprising in view of their state socialist background, and the very low requirements of the Soviet market they were used to. It also differs from the Polish practice, where enterprises exporting to Soviet Union realized very late that with growing payment difficulties they should shift to other markets. A survey of 28 companies in the machine industry in Hungary, which were previously large exporters to the Soviet Union, nonetheless reveals several limitations, indicating that adjustment was not very profound. The new activities in the western market are mostly restricted to very few countries and both technical backwardness and insufficient knowledge of marketing techniques (including language knowledge) provide strong barriers to western exports. In addition, the companies are hardly or not involved with restructuring their productive capacity. Similar to developments in Poland, the companies are reluctant to dismiss (large) parts of the workforce, even when they are facing large decline of sales. Interestingly, an exception is formed by those enterprises which have been decentralized and/or transformed into a corporation (Viszt and Ványai, 1991; see also Tardos *et al.*, 1991, pp. 193–5).

During 1989 and 1990 shortages decreased in Hungary and for most products they eventually disappeared. This did not happen as quickly as in Poland, which is clearly due to the fact that bureaucratic control was abolished only gradually in Hungary, and that monetary policy and exchange rate policy aimed at gradually strengthening trust in the forint, instead of doing it at one stroke, as the Polish authorities attempted with the zloty. To put it in terms of Figure 5.5: in Poland we see a quick movement from A to E and then back to C in a few months' time, whereas in Hungary there is gradual movement from A to C over a period of two to three years.

Assessment

The available evidence of state enterprise behaviour in Hungary and Poland suggests that the degree of structural behavioural change was low in the first years of the transition. Most of the change is a marginal adaptation of previous behaviour, and is implemented in an *ad hoc*, emergency manner. The supply response of the firms to economic liberalization and the shock of a sudden fall in demand comes pretty close to applying unchanged routines to radically different circumstances. On the one hand, the short-run supply response to economic liberalization is perverse, leading to a fall in output and a rise in prices with a disproportionate growth of average cost, as is reflected in the higher labour/output ratios. On the other hand, the ability to set off a sudden fall of demand by adapting supply and by entering new markets is weak, although not completely absent. During the previous reform period the latter ability was already somewhat more strongly developed in Hungary than in Poland, as a result of a more stable environment, a greater degree of trust and the much longer time period through which agents were exposed to a reformed system (Swaan and Lissowska, 1992). The available evidence on the first years of the transition suggests that the difference has continued to exist at about the same order of magnitude, with significant, but no spectacular improvements taking place in both countries. Accordingly, the low capability of managers to absorb changes in costs and demand has reinforced the first-round negative effects of the disintegration of the system, such as the reduction of state subsidies and the collapse of CMEA trade.

The available evidence also suggests that the impact of the Polish shock therapy on enterprise performance has been extremely weak. On the positive side, the programme succeeded very quickly in establishing a unitary currency that enjoyed the trust of producers and consumers. This encouraged the use of monetary assets as a store of value, rather than physical assets, and made an end to the process of shortages breeding shortages in general and shortage-preserving supply behaviour in particular. This is indeed a result of major importance, both in view of the dramatic (and longstanding) degree of shortages prior to the stabilization programme, and in consideration of the repeated failures during the last two decades or so to end this annoying situation. These positive results do not, however, alter the fact that the supply response of enterprises as a whole was disappointing, to say the least. The perverse, effort-minimizing supply response was very strong, and the ability to absorb changes in costs and demand was even weaker than in Hungary.

These developments on the level of enterprises are also reflected in macroeconomic performance. The first years of the transition were characterized by a sharp fall of production. Especially in Poland, but also in Hungary this was much stronger than expected. In addition, inflation continued to be very high in Poland, in spite of the strict and consistent stabilization programme (see Table 5.1).

Clearly, the fall in output is not only due to the supply response of state enterprises, but is also related to contingent reasons, such as the collapse of the Soviet market during 1990 and 1991, the most important trade market of the two countries.

Table 5.1   Basic statistics for Hungary and Poland, 1989–91 (percentage change)*

	HUNGARY			POLAND		
	1989	1990	1991[†]	1989	1990	1991[†]
GDP	–0.2	–4.0	–8 to –7	–0.2	–14.9	–10 to –8
Inflation (Cons.pr.)	17.0	29.0	36 to 37	243.8	617.8	70
Convert. curr. trade						
Exports	4.9	9.3	23	0.3	34.5	16
Imports	7.2	2.7	66	6.4	–17.5	85
Ruble trade						
Exports	–6.0	–26.1	–91	0.0	–14.5	–86
Imports	–6.9	–17.8	–91	–3.4	–38.9	–85
Unemployment (percentage of the labour force, end-of-year)	0.1	0.5	9 to 10	0.0	6	11 to 12

* In constant prices, except inflation and unemployment.
[†] Data for 1991 are end-of-year estimates.

Source: National Statistical Offices of both countries.

7. THE SLOW PROCESS OF MARKETIZATION

Given the developments described above, the question occurs how firms are able to realize price increases under a regime of restrictive monetary policy, and how they can afford at the same time to lower output and hoard labour without much structural change, without going bankrupt and without even facing losses. Or in other words: why is policy unable to make an effective break to the structural stagflationary pressure of the economy? This question is relevant for both countries, but more for Poland, as the demand and price shock was much stronger there. Two groups of factors may explain these unexpected developments: money creation by enterprises and the low degree of effective competition in the economy.

Money Creation Beyond the Control of the Monetary Authorities

Broad money has been increasing quickly in both countries, especially through the growth of trade credit (Sobota, 1991; Sándor, 1991; Várhegyi, 1991). Often this is granted ex post by simply not insisting on delayed due payments.

Bankruptcy proceedings are instituted among state companies rarely or not at all. In Hungary the amount of payments due by companies as a proportion of their bank deposits varied between *c*. 0.25 and *c*. 0.5 during 1989 (Várhegyi, 1991, p. 135). In addition to this, enterprises may sell off secondary liquidities as a reply to monetary restrictions. During the first months of 1990 Polish enterprises did this on a large scale with their foreign currency accounts (Winiecki, 1990, p. 775). Even worse, enterprises may start eating up their (working) capital, either as a final desperate move, or as a conscious action of the employees and the incumbent management in anticipation of a change of ownership. As extensive discussions at a conference of Hungarian monetary experts make plain (Tardos *et al.*, 1991), even strong commitment by the monetary authorities cannot stop these kind of developments – at best they can limit their impact to a moderate extent. For instance, despite wide agreement among banks and policymakers on the need to start bankruptcy proceedings against a small group of obstinate debtors, it proves very difficult to do so, as these debtors do not owe anything to banks or other centrally controlled institutions, while their actual creditors are unwilling to undertake anything at all.

The Low Degree of Effective Competition

A second reason why firms face limited constraints on effort-minimizing endeavours is the low degree of effective competition in the economy. As already noted, the establishment of new private firms both by domestic actors and by foreign firms is occurring more quickly in trade and services than in manufacturing industry. The evidence suggests that in large parts of manufacturing industry competition at first will continue to be mainly of an inter-sectoral nature, and not so much between firms producing the same type of product – similar to the situation in the reformed planned system of Hungary during the 1980s (see Swaan and Lissowska, 1992 on this point). As far as entry occurs, this does not immediately weaken or threaten the position of existing state firms. One of the most important lessons of the first years of the transition is that well functioning markets do not arise at one stroke, but only gradually, and at a highly uneven pace throughout the economy (see for instance Svejnar, 1991, pp. 131–2).

From an evolutionary perspective, however, these findings are hardly surprising in an economy where there are not just some small gaps left open, but where markets for many products have been virtually non-existent and where the scarce resource 'economic competence' is supplied at an unusually low level (on the concept of economic competence as a scarce resource see Pelikan, 1989, 1991). The few actors endowed with sufficient economic competence first enter easy markets, and only move on to more difficult markets when new entrants make these markets less attractive or when they themselves have sufficiently enlarged their economic competence to engage in the more difficult activities. The degree of difficulty of a market depends upon such things as capital requirements (in view of the underdeveloped banking system), organizational complexity and the speed at which profits can be gained, and runs from simple arbitrage through street trade, retail trade and services, wholesale trade and commercial services to more complex activities in manufacturing industry. The lower the supply of economic competence and the higher the number of empty markets, the more slowly will this process of market establishment spread throughout the economy. By 1990, for instance, much of economic competence in the Soviet Union's private sector was engaged in retail arbitrage, whereas in Hungary it had moved on to complex commercial services and in some exceptional cases had even entered manufacturing industry.

Surprisingly, for many products even the impact of import competition is strongly limited in the short run. Due to the low export performance of these economies, the exchange rate of foreign currency is high in terms of purchasing power. The degree of price competition implied by import liberalization is accordingly low, as is supported by calculations of the Hungarian Price Office (Bodócsi, 1989). In addition, most imported goods are no effective substitute for the kind of products demanded by domestic purchasers (cf. Soós, 1991, p. 251).

The Limited Effectiveness of Economic Policy

The foregoing argument as to why enterprises face limited constraints on effort-minimizing endeavours has some implications for the effectiveness of economic policy, both marketization policy and macroeconomic policy. Let us consider each in turn.

First, while it is obvious that policy of various kinds is necessary to bring about mature markets (see for instance Svejnar, 1991, pp. 132–6), it is less generally acknowledged that policy is not the only factor explaining the speed of the marketization process. This is similar to what was said in section 4 about the possibilities and limitations of privatization as a policy instrument to influence behaviour. Our argument as to how economic competence gradually flows over from one market to the other implies that there is a strong interrelation between the degree of effective competition in the economy on the one hand and market behaviour and the development of economic competence on the other. Accordingly, the marketization process potentially has a strong self-reinforcing power. The more firms are behaving in a (quasi) market-oriented way, the stronger (inter-sectoral) competition will be, which in turn provides an incentive for firms to increase their efforts. As a result, economic competence develops over time as an outcome of the interactive process of competition and behaviour. Especially in manufacturing industry, competition will at first be between producers of different products rather than between firms operating in the same market. Note that this argument is in fact an extension of the familiar paradigm of industrial organization studies, which sees structure and conduct in mutual interaction and no longer as a one-way causal chain (cf. Scherer, 1980, pp. 3–7).

Secondly, and even more serious, is the point that the effectiveness of macroeconomic policy is greatly weakened by the behavioural characteristics of post-socialist enterprises and the slow process of marketization. With structural stagflationary pressure (see section 5), the scope of manoeuver for policymakers is very narrow. On the one hand, the possibilities for combating inflation effectively through monetary policy are strongly limited. On the other hand, measures that push up inflation or reduce output should be applied very carefully, or indeed avoided completely (see also Soós, 1991). It is relatively easy to create high inflation, or to bring about a strong contraction of the economy, but as a result of the supply response of enterprises and the weak recovery mechanisms in the economy as a whole, it is very difficult to get the economy back on the track of low inflation or at the previous output level. This leads not only to the conventional recommendation that loosening monetary discipline should be avoided wherever technically possible, it also means that shock policies should be applied much more carefully than is generally assumed. Not only is the state sector unable to absorb the demand shock, the growth of the private sector will also be hampered by the depression (see also Murrell, 1990, p. 11). Private firms will not be exempt from the effect of the falling purchasing power of the population, whatever preferential treatment they may get from the government. Furthermore, much private enterprise in the formerly centrally planned economies is closely intertwined with the state sector, due to its origin in the second economy. It was noted above that not all of the output fall in the state sector due to stabilization policies can be welcomed as a sign that wasteful production is decreasing. This is especially so when wholesale and retail trade are not well developed. There is strong indication that this has reinforced the negative impact of the shock therapy in Poland in 1990 (see for instance Dabrowski *et al.*, 1991, p. 19). Whereas many observers welcomed the unusually widespread street trade as a sign of marketization, it was rather a sign of disintegrating of existing retail markets, which reinforced the fall in output.

The main argument developed in this chapter is summarized in Figure 5.6. This illustrates that market behaviour in previously centrally planned economies is not a direct result of privatization, the establishment of proper market institutions and monetary stabilization, the three factors that are usually identified as the key issues in understanding economic performance in

Figure 5.6   Policy issues and their impact on performance in the transition process: an evolutionary view

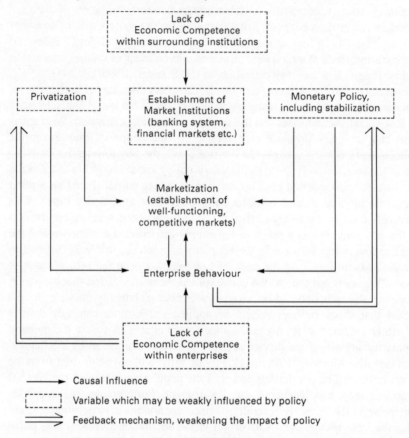

Note: In the long run, there clearly is positive feedback from marketization to economic competence within enterprises. This is not represented here because it is at first dominated by the negative feedback mechanisms.

economies in transition. The argument developed here contrasts with this conventional view in three respects. First, we pointed to the importance of economic competence as a fourth issue influencing market behaviour. As the level of economic competence is low and grows only slowly, this factor will at first dominate over the potential progress made with respect to the other three issues. Secondly, we pointed to the limitations of economic policy as a means of influencing privatization, marketization and even monetary stabilization. Thirdly, we drew attention to feedback mechanisms between economic competence and market behaviour on the one hand and privatization, monetary stabilization and marketization on the other.

Hungary as an Example?

Let us return from the general argument on economic transition to the actual developments in the two countries under investigation. Comparison of the transition process in Poland in the years 1988–90 with that in Hungary gives the interesting result that shock therapy is not the only way to bring about economic liberalization. What is more, gradual liberalization in Hungary, which followed a reform period of two decades, had a more favourable impact on both enterprise behaviour and macro performance than did the shock therapy in Poland. To be sure, this can be attributed partly to the very unfortunate developments in Poland in the decade preceding the disintegration of the system.The economy was in stagnation throughout the 1980s, as an after-effect of the crisis at the beginning of the decade, and, the Polish reforms of 1982 had been preceded by various unsuccessful reform experiments in earlier periods. However, even if one takes this into account, the foregoing conclusion is very disquieting, precisely because the shock therapy was designed to end the sequence of ill-fated reforms.

Does this mean that the Hungarian example of first reforming the centrally planned system and then liberalizing quickly, but gradually, can be and should be copied by other countries, or that Poland would have been better off if it had done so? Unfortunately, there are strong limitations to both the desirability and the feasibility of following the Hungarian example (see also Mizsei, 1988; Csaba, 1989; Bauer, 1990, and Aven, 1990, on this issue). First, the relative success or, properly speaking, the lower degree of failure of the Hungarian economic reforms was not just the result of proper policy measures, but was also helped by a set of social and economic conditions that are not always present elsewhere and that cannot be created at will (see Swaan and Lissowska, 1992 for details). Secondly, the system of indirect bureaucratic control depended on a powerful state bureaucracy supported by and entangled with a yet more powerful party bureaucracy. This kind of environment has stopped existing everywhere in Eastern Europe, implying that indirect bureaucratic control as a comprehensive system is simply not feasible, even as a short intermediary stage. Thirdly, the system of comprehensive indirect bureaucratic control was coupled with various negative effects, and some of the positive results were only reached after fifteen to twenty years. This is not really what one would expect from a successful policy package. Fourthly, more in general, the fact that behaviour and economic competence develop as a result of a learning process indicates the limitations of influencing behaviour instantaneously through a specific policy package or by creating particular institutional configurations.

Implications for Economic Research

Although this study accordingly does not lead to ready-made policy recommendations, it highlights the importance of economic competence and learning as variables which deserve more careful attention from (policy-oriented) economic research. It seems to be more fruitful to anticipate normal human constraints and to tune in to limitations of cognition, learning and behaviour, than afterwards to blame particular actors for not adapting as quickly as the policymakers expected them to. Followers of conventional policy analysis possibly would not deny the importance of learning, but they mostly take it for granted that learning will automatically be enhanced by their programme. This holds in fact for most currents on the policy spectrum, from advocates of quick stabilization and privatization to advocates of slow, state-led adjustment with industrial policy dominating, to mention just two extremes. By not taking explicit account of the fact that well-functioning economic systems are the outcome of a learning process of decades, if not centuries, the impact of measures is likely to be largely overestimated – independent of whether one tries to imitate the Japanese, the German, the Swedish, the South Korean or whatever example. We are not implying that conventional policy recommendations are utterly worthless. Rather, we would suggest that the problem of economic learning poses a challenge to general economics. A better understanding of how economic learning is taking place, and of how to enhance it in the East European context, might indeed prove a useful complement to existing policy recommendations. There appear to be strong doubts about the tenability of the conventional views of economic history as a teleological process and rational selection processes as the main driving force of economic evolution (see Dow, 1987; Seal, 1990). In view of these doubts, increased attention to individual and organizational learning is warranted in order to understand the process of economic evolution.

8. CONCLUSIONS

This chapter has been concerned with the supply response to economic liberalization in Poland and Hungary, in particular that of state-owned firms in manufacturing industry. It was argued that the degree of structural behavioural change is low in the first years of the transition. Most of the change is a marginal adaptation of previous behaviour, and is implemented in an *ad hoc*, emergency manner. The weak supply response is a consequence of the fact that individuals and organizations develop procedures and routines as a guideline for their economic actions, instead of continuously adapting and optimizing their behaviour in view of the expected outcome. This behavioural characteristic is motivated by the cognitive constraints human beings face and by the costs of acquiring full information. As a result, the speed of change is limited in the event of a suddenly changing environment (sections 2 and 4). Although this notion applies to actors in any kind of economic system, its impact is reinforced in the East European context by the sudden disruption of organizational equilibria and the low level of prevailing economic competence. As a consequence, economic liberalization leads only very gradually to improved behaviour, even if it is coupled with substantial privatization. Note that the weaknesses in enterprise behaviour are not so much related to conscious obstruction, rent-seeking or particular human defects, but are rather seen to result from normal human constraints, especially as regards the human ability of cognition and adaptation.

In particular two behavioural characteristics of post-socialist firms aggravate their supply response (section 5). On the one hand, the short-run response to economic liberalization is perverse, leading to a fall in output and a rise in prices with a disproportionate growth in average cost (see Figures 5.1–5.5). On the other hand, the ability to set off a sudden fall of demand by adapting supply and by entering new markets is weak, although not completely absent. During the previous reform period the latter ability was already somewhat more strongly developed in Hungary than in Poland, as a result of a more favourable environment to economic learning. The available evidence on the first years of the transition suggests that the difference between the two countries has continued to exist at about the same order of magnitude, with significant, but no spectacular improvements taking place (section 6). As a consequence, there is a strong structural (or behavioural) inflationary pressure in both countries.

Unfortunately, there appear to be strong limitations to the possibilities of influencing enterprise behaviour by economic policy (section 7). Privatization, monetary stabilization and marketization develop in strong interaction with economic competence and market behaviour. This implies that the speed of the transition process and the potential impact of policy are strongly limited by the initial conditions: the prevailing lack of economic competence and the behavioural routines as developed under the previous economic system (Figure 5.6). In addition, it seems neither desirable nor feasible to imitate the Hungarian reform example to its full extent in other countries. As an alternative, and as a complement to existing knowledge, we called for more explicit attention to economic competence and economic learning as objects of research in the field of general economics.

ACKNOWLEDGEMENTS

Earlier versions of this chapter were presented at the Dutch ECOZOEK-meeting (May 1991), the London School of Economics (June 1991), the Leuven Institute for Central and East European Studies (June 1991), and the Annual Conference of the European Association for Evolutionary Political Economy in Vienna (November 1991). Without implying responsibility we are particularly indebted to Guido Biessen, Andrzej Byrt, Keith Cowling, Michael Ellman, Saul Estrin, László Géza, Marek Góra, Attila Havas, Marvin Jackson, Kamilla Lányi, Jan Larosse, Krzysztof Markowski, Claude Menard, Agnes Nagy, Mieczys-ław Szostak and Zbigniew Zajda for remarks, criticism and suggestions of various kinds. Sections 3 and 6 and parts of section 7 were jointly developed by both authors, while the remaining sections are mainly the work of the first author.

REFERENCES

Aoki, Masahiko (1990), 'Toward an Economic Model of the Japanese Firm', *Journal of Economic Literature*, **28**, (1), 1–27.
Aven, Peter A. (1990), 'Economic Reform: Different Results from Similar Actions, Paper presented to the first conference of the European Association for Comparative Economic Studies, Verona, September.
Balcerowicz, Leszek (1989), *Systemy Gospodarcze: Elementy Analizy Porownawczej* (Economic Systems: Elements of Comparative Analysis), Warsaw: Central School of Planning and Statistics, Monografie i Opracowania No. 281.
Bauer, Tamás (1990), 'The Microeconomics of Inflation under Economic Reforms: Enterprises and their Environment', paper presented to the EDI/World Bank Seminar 'Managing Inflation in Socialist Economies', Warsaw, March.
Blanchard, Olivier, Rudiger Dornbusch, Paul Krugman, Richard Layard and Lawrence Summers (1991), *Reform in Eastern Europe*, Cambridge, MA: MIT Press.
Bodócsi, András (1989), 'Az importliberalizálás és az árak: csodák márpedig nincsenek' (Import liberalization and Prices: Still No Miracles), *Figyelö*, **33**, (35), 31 August, 9.
Boguszewski, Piotr (1991), 'Ceny' (Prices), *Zycie Gospodarcze*, **46**, (20), 19 May, Supplement of the Institute of the National Economy IGN, p.III.
Burkett, John (1986), 'Search, Selection and Shortage in an Industry Composed of Labor-Managed Firms', *Journal of Comparative Economics*, **10**, (1), 26–40.
Caselli, Gian Paolo and Gabriele Pastrello (1991), 'The 1990 Polish Recession: A Case of Truncated Multiplier Process', *Most*, **1**,(3), 51–68.
Crane, Keith (1991), 'Institutional Legacies and the Economic, Social and Political Environment for Transition in Hungary and Poland', *American Economic Review*, **81**, (2), *Papers & Proceedings*, 318–22.
Csaba, László (1989), 'Some Lessons from Two Decades of Economic Reform in Hungary', *Communist Economies*, **1**, (1), 17–29.
Csanádi, Mária (1987), 'A döntési mechanizmus szerkezetéröl' (On the structure of the Mechanism of Decision-making), *Társadalomkutatás*, **4**, (December), 5–27.

Csanádi, Mária (1989), 'A pártállam-rendszer szerkezete, kohéziója és szétesé se Magyarorszá g példáján' (The Structure, Cohesion and Disintegration of the Party-state System: the Case of Hungary), *Gazdaság*, **23**, (4), 5–36.

Csanádi, Mária (1990), 'Beyond the Image: the Case of Hungary', *Social Research*, **57**, (2), 321–46.

Cyert, Richard M. and James G. March (1963), *A Behavioural Theory of the Firm*, Englewood Cliffs, NJ: Prentice-Hall.

Dabrowski, Janusz M., Michał Federowicz and Anthony Levitas (1991), *Report on Polish State Enterprises in 1990*, Gdansk: Research Center for Marketization and Property Reform, mimeo.

Dembinski, Pawel H. (1991), *The Logic of The Planned Economy: The Seeds of the Collapse*, Oxford: Oxford University Press.

Dembinski, Pawel and Jacques Morisset (1990), 'IMF Stabilization Policies in Latin America and Eastern Europe: a Tentative Assessment', Paper presented to the first conference of the European Association for Comparative Economic Studies, Verona, September.

Dow, Gregory K. (1987), 'The Function of Authority in Transaction Cost Economics', *Journal of Economic Behaviour and Organization*, **8**, (1), 13–38.

Ellman, Michael (1989), *Socialist Planning*, 2nd ed, Cambridge: Cambridge University Press.

Ellman, Michael (forthcoming), 'General Aspects of Transition', in M. Ellman, E. Gaider and G. Kolodko, *Economic Transition in Eastern Europe*, De Vries lecture No. 2, Oxford: Basil Blackwell.

Górniak, Jarosław and Jan Jerschina (1991), 'Out of Corporatism towards ... Neocorporatism?', Paper presented to the annual conference of the European Association for Evolutionary Political Economy, Vienna, November.

Hare, Paul and Irena Grosfeld (1991), 'Privatization in Hungary, Poland and Czechoslovakia', London: Centre for Economic Policy Research, Discussion Paper No. 544, April.

Heiner, Ronald A. (1983), 'The Origin of Predictable Behaviour', *American Economic Review*, **73**, (4), 560–95.

Hunya, Gábor (1991), *Speed and Level of Privatization of Big Enterprises in Central and Eastern Europe - General Concepts and Hungarian Practice*, Vienna: Wiener Institut für Internationale Wirtschaftsvergleiche, Forschungsberichte No. 176, November.

Inzelt, Annamária (1988), *Rendellenességek az ipar szervezetében* (Anomalies in the Structure of Industry), Budapest: Közgazdasági és Jogi Könyvkiadó.

Karpinska-Mizielinska, Wanda (1991), 'Dyrektor a warunkach transformacji' (The Director in Conditions of Transformation), *Zycie Gospodarcze*, **46**, (20), 19 May, Supplement of the Institute of the National Economy IGN, p.I.

Kolinska-Flakiewicz, D. (1991), 'Zaopatrzenie i produkcja' (Inputs and Production), *Zycie Gospodarcze*, **46**, (24), 16 June, Supplement of the Institute of the National Economy IGN, p.II.

Kolodko, Grzegorz W. and Walter W. McMahon (1987), 'Stagflation and Shortageflation: A Comparative Approach', *Kyklos*, **40**, (2), 176–97.

Kolodko, Grzegorz W., Danuta Gotz-Kozierkiewicz and Elzbieta Skrzeszewska-Paczek (1991), *Hiperinflacja i stabilizacja w gospodarce postsocjalistycznej* (Hyperinflation and Stabilization in a Post-Socialist Economy), Warsaw: Instytut Finansow.

Kornai, János (1980), *The Economics of Shortage*, Amsterdam: North Holland.

Kornai, János (1985), 'Gomulka on the Soft Budget Constraint: a Reply', *Economics of Planning*, **19**, (2), 49–55.

Kornai, János (1986), 'The Hungarian Reform Process: Visions, Hopes and Reality', *Journal of Economic Literature*, **24**, (4), 1687–737.

Kornai, János (1990), *The Road to a Free Economy: Shifting from a Socialist System, the Case of Hungary*, New York: W.W Norton.

Kornai, János (1991), *'The Principles of Privatization in Eastern Europe'*, Cambridge, MA: Harvard Institute of Economic Research, Discussion Paper No. 1567, forthcoming in *De Economist*.

Kotowicz, Joanna (1991a), 'Progi i bariery' (Barriers), *Zycie Gospodarcze*, **46**, (20), 19 May, Supplement of the Institute of the National Economy IGN, p.I.

Kotowicz, Joanna (1991b), 'Pobudzanie zdolnosci rozwojowej' (Promoting New Capacity Creation), *Zycie Gospodarcze*, **46**, (24), 16 June, Supplement of the Institute of the National Economy IGN, p.III.

Kowalik, Tadeusz (1991a), 'Privatization and Social Participation: the Polish Case', Paper presented to the UNRIDS/ISS Workshop on Participation and Changes in Property Relations in East-Central Europe and the Soviet Union, The Hague, May.

Kowalik, Tadeusz (1991b), 'Marketization and Privatization: the Polish Case', *The Socialist Register*, **27**, 259–78.

Laky, Teréz (1976), 'Attachment to the Enterprise in Hungary: Societal Determination of Enterprise Interest in Development', *Acta Oeconomica*, **17**, (3–4), 269–84.

Laky, Teréz (1980), 'The Hidden Mechanism of Recentralisation in Hungary', *Acta Oeconomica*, **24**, (1-2), 95–109.

Laky, Teréz (1991), 'Small Business Organizations in the Hungarian Economy', The Hague: Institute of Social Studies, Industrialization Seminar Paper 91–2/5.

Lissowska, Maria (1990), 'Recent Changes in the Behaviour of Polish Enterprises Compared to Classical Socialist and Free-market Systems', Paper presented to the first conference of the European Association for Comparative Economic Studies, Verona, September.

Loasby, Brian (1976), *Choice, Complexity and Ignorance*, Cambridge: Cambridge University Press.

McKinnon, Ronald I. (1991), 'Financial Control in the Transition from Classical Socialism to a Market Economy', *Journal of Economic Perspectives*, **5**, (4), 107–22.

Mizsei, Kálmán (1988), 'Is the Hungarian Economic Mechanism a Model to be Emulated?', *Eastern European Economics*, **26**, (4), 58–71.

Murrell, Peter (1990), '"Big Bang" versus Evolution: East European Economic Reforms in the Light of Recent Economic History', *PlanEcon Report*, **6**, (26), 29 June, 1–11.

Nelson, Richard R. and Sidney G. Winter (1982), *An Evolutionary Theory of Economic Change*, Cambridge, MA: The Belknap Press of Harvard University.

Ouchi, William G. (1981), *Theory Z: How American Business Can Meet the Japanese Challenge*, Reading, MA: Addison-Wesley.

Pelikan, Pavel (1989), 'Evolution, Economic Competence, and the Market for Corporate Control', *Journal of Economic Behaviour and Organization*, **12**, 279–303.

Pelikan, Pavel (1991), 'The Dynamics of Economic Systems, or How to Transform a Failed Socialist Economy', Paper presented to the annual conference of the European Association for Evolutionary Political Economy, Vienna, November.

Sándor, László (1991), 'A vállalati sorban állások okai és kezelésük lehetőségei'

(Reasons and Possible Treatment of Postponement of Payments by Companies), in Márton Tardos *et al.*, *Ki fizet a végén? Vita a magyar gazdaság pénzügyi helyzetéröl* (Who Will Pay in the End? Discussion on the Financial Situation of the Hungarian Economy), Budapest: Institute of Economics, Hungarian Academy of Sciences, pp. 136–43.

Scherer, F.M. (1980), *Industrial market structure and economic performance*, Boston: Houghton Mifflin.

Schotter, Andrew (1986), 'The Evolution of Rules', in Richard N. Langlois (ed.), *Economics as a Process: Essays in the New Institutional Economics*, Cambridge: Cambridge University Press, pp. 117–33.

Seal, W.B. (1990), 'Deindustrialisation and Business Organisation: an Institutionalist Critique of the Natural Selection Analogy, *Cambridge Journal of Economics*, **14**, (3), 267–75.

Simon, Herbert A. (1976), *Administrative Behavior* (1947), 3rd ed., New York: The Free Press.

Smuga, Tadeusz (1991a), 'Place' (Salaries), *Zycie Gospodarcze*, **46**, (20), 19 May, Supplement of the Institute of the National Economy IGN, p.III.

Smuga, Tadeusz (1991b), 'Zatrudnienie' (Employment), *Zycie Gospodarcze*, **46**, (24), 16 June, Supplement of the Institute of the National Economy IGN, p.III.

Sobota, J. (1991), 'Dluznicy i wierzyciele' (Debtors and Creditors), *Zycie Gospodarcze*, **46**, (20), 19 May, Supplement of the Institute of the National Economy IGN, p.IV.

Soós, Károly Attila (1991), 'Liberalization and Stabilization', in András Köves and Paul Marer (eds.), *Foreign Economic Liberalization: Transformation in Socialist and Market Economies*, Boulder: Westview Press, pp. 247–53.

Stark, David (1990), 'Privatization in Hungary: From Plan to Market or from Plan to Clan?', *East European Politics and Society*, **4**, (3), 351–92.

Stark, David (1991), 'Privatizációs stratégiák Közép-Kelet-Európában' (Privatization Strategies in East Central Europe), *Közgazdasági Szemle*, **38**, (12), 1121–42.

Svejnar, Jan (1991), 'Microeconomic Issues in the Transition to a Market Economy', *Journal of Economic Perspectives*, **5**, (4), 123–38.

Swaan, Wim (1989), 'Price Regulation in Hungary: Indirect but Comprehensive Bureaucratic Control, *Comparative Economic Studies*, **31**, (4), 10–52.

Swaan, Wim (1990), 'Price Regulation in Hungary, 1968–1987: a Behavioural-Institutional Explanation, *Cambridge Journal of Economics*, **14**, (3), 247–65.

Swaan, Wim (1991), 'Prices and Market Behaviour in Hungary in the Early Stages of the Transition to a Market Economy', *Soviet Studies*, **43**, (3), 507–33.

Swaan, Wim and Maria Lissowska (1992), *Economic Reforms and the Evolution of Enterprise Behaviour in Hungary and Poland during the 1980s*, Leuven: Leuven Institute for Central and East European Studies, Working Paper No.4.

Szalai, Erzsébet (1991), 'Integration of Special Interests in the Hungarian Economy: The Struggle between Large Companies and the Party and State Bureaucracy', *Journal of Comparative Economics*, **15**, (2), 284–303.

Tardos, Márton, et al. (1991), *Ki fizet a végén? Vita a magyar gazdaság pénzügyi helyzetéröl* (Who Will Pay in the End? Discussion on the Financial Situation of the Hungarian Economy), Budapest: Institute of Economics, Hungarian Academy of Sciences.

Várhegyi, Éva (1991), 'A monetáris politika eredményei és korlá tai' (Results and Constraints of Monetary Policy in Hungary), in: Márton Tardos *et al.*, *Ki fizet a végén? Vita a magyar gazdaság pénzügyi helyzetéröl* (Who Will Pay in the End?

Discussion on the Financial Situation of the Hungarian Economy), Budapest: Institute of Economics, Hungarian Academy of Sciences, pp. 123–35.

Viszt, Erzsébet and Judit Ványai (1991), 'A túlélés kényszére (The Need to Survive), *Figyelö*, **35**, (10), 7 March, 10.

Winiecki, Jan (1989), 'Large Industrial Enterprises in Soviet-type Economies: The Ruling Stratum's Main Rent-Seeking Area', *Communist Economies*, **1**, (4), 363–83.

Winiecki, Jan (1990), 'Post-Soviet-Type Economies in Transition: What Have We Learned from the Polish Transition Programme in Its First Year', *Weltwirtschaftliches Archiv*, **126**, (4), 765–90.

Winiecki, Jan (1991), The Inevitability of a Fall in Output in the Early Stages of Transition to the Market: Theoretical Underpinnings, *Soviet Studies*, **43**, (4), 669–76.

PART THREE

The Political Economy of Mixed Economy
Emergence in Europe

6. Transition from Command to Market Economies in Central and Eastern Europe: First Experiences and Questions*

Kazimierz Laski

1. INTRODUCTION

The collapse of the system of 'real socialism' in Central and Eastern Europe started a process of transition from totalitarian party-states and command economies towards democratic systems and market-oriented economies. The beginning of this process (the – partly – free elections in Poland and the first non-communist government in this part of the world, the street demonstrations in Leipzig with citizens proclaiming 'We are the people', leading to reunification of Germany, the Velvet Revolution in Prague raising Václav Havel, the symbol of spiritual resistance against the communist dictatorship, to the presidential office at Hradcany Castle and similar, though less spectacular developments in Hungary) triggered a real explosion of hope – and even enthusiasm – on the part of the population at large in the Central and East European countries. People believed that the removal of the odious communist dictatorship and of the indolent command economy would very soon bring about a viable democratic regime and a flourishing western-type market economy. As soon as it became evident that democracy means more than just free elections, and that the way towards a market economy and prosperity would be rough and protracted, disappointment and disillusionment spread. The prevailing popular frame of mind has been properly called the 'post-revolutionary hangover'. The explanation of this hangover can be found if we have a look at the relevant economic data in Table 6.1. The GDP which in 1990 had already declined in Eastern and Central Europe (including Yugoslavia) by about 8 per cent sank by another 15 to 16 per cent in 1991. The GDP of the Soviet Union in 1991 registered a decline of about 17 per cent. There is no example in modern history of a fall of GDP of this size in a peaceful period. It is an important task of economic research to identify the

Table 6.1   The dynamics of GDP (% in relation to previous year)

	1990	1991
Bulgaria	−11.8	−20 to −25
Poland	−11.6	−8 to −10
Romania	−7.3	−17
Czechoslovakia	−2.0	−16
Hungary	−4.3	−7 to −9
Central and Eastern Europe	−8.4	−13 to −15
Yugoslavia	−8.5	−25
Central and Eastern Europe and Yugoslavia	−8.4	−15 to −16
USSR	−2.0	−17
Whole region	−3.8	−16 to −17

Source: 1990: national sources, *1991*: WIIW.

causes of the resulting disappointment and to find out whether it could be avoided or at least reduced to a less intensive level.

The existing hardships in the economies in transition (EIT) are mainly a heritage of the communist past. Another important factor is the collapse of the COMECON, and related losses of markets for, and suppliers to, EITs almost from one day to the next. Although both factors play an undeniable role, they are very often overemphasized by ruling groups in order to divert attention from economic strategies and policies which, to a considerable degree, are also responsible for the present situation and lack of perspectives. It is the firm conviction of this writer that, if these policies were different and mistakes avoided, the situation would be better in the sense that hardships would not go beyond the level determined by the heritage of the past and by external circumstances.

We start this chapter by investigating the sequencing of the transition towards a market economy (the alternative of a shock versus a more gradual therapy). Then we go on to stabilization and recession as necessary phenomena during the transition from a command to a market economy. The relation between stabilization policy and growth is analysed in the next section. Finally we will devote some thoughts to ideological matters.

2. SHOCK THERAPY VERSUS GRADUALISM

The EITs are confronted with three main tasks: (a) stabilization and intro-duction of market clearing prices; (b) privatization; and (c) restructuring and growth. While the first goal should be tackled at the very beginning of the transformation process, the two remaining tasks require years rather than months or days. From this point of view the whole discussion concerning the sequencing of the transition is beside the point.

Proponents of a shock therapy frequently argue that gradual changes in the past were always absorbed and neutralized by the existing structure of command economies. But they forget that previous blueprints of change were reforms inside a socialist system (like the well-known New Economic Mechanism in Hungary since 1968, and the hesitant reform attempts in Poland, Czechoslovakia and other countries). These reforms were not aimed at abolishing central planning (nor the prevalence of collective ownership of production factors) but at improving it. Market co-ordination, mostly limited to current decisions, had to substitute for administrative co-ordination, and simply represented a more efficient instrument of central planning (Brus and Laski, 1989, Ch. 7). All these reforms failed, not because they were gradual, but because command economies proved incapable of being reformed. The present EITs are not confronted with reforms as in the past, but with a systemic transformation (Altmann *et al.*, 1991, p. xi). Their target is the dis-banding of the command economy, not its improvement; therefore the former arguments against gradual changes do not hold water.

It is simply out of the question to introduce a market economy at one stroke in countries that have lacked market institutions and environment as well as appropriate human attitudes for almost half, and in one case even for three quarters of a century (Oppenheimer, 1991, p. 59). This is somehow overlooked in numerous metaphors now so popular in some EITs. One of these says that the command and capitalist economies are separated by a kind of abyss, and that it is not advisable to try to leap across an abyss other than by one mighty jump. This sounds quite convincing. However, Peter Wiles draws our attention to the fact that the relation between the two systems should rather be described as a precipice with capitalism at the top and command economy at the bottom. To try to jump to the top instead of systematically climbing the hill would be both exhausting and fruitless (Wiles, 1991, p. 88). The road to a market economy will require much effort and much time, but stabilization and price liberalization have to start the process, and the sooner the better. This is our next topic.

3. STABILIZATION AND RECESSION

3.1 From 'Suction' to 'Pressure'

To understand the reasons why a stabilization policy is necessary and why related recession is unavoidable, we should start by a somewhat more general approach. It deals with an important asymmetry between the transition from a command towards a market economy and the reverse process, i.e., the transition from a market towards a command economy. This asymmetry is closely related to basic features of each system.

The market economy is a demand-constrained system. Given the production capacity and the price–wage relation, the actual national income is determined by effective demand. As a rule, effective demand stays behind potential supply (or potential national income), resulting in some reserve production capacity and some unemployment. While certain factors of production lie idle, others are used in a rather efficient way. The economy under these conditions is said to work under 'pressure' (Kornai); the market is character-ized as a 'buyers' market'.

The command economy is a supply-constrained system. In this system factors of production, including labour, are utilized very intensively, although in a rather inefficient way. Indeed, effective demand can always be (and is) generated by a fiat of the Central Planning Board which in addition deter-mines – at least in principle – the price–wage relation, adjusting it to the expected uses of final output. In a command economy, demand as a rule is ahead of potential supply, creating a permanent state of 'suction' (Kornai). Under these conditions the market becomes a 'sellers' market', and the economy is characterized by permanent, more or less intensive, shortages.

The passage from a market economy towards a command system, seen from this point of view, implies a drastic increase in effective demand and the substitution of a 'buyers' market' by a 'sellers' market'. The previously idle factors of production, especially labour, as proved by the experience of socialist countries, can – under these conditions – be activated, and the others, which were not fully utilized, more intensively employed. This leads to a quick increase in production, employment and consumption. These short- (or even medium-) term gains are overcompensated by losses in efficiency and creativity in the long run; however, they make the transition to a command economy rather attractive. They were quite an important factor in the initial successes of central planning, sustaining illusions con-cerning its alleged superiority over the capitalist economies.

The transition from a command economy to a market one requires the substitution of 'pressure of supply' for 'suction of demand'. This substitution implies a limitation of effective demand to a level below that of potential supply, resulting in some reserve capacity and unemployment. This allows for a necessary degree of flexibility of production (in the sense of the ability to adjust the structure of supply to that of demand). Some decrease in actual national income caused by cuts in total demand is necessary, if the economy has to be exposed to the demand constraint. In this sense some recession, implying immediate losses in production, employment and consumption, must be part and parcel of every programme to transform a command economy into a market one. These short- (and even medium-) term losses should be overcompensated by an increase in efficiency and creativity in the long run, but they make the transition to a demand-determined market system quite difficult.

3.2 Controlling Effective Demand

The driving force of the market mechanism is the price mechanism. This mechanism requires scarcity prices equilibrating demand and supply. A seriously meant transition towards market co-ordination is thus bound to start with the suppression of price controls and administrative price-fixing. This would, as a rule, cause substantial price increases because repressed inflation becomes open, and – additionally – because the lifting of price controls is usually coupled with the cutting of numerous subsidies. However, not all subsidies must and should be abolished at once (basic foodstuffs in some cases, rents in most cases, etc.). Thus the introduction of market clearing prices does not necessarily mean full and immediate price liberalization. In that sense, elements of gradualism should be present even in the first phase of transition.

Whatever the policy chosen with respect to price liberalization, an acceleration of inflation may be expected. In order to avoid an uncontrolled inflationary process, price liberalization must be accompanied by a stabilization programme. As excess demand is the rule in a command economy, internal equilibrium can in the short run be achieved only by reducing demand. The existing disequilibria mostly have their source in the sector of state enterprises, in the state budget and in monetary policy. The therapy must therefore start here.

The soft budget constraint of state enterprises must be hardened. Only in this way will it be possible to control and restrict their insatiable demand on resources (investment, labour, material inputs) and abolish the very cause of the shortage economy. At the same time the artificial concentration of production should be lessened. The dissolution of different associations of enterprises, representing true monopolies, is advisable in order to create better competitive conditions on the market. The creation of smaller units would also facilitate privatization.

Government budget deficits play a weighty part in creating excess demand. In order to cut these deficits to a tolerable level, expenditures (e.g. defence, subsidies) have to be cut and the revenues adjusted. As far as private households are concerned, their current incomes must be adjusted – at expected prices – to current consumer goods supplies. Therefore some kind of income policy restraining uncontrolled money wage increases seems unavoidable.

At the same time a solution must be sought to the problem of monetary overhangs (representing partly forced savings of the past), which exist everywhere, though to a varying extent in the individual countries. In countries with high inflation, or even hyperinflation, the real value of cash balances has been so strongly reduced that the monetary overhang may no longer exist. Money has to fulfil its basic function not only as a medium of exchange but as a store of value. Thus an effective monetary and credit policy is everywhere a necessary – though not sufficient – precondition for a successful stabilization of the economy. The separation of commercial banks from the central bank, and the autonomy of the central bank in determining the money supply, are important elements of the reform of the banking system. Under existing circumstances a prudent monetary policy, clearly marking an end to the irresponsible monetary expansion of the past, cannot be avoided.

Internal stabilization should be accompanied by a gradual reintegration of the East into the world economy. The first important measure here is the introduction of a unified exchange rate (necessitating substantial devaluation in most countries) linked with some internal convertibility of the currency, mainly for goods and services, and limited to firms only. A full currency convertibility, however, should be approached step by step – in concurrence with the transition to free market conditions in other fields. The arguments for a gradual approach to convertibility are forcefully presented by Levcik (1991). On the other hand, internal stabilization of the economy without some liberalization of foreign trade and without taking account of world market conditions does not make sense, because the achieved internal equilibrium would not be adjusted to these conditions. We will return to this topic later.

All these measures should be started concurrently, giving a clear signal that a new market order is being introduced. In this sense, but only in this sense, they represent a shock therapy; it is necessary, especially in countries with high (open or repressed) inflation, in order to break the inflationary expectations of the economic actors – mainly enterprises and private households. This therapy is not free from dangers. The reduction of global demand together with a tight monetary and credit policy, as well as some opening to the outside world, would provoke a fall in production and employment. It may also create a heavy burden on the population in terms of reduced real wages. This policy can work, if the population is ready to accept sacrifices in the form of unemployment and lower standards of living as a necessary price for abolishing the hated and inefficient communist regime. But the ability of the population to sacrifice the present for the sake of the future should not be overestimated, nor the duration of time during which the readiness to accept painful measures prevails. Thus even under propitious conditions the exposure of the economy to market forces should not exceed certain limits and must be accompanied by various government measures softening the blow of the shock therapy and creating general conditions for its success in the foreseeable future.

From the macroeconomic point of view the most important task is that of controlling and influencing total effective demand, and in the first place such factors as investment, budget deficit, and export surplus. Indeed, these three factors determine the savings of both the enterprise and private household sectors, and, given the share of savings in the gross domestic product (GDP), also its volume. It is known that ex post (gross) savings S, defined as above in the text, can be specified as follows:

$$S = I + E + D \tag{1}$$

where I denotes (gross) investment in the enterprise sector, E stands for the difference between exports and imports (trade surplus including net non-factor services) and D represents the budget deficit, i.e. the difference between government expenditures (on goods and services) and revenues. Further, we define the rate of savings, (the share of savings in GDP) as

$$s = S/GDP$$
or
$$GDP = (1/s)S. \tag{2}$$

From (2) we get: if s = constant

$$\Delta GDP = (1/s)\ \Delta S \tag{3}$$

and in general case: if s ≠ constant

$$\Delta GDP = GDP(gS - gs), \tag{4}$$

where all aggregates are measured in constant prices.

In (3) the term (1/s) denotes the multiplier measuring the impact of changes in savings S, i.e. of the sum of investment, deficit spending and export surplus upon the GDP. In (4) the terms gS and gs denote the rate of growth of S savings and of s the rate of saving, respectively. The formula (4) cannot be used when the yearly changes in S and s are not small. In the latter case we get from (2)

$$1 + gGDP = (1 + gS)/(1 + gs)$$

where gGDP denotes the rate of growth of GDP. By simple manipulations we get

$$\Delta GDP = GDP(gS - gs)/(1 + gs) \tag{5}$$

the formula which can be used when yearly changes of S and s are not small.

Let us assume that before the stabilization plan is being started the economy is characterized by rather high deficit government spending and the plan intends to cut this deficit. Let us assume, on the other hand, that the plan does not foresee an increase in the sum of both investment and foreign trade surplus. Under these conditions the cuts in deficit spending should be adjusted to the expected changes in the saving propensity of the economy. If it is expected that, for example, the overall propensity to save (which depends on the distribution of value added net of taxation between profits and wages, and specific propensities to save out of these incomes) would not decrease (i.e., that it would remain constant or even increase), then cuts in deficit spending would cause a multiplied reduction of the GDP. Thus, the size of the cuts in deficit spending must be calculated so that the resulting drop in aggregate demand would not go beyond that necessary to create enough 'pressure' on the supply side of the economy. A policy of 'sound' finance aiming at balancing the budget (or even creating a budget surplus) as fast as possible would under these conditions provoke only a sterile recession, avoidable unemployment, and the danger of a cumulative process involving further cuts in investment and output. *Mutatis mutandis*, the same applies to monetary and credit policies. They should be adjusted to the existing situation and aims, and not blindly follow some dogmatic prescriptions.

3.3 The Polish Stabilization Plan 1990 – an Illustration of the Method

The stabilization plan for 1990 represented a completely new approach to the problems facing Poland, and the reaction of the economy to the measures envisaged was quite uncertain. Nevertheless, some estimates had to be made, and have been made, with respect to prices, output, employment, government budget and foreign trade.

According to the stabilization plan the rate of inflation between December 1990 and December 1989 should not have exceeded 140 per cent. The highest price increase, of about 45 per cent, was expected in January 1990, to be followed by the slowing down of inflation in February and March. Already in the second quarter of the year inflation was to be reduced to about 1–2 per cent per month.

The sharply limited increases in money wages, with anticipated inflation, were to lead to a reduction in real wages. According to the scenario of the plan, real wages should fall by about 15–20 per cent between 1989 and 1990, with most of the reduction taking place in the first quarter of the year. At the same time real consumption was to fall only insignificantly, because it was assumed that part of money incomes in 1989 was not supported by adequate supplies of goods and services. Thus losses in real wages were to be mostly of a statistical nature.

The anticipated decline in industrial output amounted to about 5 per cent, and in national income to about 3.1 per cent. Unemployment was to reach the level of about 400,000, representing some 3 per cent of total employment. The government budget was to be balanced, at least towards the end of the year.

In foreign trade in convertible currencies, with exports more or less constant, an increase in imports of about US $1.0 billion was expected, thus changing the surplus in the trade balance of 1989 into a trade deficit of about US $0.8 billion in 1990. In trade with the Council For Mutual Economic Assistance (CMEA) countries the export surplus in the trade balance was expected to decrease to about 0.54 billion transferable roubles.

One of the main achievements of the stabilization plan in 1990 was the restoration of the basic money functions to the zloty. Hyperinflation was replaced by inflation. Prices reached the market clearing level, and most of the shortage phenomena, typical of a command economy, disappeared. There was some improvement in the structure of prices, caused by the cutting down on subsidies, and by their exposure to the demand constraint. The exchange rate of the zloty to the US dollar was kept constant over the whole year, the government budget closed with some surplus, and in both convertible and non-convertible currencies a considerable trade surplus was achieved.

The goals of the stabilization plan, however, were not met and, what is more important, the costs of these achievements were much higher than anticipated (for more on this topic see Kolodko, 1991 and Kolodko and Rutkowski, 1991). Table 6.2, in which some goals and results of the plan have been confronted, shows that in 1990 GDP fell by 12 per cent, almost four times stronger than anticipated. The same applies to industrial output (including private industry), where the real decline was almost five times stronger than anticipated. Prices of consumer goods increased by 250 per

Table 6.2   Polish stabilization plan 1990: goals and results (average rate of growth p.a. in % unless otherwise stated)

	Assumption (1)	Results (2)	(2) : (1) (3)
GDP	−3.1	−12	3.9
Industrial output	−5	−23.3	4.7
Consumer prices			
December 1990 over December 1989	140	249	1.8
IV. quarter 1990	1.5*	5.5*	3.7
Real wages	−15 (−20)	−28.1	1.6
Unemployment (thousands)	400	1,126	2.8
Trade balance			
in US$ billion	−0.8	2.2	−2.75
in TR billion	0.5	7.1	14.2

*Average rate of growth per month, in per cent

Source: Kolodko (1991), p. 9; Kolodko and Rutkowski (1991), p. 161; Rocznik Statystyczny (1991).

cent instead of expected 140 per cent from December 1989 to December 1990. The monthly rate of growth of the consumer price index in the fourth quarter of 1990 was still 5.5 per cent instead of 1.5 per cent as fixed in the stabilization plan. Real wages decreased by 28 per cent instead of 15–20 per cent as assumed in the plan;[1] and unemployment reached 1.126 million at the end of the year – almost three times the assumed number. Only in foreign trade were the results better than expected. In trade in convertible currencies exports expanded considerably, and although imports also increased, a significant trade surplus of US$2.2 billion was registered. A big surplus (of transferable rouble (TR) 7.1 billion) was registered in trade in non-convertible currencies, especially with the Soviet Union. Here, however, exports decreased slightly while imports fell dramatically. It should be stressed that the large trade surplus, in the face of a sharply declining GDP, additionally limited internal absorption. Indeed, private households' consumption decreased in 1990 by 24 per cent against about 1 per cent foreseen in the plan.

There are several important causes of the negative features of the development in 1990 and of the visible gap between the goals and the results of the stabilization plan. Perhaps the most important was the excessive concentration on monetary and fiscal policy with almost complete neglect of the sphere of production. In the domain of monetary policy two serious mistakes have been made. The drastic rise of the interest rate at the beginning of 1990 gave an initial impetus to the sharp decline in production. The devaluation of the zloty was also higher than economically justified. Indeed the exchange rate could be kept constant although the internal price level increased by 250 per cent from the beginning to the end of the year. This is the best proof that the devaluation was excessive, and it resulted in an initial acceleration of inflation. As far as fiscal policy is concerned, it was a serious fault to tolerate a sizeable budget surplus over most of the year. This factor additionally constrained the level of effective demand. Only at the end of the year was the budget surplus reduced.[2]

The main cause of the excessive recession, however, was the stabilization plan itself. If data implied in the plan concerning investment, export surplus and budget deficit were aggregated, the resulting savings for 1990 could be approximated. If – additionally – an assumption were made concerning the propensity to save expected for 1990, the approximate level of GDP could be found. The resulting estimate could not but show that the recession administered by the plan had to go much further than anticipated in the same plan.[3]

Table 6.3   GDP in Poland (trillion zloty, constant prices of 1989)

		1989 (1)	1990 (2)	(2)–(1) (3)	(3) : (1) (4)	1990 (5)*
Gross domestic product	Y	118.3	104.2	−14.2	−12%	
Investment of the business sector (including changes in inventories)	I	38.6	32.7	−5.9	−15.3%	−3.9
Export surplus	E	4.6	7.2	2.6	56.5%	−5.6
Budget deficit	D	3.6	−0.3	−3.9	−108.3%	−3.6
Savings of the business sector and private households	S	46.8	39.6	−7.2	−15.4%	−13.1
Rate of savings (5 : 1)	s	39.6%	38.0%	−1.6[†]	−4.0%	

*Changes in I, E and D as forecast in February 1990.
[†]Percentage points.

Source: Own estimates based on data from the Central Planning Commission, Warsaw.

The reduction of savings (in 1990 compared to 1989) implied in the plan was equal to Zl 13.1 trillion (see column 5 of Table 6.3). This reduction would provoke – at a constant saving rate – a dramatic decrease of the GDP amounting to

$$\Delta GDP = (1/0.396)(-13.1) = -33.1 \text{ trillion Zl}$$

or to a relative decline of about 28 per cent. In reality the decline of savings was much smaller; they decreased by Zl 7.2 trillion against 13.1 adopted implicitly in the plan. As could be expected (because of the decline of the GDP and of the extreme devaluation of the zloty), the trade deficit (of Zl 1 trillion) did not materialize, and instead a quite important trade surplus was recorded (of Zl 7.2 trillion). Thus – in relation to 1989 – the export surplus increased by Zl 2.6 trillion instead of the expected decline by Zl 5.6 trillion. This factor alone corrected the savings foreseen in the plan by Zl +8.2 trillion. This was also the main cause of the gap between the factual and the implied decline of the savings, because investment and budget deficit declined more or less according to the assumptions of the plan.

We must, however, come back to the assumption concerning the constancy of s, the rate of savings. At the beginning of 1990 nobody knew for sure how the rate of savings would change and in what direction, if at all. However, factors which influence these changes were known and could and should have been analysed. First, because the share of the sum of direct and indirect taxes in GDP in 1990 (according to the budget projections) was to increase by almost 4 percentage points, the share of value-added after taxation would correspondingly decrease. Given the distribution between wages and profits, and the propensity to save out of these incomes, this factor should have diminished the coefficient s. Secondly, it could be expected that the propensities to save out of wages (and in the case of peasants, out of their earnings) would probably decrease, because forced savings would disappear and real income would decline. Under these conditions the second factor should have acted in the same direction as the first one, although it should be stressed that the private households' propensity to save in Poland was rather low. Thirdly, it could be expected that the distribution of value-added after taxation between wages and profits would change and the share of profits would probably increase. Indeed, when subsidies are strongly reduced, profits correspondingly increase, even if prices increase only by the amount of subsidies withdrawn. But it was known that prices would also increase in relation to unit labour costs, because real wages were expected to decline in absolute terms and in relation to labour productivity, creating room for additional profits. As the propensity to save out of profits is much higher than that out of wages – and out of profits in state-owned enterprises almost equal to one – this redistribution of value-added towards profits would increase the value of the coefficient s. Taken together the first two factors seemed to act in one direction, the third one in an opposite one. As there existed forces acting in different directions, it was safe to assume in the plan that changes in the coefficient s would at least not be very large.

This proved to be the case. The rate of savings decreased by 1.6 percentage points, i.e. by 4 per cent, reaching in 1990 the level of 38 per cent. This decline somewhat softened the blow to the GDP provoked by the fall of S, but was too weak to play a more important role. The relative stability (or the change) of the rate of saving – if it can be estimated – means that there is a simple method of evaluating the joint influence of different measures affecting investment, export surplus and budget deficit upon the GDP. The real problem is that this kind of calculation was not made at all by the authors of the stabilization plans, and they did not seem to be particularly interested in their results either. This applies not only to Poland, but to other countries starting or preparing stabilization plans as well. The theoretical basis of the stabilization policy now practised in EITs is the quantity theory of money, and a complete neglect of the theory of effective demand.

3.4 Pitfalls of Conventional Stabilization

The conclusions drawn from the quantity theory of money, although appealing to everyday intuition, may be quite a poor guide in practical policy matters. The conventional stabilization policy uses as its most important instrument credit restriction. The so-called financial programming assumes, as the quantity theory of money always does, that the velocity of circulation of money is roughly constant (or – at least – predictable). Then with net output (or number of transactions) constant – and given the net capital inflow from abroad – the credit restriction on public and private borrowers should slow down inflation. The logic of this approach is not flawless if net output, as usually happens, decreases. But even in this case the stabilization policy could work if aggregate demand falls more sharply than aggregate supply.

The actually observed level of (physical) net output Q is constrained either by the demand (Q^d) or supply (Q^s) side, whichever is lower, i.e.

$$Q = \text{Min} (Q^d, Q^s) \tag{6}$$

Bhaduri (1992) stresses that credit restriction, as well as a high interest rate, would negatively influence both Q^d and Q^s. Under these conditions the basic objective of stabilization policy may be lost if supply falls more sharply than demand and, thus, the excess demand gap increases instead of decreasing (the so called 'anti-stabilization' case). But even in Bhaduri's 'pro-stabilization' case the outcome is not sure.

This case is presented in Figure 6.1. On the horizontal line we measure the degree of credit availability and on the vertical one, the aggregate net output, demand or supply determined.

With initial lax credit policy (OA) there exists an excess demand gap a and the net output equals Q_a with accompanying shortage phenomena. With credit restricted from OA to OB an equilibrium net output Q_b could be achieved. The lost output $(Q_a - Q_b)$ is the cost of moving from a supply- to a demand-determined system and represents *inter alia* some reserve capacity assuring the necessary flexibility of supply with respect to demand.[4] If, however, the credit availability is, e.g., limited to OC (OC<OB) an excess supply gap c materializes with net output Q_c and available loss of net output $(Q_b - Q_c)$.

Figure 6.1   Credit availability and inflation

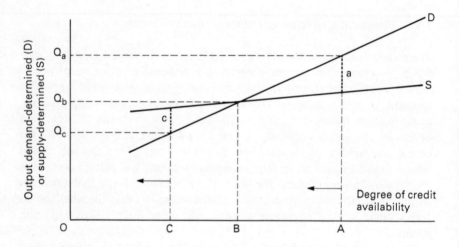

This configuration seems quite characteristic of the situation in Poland after two years of stabilization policy. The GDP which sank by 12 per cent in 1990 decreased by another 8 to 10 per cent in 1991. Inflation, though slowing down, was, however, quite high in 1991 (70.3 per cent p.a., that is 4.5 per cent per month).[5] For the conventional stabilization policy the supply of money determines the price level. If, thus, inflation is still high monetarists would conclude that the credit restriction did not go far enough and require that the conventional stabilization policy be blindly continued *coûte que coûte* till inflation is eradicated. This requirement is symbolized by the arrow and would, if followed, provoke a further decline of Q and a further increase of the excess supply gap. It should be added that losses of net output may partly be irreversible if the capacities concerned are destroyed (existing supply of specialized intermediary inputs gets lost, workers with special skills change jobs, some factories are closed down etc.). In all these cases the restoration of effective demand would not restore the partly lost potential net output.

There exists some logic in the monetaristic approach. If the quantity of money determines the price level there is no place left in this theory for other factors, namely for costs. Most prices in a modern society, excluding agriculture and raw materials, are, however, cost not demand determined. Thus at the level of credit availability OB and at net output Q_b prices need not remain constant if direct costs increase. With a given mark-up ratio those prices would rather increase *pari passu* with costs. The same applies to a level of credit availability OC with an excess supply gap *c*. Although aggregate demand here is below potential supply, prices would not remain constant or even fall, if costs are on the rise. It should be added that the stabilization policy itself exerts a strong influence upon costs. The most important factors met in all stabilization policy cases are drastic increases in prices of energy and of the working capital (in the form of exorbitant levels of interest rates). The strong devaluation of national currencies also plays a role via increased costs of imported inputs. Last but not least unit real labour costs very often increase too.

As a matter of principle money wages are very often indexed during stabilization policies with an indexation coefficient allowing only partly compensating for the inflation. It is thus required that

$$\frac{\Delta w}{w} = \omega \frac{\Delta P}{P}, \ 0 < \omega < 1 \tag{7}$$

where w, P and ω denote money wages, price level and the indexation coefficient, respectively. Under these conditions the real wage rate $w_r = (w/P)$ must decrease if inflation persists:

$$\frac{\Delta w_r}{w_r} = \frac{\Delta w}{w} - \frac{\Delta P}{P} = \omega \frac{\Delta P}{P} - \frac{\Delta P}{P} = (\omega - 1)\frac{\Delta P}{P}; \tag{8}$$

thus

$$\frac{\Delta w_r}{w_r} < 0 \qquad \text{if } \frac{\Delta P}{P} > 0. \tag{9}$$

Non-increasing real wages should decrease, or at least keep constant, unit real labour costs. This implies, however, non-decreasing labour productivity. Indeed unit real labour costs denoted by $u_r = w_r/q$ where q stands for physical labour productivity would change by

$$\frac{\Delta u_r}{u_r} = \frac{\Delta w_r}{w_r} - \frac{\Delta q}{q} \tag{10}$$

If $(\Delta q/q) = 0$ then the non-full indexation of nominal wages would provoke a decline of u_r. It is, however, characteristic that in all countries undergoing stabilization in EITs the drastic cuts in output, especially in industry, are not compensated by parallel cuts in employment, mainly for social reasons, as unemployment should not increase too quickly. Thus redundant labour in enterprises increases further and labour productivity decreases. We have then often

$$\frac{\Delta u_r}{u_r} > 0 \text{ if } \frac{\Delta w_r}{w_r} - \frac{\Delta q}{q} > 0 \ \text{ i.e. } \ \frac{\Delta w_r}{w_r} > \frac{\Delta q}{q} \tag{11}$$

Unit real labour costs increase if real wages decrease but more slowly than labour productivity does. All these phenomena took place during the stabilization plan in Poland in 1990 and 1991. Characteristic of 1991 was the decline of the mark-up ratio, resulting in the fall of prices in relation to costs, thus rentability. This proves additionally that we had in this case a cost-push but not a demand-pull inflation. But still the stabilization policy addresses demand-pull inflation as the main danger. An erroneous diagnosis of the real causes of the existing situation leads to the continuation of an erroneous policy.

4. STABILIZATION AND GROWTH

Stabilization is not an aim in itself, it is required as a condition for the resumption of growth. Stabilization of the economy is principally a short-term goal; it has to be achieved at given production capacities. Growth of the economy is principally a long-term goal; it implies expanding production capacities, due mainly to investment. Growth following successful stabilization is the more important, the greater the costs in terms of lost output of the stabilization programme. It should be stressed that these costs are in the case of EITs much higher than in other countries that have under-gone similar treatment.[6] Indeed, the negative growth rates p.a. in Central and East European countries, as already said, have reached levels unknown elsewhere since the times of the great crisis of 1929–33.

An additional factor is the low level of GDP per capita in the EITs compared with other European countries. In the past six years the gap between Czechoslovakia, Hungary and Poland on the one hand, and Austria on the other, measured by GDP per capita, increased by about one third. The

Table 6.4   *Extrapolation of benchmark (1985) GDP per capita according to the Physical Indicator Global (PIG) method (current international dollars)*

Year	1985	1986	1987	1988	1989	1990	1991
Bulgaria	7 474	8 021	8 265	8 495	8 871	8 384	6 909
Czech and Slovak Federal Republic	8 153	8 516	8 844	9 275	9 752	9 832	9 114
GDR	8 993	9 365	9 813	10 250	10 896	9 383	6 765
Hungary	7 431	7 800	8 100	8 570	8 815	8 887	8 696
Poland	6 441	6 740	6 771	7 080	7 268	6 640	6 155
Romania	5 852	6 184	6 283	6 570	6 716	6 066	4 998
USSR	7 328	7 744	8 002	8 368	8 781	8 945	8 292
Yugoslavia	6 002	6 370	6 478	6 653	6 829	6 455	5 319
USA	12 870	13 482	14 223	15 196	16 137	16 947	17 804
Austria	10 682	11 080	11 633	12 476	13 535	14 641	15 532
USA = 100							
Bulgaria	58.1	59.5	57.4	55.9	55.0	49.5	38.8
CSFR	63.3	63.2	62.2	61.0	60.4	58.0	51.2
GDR	69.9	69.5	69.0	67.5	67.5	55.4	38.0
Hungary	57.7	57.9	56.9	56.4	54.6	52.4	48.8
Poland	50.0	50.0	47.6	46.6	45.0	39.2	34.6
Romania	45.5	45.9	44.2	43.2	41.6	35.8	28.1
USSR	56.9	57.4	56.3	55.1	54.4	52.8	46.6
Yugoslavia	46.8	47.2	45.5	43.8	42.3	38.1	29.9
USA	100.0	100.0	100.0	100.0	100.0	100.0	100.0
Austria	83.0	82.2	81.8	82.1	83.9	86.4	87.2
Austria = 100							
Bulgaria	70.0	72.4	70.2	68.1	65.5	57.3	44.5
CSFR	76.3	76.9	76.0	74.3	72.1	67.2	58.7
GDR	84.2	84.5	84.4	82.2	80.5	64.1	43.6
Hungary	69.6	70.4	69.6	68.7	65.1	60.7	56.0
Poland	60.3	60.8	58.2	56.8	53.7	45.4	39.6
Romania	54.8	55.8	54.0	52.7	49.6	41.4	32.2
USSR	68.6	69.9	68.8	67.1	64.9	61.1	53.4
Yugoslavia	56.4	57.5	55.7	53.3	50.5	44.1	34.2
USA	120.5	121.7	122.3	121.8	119.2	115.8	114.6
Austria	100.0	100.0	100.0	100.0	100.0	100.0	100.0

Sources: *Handbook of Economic Statistics* (1990), Havlik (1991, Table 11). Data for 1990 and 1991 are own preliminary estimates.

Table 6.5 Alternative estimates of per capita GDP (GNP) (in current dollars and %)

Method/Source	International Comparison Project 1989			CIA 1989			Physical indicators 1990			Purchasing Power Parities 1990			Exchange rates 1990		
Year	$	USA =100%	Austria =100%	$	USA =100%	Austria =100%	$	USA =100%	Austria =100%	$	USA =100%	Austria =100%	$	USA =100%	Austria =100%
Bulgaria	.	.	.	5 690	27.2	.	8 380	49.5	57.3	5 430	25.0	37.7	6 290	28.9	30.5
Czechoslovakia	.	.	.	7 900	37.8	.	9 830	58.0	67.2	7 940	36.5	55.1	2 810	12.9	13.6
GDR	.	.	.	9 670	46.3	.	9 380	55.4	64.1	8 500	39.1	59.0	8 820	40.6	42.8
Hungary	6 200	30.0	45.2	6 090	29.2	.	8 890	52.4	60.7	5 920	27.2	41.1	3 160	14.5	15.3
Poland	4 980	24.1	36.3	4 560	21.8	.	6 640	39.2	45.4	3 910	18.0	27.2	1 740	8.0	8.4
Romania	.	.	.	3 440	16.5	.	6 070	35.8	41.4	2 950	13.6	20.5	1 540	7.1	7.5
USSR	.	.	.	9 230	44.2	.	8 490	52.8	61.1	5 060	23.3	35.1	5 660	26.0	27.4
Yugoslavia	5 320	25.7	38.8	5 460	26.1	.	6 455	38.1	44.1	5 140	23.6	35.7	.	.	.
USA	20 690	100.0	150.9	20 890	100.0	.	16 950	100.0	115.8	21 730	100.0	150.9	21 730	100.0	105.4
Austria	13 710	66.3	100.0	.	.	.	14 640	86.4	100.0	14 400	66.3	100.0	20 620	94.9	100.0

Sources: Havlik, (1991, p. 37).

same conclusions apply for other Central and East European countries. Havlik's estimation (see Table 6.4), based upon the physical indicator global (PIG) method, gives a proper ranking, but seems to exaggerate the absolute levels of output of the Central and East European countries. More reliable from this point of view are the data estimated by the purchasing power parities (PPP) method (see Table 6.5). According to this method the GDP per capita in Czechoslovakia, Hungary and Poland in 1990 reached 55 to 27 per cent of the Austrian level. Completely unreliable, on the other hand, are calculations based on exchange rates of national currencies against the US dollar. According to this method Czechoslovakia and Hungary in 1990 achieved about 15 per cent and Poland only 8 per cent of the Austrian level. These figures are rather an index of the intensity of the devaluation of national currencies than a measure of their output level. The relation between the level of development and the disparity between the exchange rate and the purchasing power of national currency, as well as additional data about the relative position of Poland in recent history, can be found in Table 6.6.

This, however, is not our present topic. The important point for our further analysis is the fact that EITs remain far behind the average European level and that this lag becomes larger. The falling back of these countries means not only absolute and relative losses in their standards of living, but also

Table 6.6   GDP in US dollars per capita

	according to ICP		according to exchange rates	
	(1)	(2)	(3)	(1) : (3)
		Austria=100		
FRG (1988)	13 876	111.3	19 593	70.8
Italy (1989)	13 709	110.0	15 127	90.6
Netherlands (1989)	13 668	109.6	15 084	90.6
France (1987)	12 913	103.6	16 370	78.9
Austria (1988)	12 467	100.0	16 682	74.7
Great Britain (1987)	12 294	98.6	12 054	102.0
Spain (1989)	10 082	80.9	9 712	103.8
Greece (1987)	6 707	53.8	5 293	126.7
Portugal (19870	5 864	47.0	3 572	164.2
Poland (1989)	4 939	39.6	2 171	227.5
Poland (1991)	3 400	27.3	2 180	156.0

Source: Zienkowski (1991).

increased difficulties in their efforts to join the European Community in the future. An enlargement of the Community would quite certainly be opposed the more strongly by its rich members, the more the EITs become the poorhouse of Europe.

It is clear that EITs desperately need growth, the sooner the better. These countries are told that successful stabilization, resulting in strongly reduced price inflation, a balanced government budget and competitive real exchange rate would not only promote a more efficient static allocation of resources, but would also create a sound base for future growth. This is more or less the economic strategy of the IMF as exemplified e.g. in the paper by Khan and Knight (1985). In their model the most important factors that should bring about growth – and that relatively quickly (in less than two years) – in the aftermath of the stabilization shock are an increase in the export surplus due to real devaluation (and gains in competitiveness), and – foremost – an increase in investment. Dornbush (1990), analysing these factors, reveals the weak points of the model: foreign demand is assumed to be perfectly elastic, reduced real wages would not affect the inflationary process itself (by provoking wage compensations which would start a vicious circle where devaluation brings inflation, and inflation necessitates further devaluation), investments are treated exogenously and are not linked to credit conditions, especially high interest rates advocated to mobilize savings. The model also completely disregards the issue of income distribution. Dornbush (1990, pp. 12–13), concludes:

> All the serious issues in stabilization are, in fact, glossed over, strategically assumed away or made exogenous. As a result one is left with a strikingly optimistic outlook. The reality, however, is that attempts to implement these measures fail more often than not. They fail either because the income distribution issues produce a serious inflation and recession problem, or because the financing for supply side policies that raise growth cannot be marshalled, or they fail because the trimming back of credit growth and the devaluation produce a deep recession and no investment boom, not in the first and not for many years. ... In summary then, the IMF model fails to recognize critical empirical linkages and assumes away the key issues of what mechanism brings about the resumption of investment. Disappointingly, it does not teach us anything about adjustment and the return of growth.

Dornbush illustrates his criticism by the example of Bolivia. I am going to continue quoting him on this subject, not only because the case is interesting *per se*, but also because Jeffrey Sachs – the famous adviser to some EITs – gained his credentials, especially in Poland, as the author of the successful Bolivian stabilization:

Bolivia has tamed hyperinflation, stabilized public finance and administered a heavy dose of supply side economics. The easy work is done, and now the country waits for recovery and growth: Per capita income ... is no longer plummeting, but it has fallen desperately low and there is no assurance, 4 years after stabilization, of a major turn of events. Per capita income continues to fall. Moreover, in November 1989, social conflict erupted into the open when the government declared a state of siege and once again jailed striking union leaders. The Bolivian government may have won the war on inflation, but they have now lost the peace. Bolivia's case is so important because there is consensus that the country implemented all those reforms that should be accomplished, did so firmly and by now many years ago. The case confirms the suspicion that stabilization may not be enough. (Dornbush, 1990, p. 4)

The basic problem in a market economy is its tendency to cumulative developments. In an economy in recession, employment is low, and so is output. Capacity is only partly utilized. Therefore investment is low and so are profits. Because of the poor outlook for the future, investment decreases further, and so do profits. Of course, recession caused by a stabilization programme sooner or later comes to an end. If it is successful, inflation is also pushed down to a tolerable level. But the achieved equilibrium is characterized by a low level of employment and output, by low profitability of firms, by low utilization of capacity, and by lack of perspectives for the future resulting in continued low investment.

In a booming economy the cumulative tendency is present too, but now it works in an opposite direction. Employment is high, and so is output. Capacity is fully utilized, investment is high, and so are profits. Thus, perspectives for the future are good, and result in continued high investment.

The problem with stabilization is how to get from the former cumulative tendency to the latter, from the vicious circle of stagnation to the virtuous circle of growth. One cannot exclude the possibility that spontaneous market forces could in the end solve the problem, but one has to wait for years, and success is not certain. At the recent congress of the European Economic Association, the Minister of Finance of Mexico and an economist from Chile, both coming from countries where the economic situation has lately improved considerably, said that the experience of their countries proves that the lag between stabilization and growth amounts to about ten years. This is a terribly long period for EITs, especially in view of the losses in output and standards of living recorded till now.

One could object that all these examples are taken from developing countries. But in EITs, although their economic development level is higher, there exist additional factors which make their passage to growth even more, not less, difficult. The main problems are the very high share of the public sector, unclear ownership relations, and the lack of entrepreneurs able to make responsible economic decisions, especially investment decisions. Under these conditions some additional factor to help start the cumulative growth tendency may be helpful, if not absolutely necessary, and the first candidate to take on this role is the state.

The general mood in the economic profession is rather against the state. It has become fashionable to call for 'the minimal' state. It is said that state intervention harms rather than helps. Even if this were true in the case of 'fine tuning', when the problem is limited to small deviations from full employment (but that is yet far from having been proved), the conclusion would not automatically apply to big problems, when large and persistent unemployment occurs. This point was forcefully made by Assar Lindbeck (1991, pp. 31–2) in his presidential address at the Annual Congress of the European Economic Association:

> In the context of a non-market clearing labor market, it is certainly reasonable to regard unemployment, in particular highly persistent unemployment, as a major macroeconomic distortion. There is therefore a potential case for policy actions, provided such actions do not create more problems than they solve. Experiences in many countries suggest that the latter reservation is not a trivial one. ... For reasons like these, I am perfectly willing to subscribe to the prevailing skepticism about 'fine tuning' of monetary and fiscal policy actions, if such policies are interpreted as very ambitious attempts to counteract even modest fluctuations in aggregate employment and unemployment. However, these objections to stabilization policy activism are less important when there are what may be called major macroeconomic 'level problems', i.e. situations when the economy is either clearly overheated, as for instance in the US in the mid-1960s, or when unemployment is far above the long-run term trend, as in several EC countries in the mid-1980s. In cases like these, it does not matter much if the size and timing of the policy actions are far from perfect from a cyclical point of view. Thus, even though it may be advisable to avoid 'fine tuning' in monetary and fiscal policy, there may be a strong case for 'coarse tuning', e.g. policies designed to avoid serious macroeconomic 'level problems'.

Lindbeck had in mind western countries and their big problems. But they are minor in comparison with the big problems of the EITs. To require a 'minimal' state under these conditions is more than irresponsible.

So far we have concentrated on global problems. But the need for state activities is also created by structural problems facing the formerly socialist countries on their way to a market economy. The share of services in total employment and output has to increase; that of agriculture must be diminished. The industrial sector must be basically restructured and modernized in order to reduce its high material and energy intensity. The opening of the so far isolated economy to the outside world, and the expansion of export capacities, are further fundamental requirements. Last but not least, the environmental situation, which is critical almost everywhere, must be dealt with.

To believe that all these problems can be solved by spontaneous market forces is a dangerous illusion.

Foreign trade is a good example of an area where macroeconomic and industrial policies must work together. The structure of production inside command economies came into existence almost without any consideration for world market conditions and international division of labour. The abrupt exposure of such economies to world competition, as clearly illustrated by the example of the former GDR, may be quite a dangerous experiment. In this situation the introduction of a unique exchange rate and the liberalization of foreign trade should be accompanied by a selective tariff policy, sheltering those branches of production which can become competitive in the future, or those which will eventually be liquidated, but only gradually, after the necessary conditions have been created. Different quantity restrictions, tolerated even in most developed countries, should also be used when necessary.

The strengthening of the position of the former socialist countries in the world economy is a major problem on their way from a command to a market economy. These countries require an active policy, facilitating imports of modern technology, and promoting exports and changes in export structure towards manufactures, especially machines and equipment of an up-to-date technological standard. This policy cannot simply follow the conclusions of the conventional theory of comparative advantage of the Ricardo and Heckscher-Ohlin type, consisting in free trade policy. It should rather concentrate on a factor which is missing in all these static theories, namely on technical progress.

Luigi Pasinetti (1988) provides an example of two countries: one developed, the other one underdeveloped, but both having exactly the same structure of prices. Under these conditions, foreign trade in the pure form is not of interest to either country. Let us imagine, however, that labour productivity in the developed country is ten times higher than that in the less developed one. From the point of view of the latter country, international trade linked with the process of learning from the former is an extremely interesting proposition. The main role of international interaction in this case lies not so much in the choice of an optimal point on the production possibility curve, but predominantly in the shift of this curve outward from the origin of the co-ordinate system. Pasinetti concludes that the major and primary source of international gains is international learning, not international trade (1988, pp. 139–47). This is a rather fundamental proposition, not only for less developed countries, but particularly for the former socialist countries when they turn towards a more market-oriented economy, because it shifts their attention from pure static to dynamic problems, and from free trade policy prescriptions to efforts of learning and adopting technical knowledge from abroad.

There is one important problem with this approach. In the case of static equilibrium theories there exists a well defined set of unambiguous policy prescriptions on what to do, and especially what not to do, in order not to hinder the benevolent action of the 'invisible hand' of the market. What, however, should be done in order to break a lethargic industrial structure, to develop industries which do not yet exist, to teach skills which are not available in the country, to create a social climate propitious for entrepreneurship, innovation, and risk-taking? These questions are much easier asked than answered (Datta-Chaudhuri, 1981, pp. 76–7).

The action of market forces is absolutely necessary. Thus a sound policy may and should support (not replace) the market mechanism. It is known that Japan (and later on most of the newly industrialized countries) followed two basic rules in its policy of selecting and supporting export-oriented industries. First, the selected industries should be those that are the most promising from the point of view of the expected rate of growth of labour productivity; as a rule these are young industries where the potential for further technical progress is still unexploited. Secondly, export promotion should concentrate mainly on goods that are characterized by an expected high income elasticity of demand. These two rules have not much in common with the traditional theory of comparative advantage and with the postulate of state abstention from foreign trade. They seem, however, to deliver the results, although mistakes cannot be avoided.[7]

Government intervention can be – but is not necessarily – benevolent. Import substitution (supported by import restrictions creating a climate favourable for private domestic and foreign investment) can make sense in well-chosen industries, first of all in larger countries. But this strategy is of limited applicability. If used indiscriminately for all industries and for all time, an artificial production structure would be created and ossified; consequently it could survive only as long as the protection lasts. Additionally, vested interests of protected industries (usually within the state sector) would be articulated and would demand the perpetuation of protection, endangering the achievement of original policy targets of the whole manoeuver. Thus, state support has to be strong enough to assist the development of promising firms, but not so strong as to let firms survive which cannot become self-supporting after a while. This is easier said than done. However, there exists no other solution.

The same applies to export promotion policy. Export capacities can develop only concurrently with an industrialization programme. Nobody – and rare exceptions (e.g. transnational companies) only support the general rule – is going to invest in capacities oriented towards export only. Thus the creation and enlargement of the internal market is a precondition for successful export promotion. Efficient import substitution and export promotion must be flexible and selective; they must also be part and parcel of an integrated industrialization policy if they are to be successful.

Many professional economists and international institutions tend to think in terms of two standard concepts. 'In the field of economic development, two mutually exclusive sets of associated ideas are often set against each other: one set consists of capitalism, free trade and export promotion and the other, socialism, State intervention and import substitution' (Datta-Chaudhuri, 1981, pp. 76–7). This opposition is simply wrong. On the one hand, socialist countries failed completely, not because they were interventionist, but because they killed private entrepreneurship, the very medium which their intervention should have moulded. On the other hand, Japan and the NICs are examples of highly interventionist states, promoting capitalist development through selective intervention in both export promotion and import substitution.

5. SOME IDEOLOGICAL CONSIDERATIONS

Economics is a mixture of ideology and science intertwined. It is not at all easy to separate one from the other. Does the ideological attitude of an economist simply follow his scientific convictions, or are the latter no more than a scientific decoration of the former? In normal circumstances it is very difficult to say what prevails in a given case: ideology or science. Under special conditions, however, this is not impossible. Assume, for example, the following proposition of Joan Robinson: that an economist changes his political attitude from one day to another. If after this change his previous economics disappears completely, we are entitled to conclude that there was nothing but ideology in it. If, conversely, our economist still supports some elements of his economics, this part is certainly non-ideological (although not necessarily true).

What Joan Robinson saw as an abstract experiment has become an experience of a whole generation of economists in the past years. Of course, I mean here the group of economists who were critical of capitalism and had more or less pronounced socialist inclinations. They were often influenced by Marx, but also by the theory of effective demand in its more or less radical version.

The collapse of the socialist experiment in the form of a command economy could not but shatter their economics. The great majority of them stopped perceiving socialism as a closed system transcending the institutional framework of capitalism, and accepted the idea that the continuity of economic development, broken by the revolution from which the 'real socialist' economy emerged, should be restored. Thus their anti-capitalistic attitude gave way to the acceptance of industrial capitalism as an unavoidable system, and the conditions of the experiment formulated by Joan Robinson were fulfilled for a number of them.

The results – as could be expected – are mixed. Some previously radical economists revised important elements of their thinking. First of all they accepted the necessity of real markets, real money and real competition based, at least to a preponderant degree, on private ownership of economic resources. But they still believe in the existence of an overall interest of society that cannot be reduced to the sum of individual interests. They would also very often retain the basic assumptions of the theory of effective demand. They would argue that central planning was introduced as a remedy for the illnesses of capitalism, but this remedy proved worse than the malady itself. They would accept the fact that the medicine almost killed the patient and has been discarded, but they would reject the idea that the patient had been in perfect health in the first place. Thus it can be said that part of the economic thinking of this group contained more than pure ideology, in so far as it survived a change in political opinions.

The other group behaved differently. They made a full turnabout and moved from Marx and Keynes–Kalecki directly to Mises and Hayek. They not only accepted the latters' criticism of orthodox socialism, which after all had been correct, but took over their extreme liberal position identifying any economic action of the state with socialism. Say's Law has become for them as solid as it was shaky before. Of the economics of this group nothing remained after the political turnabout; it had contained no scientific elements.

The transition from a command to a market economy is based on an anti-communist and uncritically pro-capitalistic ideology (Drewnowski, 1990, pp. 5–6). This is understandable, because ideology played a decisive role in the rise of central planning and in the destruction and suffering caused by its functioning; but it may become dangerous if it leads to a doctrinaire attitude in the practical reconstruction of the economies. The generation of economists which is now directing the transition in Eastern Europe has no immediate experience of the capitalist economy in their countries before the Second World War. They know capitalism mostly from microeconomic textbooks and from superficial visits to the most developed western countries. Their consciousness has been moulded by the absurdities of the Soviet-type economy in their countries, they are inclined to identify every economic activity of the state with these absurdities, and to promote a purely capitalistic system with a marginal role of the state in economic matters. The social climate is propitious for this attitude; it is also supported by foreign experts, mostly monetarists, who in the majority of cases have no knowledge of these countries, and – as a rule – by theoretical inclinations of such potent institutions as the IMF and the World Bank. It should be added, however, that these institutions do not have an official theoretical position. They are often ready to discuss the problems with local economists and to look for solutions acceptable to both sides. A good example is Hungary, where – with full IMF approval – no shock therapy has been applied. The sad truth is that very often the ruling groups in EITs are 'plus catholique que le pape' and use the prestige of the IMF as a cover for their own extreme liberal inclinations.[8] The situation is, however, much more complicated. The transition from socialism to capitalism is without precedent (McCracken, 1990). Under such conditions it is not enough to decree the introduction of free markets and then wait for market forces to do the job. What is badly needed is to analyse the situation, to look for new solutions and, most of all, not to neglect economic policy at a time when it is needed more than ever.

NOTES

*   The first draft of this chapter was published in *The Transition from Command to Market Economies in East-Central Europe*, ed. Sándor Richter, Vienna Institute for Comparative Economic Studies, Yearbook IV, Westview Press, published in co-operation with the Vienna Institute for Comparative Economic Studies, 1992. The present version, besides some smaller changes, includes a new section on pitfalls of conventional stabilization policies. Special thanks for critical remarks are due to discussants at the 1991 conference of EAEPE in Vienna and to Leszek Kurowski and Friedrich Levcik as well as to other colleagues from the Vienna Institute for Comparative Economic Studies (WIIW).

1.   Jeffrey Sachs (1990), an important designer of the Polish shock therapy, said: 'fears of plummeting take home pay abound, though the average industrial worker earned the equivalent of $131 in October [1990] compared with $108 in October 1989'.

     Indeed, between October 1989 and October 1990 monthly industrial wages in zloty increased by a factor of about 5, while the exchange rate of the US dollar measured in zloty increased only by a factor of about 4. Jeffrey Sachs forgot, however, to add that prices of consumer goods in the same period increased by a factor of about 6. Thus, the purchasing power of one US dollar on the consumer goods market in Poland decreased by about 50 per cent.

     Between 1980 and 1991 the per capita GDP in Poland measured in US$ increased (!) from 2171 to 2180 when measured according to exchange rates, but decreased from 4939 to 3400 (i.e. by about 31 per cent) when measured according to purchasing power parities (cf. Table 6.6). The indiscriminate use of the dollar measure, according to exchange rates, as a yardstick of real changes is under these circumstances quite irresponsible.

2.   In the first half of 1990 the budget registered a surplus of Zl 6.5 trillion, while in the second half of the year the budget closed with a deficit of Zl 5.6 trillion.

3.   In February 1990 an estimate of the expected decline of GDP was undertaken by the present writer, using data for 1989 available at that time. The results were published in Laski (1990).

4.   Cf. pp. 3–4.

5.   Cf. 'Sytuacja spoleczno-gospodarcza kraju w 1991r', *Rzeczpospolita*, 6 February, 1992.

6.   For example in Israel, between 1985 and 1989, GNP did not decrease at all during a successful stabilization. Mexico, between 1984 and 1989, registered a negative rate of

GNP growth only in one year (–3.8 per cent in 1986), an even Argentina, where stabilization has failed, negative and positive rates of growth in the same period compensated each other more or less, resulting in a stagnation of GNP (Blanchard *et al.*, 1991, p. 9).

7. In Japan, in the 1950s and 1960s, the following 'four priority industries' received preferential treatment: steel, coal, shipbuilding, and electric power. In addition – and partly later – several other industries were supported, too (e.g. cars, electronics, colour films, computers, semiconductors), as growth industries. In the majority of cases the policy was most successful but in some cases failures were registered (e.g. in the coal industry and shipbuilding). The aircraft industry also failed to stand on its own feet despite substantial government assistance.

8. Having in mind exactly those people, Wyczalkowski (1991), a retired senior economist who had worked in the IMF for dozens of years, was quoted recently as making a sarcastic remark in Warsaw that IMF stands for International Monetary Fund and not for International Market Fanatics.

REFERENCES

Altmann, Franz Lothar, Hermann Clement and Aleksandar M. Vacic (1991), Introduction to 'Reforms in Foreign Economic Relations of Eastern Europe and the Soveit Union', *ECE, Economic Studies*, **2**, United Nations, New York.

Bhaduri, Amit (1992); 'Conventional Stabilization and the East European Transition', in Sándor Richter (ed.), *The Transition from Command to Market Economies in East-Central Europe, The Vienna Institute for Comparative Economic Studies, yearbook IV, In Honor of Kazimierz Laski*, Boulder, San Francisco and Oxford: Westview Press, published in cooperation with The Vienna Institute for Comparative Economic Studies.

Blanchard, Olivier, Rudiger Dornbusch, Paul Krugman, Richard Layard and Lawrence Summers (1991), *Reform in Eastern Europe*, Cambridge MA: MIT Press.

Brus, Wlodzimierz, and Kazimierz Laski (1989), *From Marx to the Market. Socialism in Search of an Economic System*, Oxford: Clarendon Press.

Datta-Chaudhuri, M.K. (1981), 'Industrialization and Foreign Trade: the Development Experience of South Korea and the Philippines,' Eddy Lee (ed.), *Export-Led Industrialization and Development*, Geneva: International Labor Organization.

Dornbush, Rudiger (1990), *From Stabilizaton to Growth*, NBER Working Paper 3302, Cambridge, MA.

Drewnowski, Jan (1990), 'Paradoksy polskiej gospodarki,' in *Trybuna, Political Quarterly*, **65**, (121), London.

Handbook of Economic Statistics (1990), Washington DC: CIA, US Government Printing Office.

Havlik, Peter (1991), '*East–West GDP Comparisons: Problems, Methods and Results*, (WIIW-Forschungberichte, 174) Vienna: Vienna Institute for Comparative Economic Studies (WIIW), September.

Khan, Mohsin, S. and Malcolm D. Knight (1985), *Fund-Supported Adjustment Programs and Economic Growth* (IMF Occasional Paper 41), Washington.

Kolodko, Grzegorz W. (1991), '*Transition from Socialism and Stabilization Policies. The Polish Experience*', Paper presented at the 32nd Annual Convention of the International Studies Association, 'New Dimensions in Internal Relations', Vancouver, 19–23 March, mimeo, p. 9.

Kolodko, Grzegorz W. and Michael Rutkowski (1991), 'The Problem of Transition from a Socialist to a Free Market Economy: The Case of Poland', *Journal of Social, Political and Economic Studies*, **16**, (2), Summer, 161.

Kornai, Janos (1980), *Economics of Shortage*, Amsterdam: North-Holland.

Laski, Kazimierz (1990), 'O niebezpieczenstwach zwiazanych z planem stabilizacji gospodarki narodowej', *Gospodarka narodowa*, (Warsaw), **2/3**, 5–9.

Levcik, Friedrich (1991), 'The Place of Convertibility in the Transformation Process', in John Williamson (ed.), *Currency Convertibility in Eastern Europe*, Washington, DC: Institute for International Economics, pp. 40–4.

Lindbeck, Assar (1991), *Macroeconomic Theory and the Labor Market*, Presidential Address at the Annual Meeting of the European Economic Association, Cambridge, UK, mimeo, pp. 31–2.

McCracken, Paul W. (1990), 'Thoughts on Marketizing State-managed Economies', *Economic Impact*, **71**, 13, Washington DC.

Oppenheimer, Peter (1991), 'Economic Reforms and Transitional Policies: Summary of Discussion', in M. Kaser and A.M. Vacic (eds), *Reforms in Foreign Economic Relations of Eastern Europe and the Soviet Union* (Economic Studies 2), New York: United Nations Economic Commission for Europe.

Pasinetti, Luigi (1988), 'Technical Progress and International Trade', *Empirica. Austrian Economic Papers*, **15**, (1), 139–47.

Rocznik Statystyczny (1991), Warsaw: Central Statistical Office.

Sachs, Jeffrey (1990), 'A Tremor, Not Necessarily a Quake, for Poland', *International Herald Tribune*, 30 November.

Wiles, Peter (1991), 'Die kapitalistische Siegessicherheit in Osteuropa', *Europäische Rundschau* 1991/3, p. 88.

Wyczalkowski, Marian (1991), quoted in '... Rada ekonomiczna', *Zycie Gospodarcze*, (Warsaw), 24 November.

Zienkowski, L. (1991), 'Poland in Europe', *Zycie Gospodarcze*, [Polish Weekly], 50.

7. The Post-Socialist Transformation Process: Systemic Vacuum, Search Processes, Implementation Problems and Social Struggle

Jerzy Hausner and Klaus Nielsen

INTRODUCTION

The fact that the market economy is more than a mere aggregation of individual exchanges is often neglected. The market is itself a social institution, necessarily supported by a network of other institutions and social norms. The post-socialist transformation process concerns among other things the marketization of the economy in a situation, where most of the crucial preconditions of a market economy are absent.[1]

The 'formal' institutional preconditions comprise among other things the distribution of property rights, the legal and financial infrastructure, the instruments and principles of state intervention in the economy, the organizational representation of the interests of the different economic agents and social groups in a capitalist economy, and the procedures to co-ordinate such interests.

The 'informal' preconditions include the predominance of abstract, impersonal relationships and the existence of a generalized morality to back trust in economic exchanges (Platteau, 1991). Similar to many Third World countries, the situation of the post-socialist countries is characterized by the prevalent personalized character of economic relations, and also partly by a deficit of trust because of the lack of a strong code of generalized morality. Various perverse effects might spring from an abrupt introduction of market economy and market-supporting institutions in such a milieu where actors are unable to separate their institutionalized roles from personalized relationships. This is evidently the case in Eastern Europe and the former Soviet Union (Platteau, 1991, pp. 57–8).

From a systems-theoretical perspective the crux of the matter is the low degree of functional differentiation of sub-systems, such as the economy, in the socialist system. The high degree of political control of all formal organizations in society made impossible the development of a minimum of sub-system autonomy through the definition of a boundary, an identity and a self-referential logic (Mayntz, 1988). This constitues a crucial deficit in modernization processes. In these terms the erosion of the socialist systems is explained as the long-term consequence of blocked innovation, low flexibility and responsiveness – in short, of the failure to modernize.

It is a complex and long-term enterprise to develop the post-socialist economic system into an autonomous, functional sub-system. The exchange communication which are characteristic of a market economy have for long been blocked or distorted by the command communications of the socialist system (Dietz, 1991). Abolition of the command economy does not imply that exchange communications rapidly and smoothly develop instead. These have to be created from below.

Thus, the marketization of the post-socialist economies requires widespread institutional change over a long period. Swift systemic changes are not feasible. The process of creating an appropriate institutional framework for the market economy, and of developing market-supporting social norms, has just begun. Furthermore various repercussions might be anticipated to block, delay or redirect the process.

The contemporary situation can best be characterized as a systemic vacuum (cf. Dietz, 1991): the previous system has collapsed but a new one has not yet emerged. Initiatives to create more room for manoeuvre for the market mechanism as well as other search processes initiated by the breakdown of the previous system coexist with remaining elements of the old system: structures, norms, habits, procedures and informal relationships. From this situation of systemic vacuum originates a set of specific implementation problems and forms of social struggle.

The topic of this chapter is partly the post-socialist transformation process in general and partly its specific form in contemporary Poland. First, a model of the post-socialist systemic vacuum and transformation processes in general is presented. Secondly, and this is the major part of the article, the dynamics of the current situation in Poland will be presented and interpreted by means of the concepts of the general model.

A MODEL OF THE POST-SOCIALIST TRANSFORMATION PROCESS

A conceptual model of the transformation processes is presented in Figure 7.1.[2] The model has a descriptive and analytical character. It is an attempt to

Figure 7.1   The post-socialist transformation process

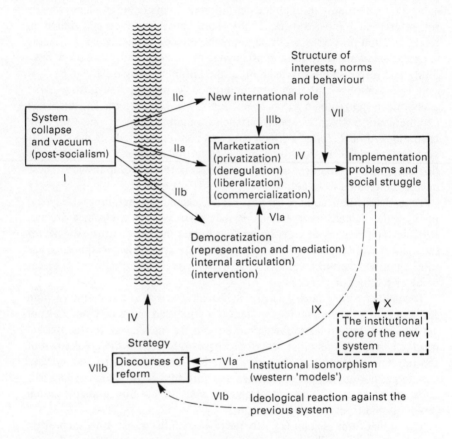

model the interconnection of phenomena which appear in the process of transformation, and to offer some initial generalizations.

The point of departure is the collapse of the socialist system and the resulting systemic vacuum (I). The systemic collapse has initiated a search for marketization in response to the breakdown of central planning (IIa) but also two other important search processes. The breakdown of the political system (one-party system; party dominance over civil society organizations) initiated a search for democratization (IIB). Furthermore, the breakdown of the Warsaw Pact and of COMECON, and the disintegration of the Soviet Union, prompted a search for a new mode of insertion into the international economy and new forms of international political co-operation (IIc).

The main focus of interest is directed at the search for marketization. We distinguish four different forms this can take: privatization, deregulation, liberalization, and commercialization.

Privatization involves the introduction of real private ownership of means of production. This is complicated by the fact that ownership was often vaguely defined in the former system with the paradoxical consequence that a first step in privatization may well be the recentralization of ownership of firms delegated by the state to management and employees during the economic reforms of the last two decades.

Deregulation involves rolling back the state through removing controls, relinquishing earlier means of intervention, and so on, to free economic agents from the constraining hand of the state. Thus it leads to greater formal freedom for economic agents to pursue their economic interests in the marketplace. This will not necessarily lead to freer, more competitive markets as unfettered market forces could lead to private monopolies.

Liberalization involves creating the conditions for free markets to operate and so entails measures to prevent the emergence or survival of monopolies. Clearly the measures involved in liberalization may contradict the desire for deregulation – and vice versa.

Commercialization is aimed at the residual public sector. It involves introducing competition and market proxies in the hope of creating greater efficiency and responsiveness to consumer or client needs. Often this is a prelude to (or even a precondition for) subsequent privatization measures.

A specific sequence of strategic stages has evolved in the process of marketization in each country. In Poland macroeconomic stabilization was the first step and the precondition for the marketization process. Deregulation was the next step followed by liberalization. Internationalization was then seen as instrumental for promoting further marketization. Commercialization of state enterprises came next as a prelude to privatization.

The process of marketization is influenced by the other dynamics (search processes) initiated by the systemic collapse. Of particular significance is the link between marketization and democratization (IIIa). The search for a democratic order has many dimensions. We distinguish three: forms of representation and intermediation; internal articulation of the state; and forms of intervention. These correspond to the input, throughput and output aspects of democracy. Efforts for marketization and democratization of the post-socialist societies are not necessarily mutually reinforcing.

There are various sites of democratic representation and intermediation: territorial (typically associated with political citizenship tied to residence within a given state territory and the right to vote in national or local elections); functional (based on function within the division of labour and typically associated with pluralist or corporatist forms of interaction between interest groups and the state); and civilian (based on identities rooted in the civil society and tied to the freedom of association and political mobilization around claims for social citizenship based on these identities). Struggles for democracy can focus on the extension and deepening of political citizenship rights, democratization through functional interest groups, or the pluralization of social citizenship and social movements. There is no guarantee that attempts to promote democratization will also promote marketization. Indeed given the opposition to market forces in some areas, democratization could institutionalize resistance.

Whatever the general forms of representation in the state, a second problem occurs in terms of the internal articulation of the different state powers and capacities associated with a particular form of state. Democratization also includes measures to secure the subordination of the state as a whole to democratically accountable bodies: a freely elected but toothless parliament which is unable to control the administration does not take democracy very far. Closely related to this issue is the question of the democratic accountability of functional organizations (e.g. trade unions or trade associations) and social movements (e.g. housing associations, friendly societies or anti-nuclear movements) to their members. Again it is not hard to envisage situations where measures to secure greater democratic accountability within the state and/or corporatist bodies hinder the pursuit of marketization.

The search for democratization also concerns the forms of state intervention; important issues are equal treatment before the law and freedom from non-authorized discretionary decisions. Securing open and fair government with due process could also block or hinder marketization like the above-mentioned forms of democratization.

The search for a new insertion in the international economy and new forms of international political co-operation also influence the process of marketization (IIIb). Internationalization is an important dimension of all forms of marketization. Indeed, opening up the economy to international competition increases pressure for various forms of marketization because it intensifies competition and the need for capitalist economic rationality. On the other hand, marketization might be blocked by pressure for protective measures if international economic relations prove highly disadvantageous; the collapse of the markets in the former Soviet Union and the former GDR, and the barriers of the European Community (EC) against products where the East European countries are internationally competitive, show that this is not a totally unrealistic scenario.

The search processes initiated by the systemic collapse are embedded in structures but they are not structurally determined. They all involve strategic choice (IV). The choice of strategy is, of course, related to the structure of economic interests, norms and behaviour in the present systemic vacuum.

However, because of the specific character of the systemic collapse we shall rather stress the importance of other political and ideological forces for the choice of – at least the initial – post-socialist transformation strategy.

The strategic dimension can be studied by investigating the discourse of reform (V). This represents the specific interpretation and priority of the different aspects of the reform process in a given country at a given point of time. Central to the idea of a discourse of reform is the understanding that policy solutions are determined as a result of discursive processes, and often through negotiations, among major economic and political groups – a process in which economists and other experts often play an important advisory role in identifying problems, proposing solutions and making final choices (Nielsen and Pedersen, 1991).

The discourse of reform in the post-socialist countries is heavily influenced by two interconnected political and ideological features: the institutional isomorphism of western 'models' (VIa); and the ideological reaction against the previous system (VIb).

The domestic discourse is in various ways penetrated by foreign institutional and policy models. The ideological inspiration of western 'models' such as Thatcherism, (neo-liberalism), the German 'social market economy', the Iberian model for development from dictatorship to democracy and European integration (Spain and Portugal), and even the Scandinavian model, are examples of one type of such influence. The IMF policy prescriptions as a precondition for financial assistance is an example of a more direct form of influence. In general, the adaptation of foreign institutional and policy models through the influence of foreign actors is called 'isomorphism', of which there are three frequently recognized types: coercive, normative and mimetic (DiMaggio and Powell, 1983; Campbell, 1992).

By coercive isomorphism is meant a process by which a less powerful unit acquires the characteristics of a more powerful one on which it is dependent for resources; either the more powerful one directly imposes its preferred structural forms and practices on the subordinate one, or the latter one is driven in the same direction in order to gain the approval and support of the former. Normative isomorphism is a process by which different units come to resemble each other via a common normative framework, for instance via the growth of professional networks that facilitate the exchange of information and dialogue by means of a common language. Finally, mimetic isomorphism is a process of simple imitation of other units which are perceived as particularly successful or legitimate. Examples of mimetic and normative as well as coercive isomorphism are easily identifiable in the current discourses of post-socialist reform

The discourse of reform is also influenced by the current idiosyncratic ideological reaction against the past which results in a tendency to '(over)negate' the features of the previous system. This ideological trend is influencing the discourse of reform in a way to further strengthen the tendency of isomorphism.

The current discourse of reform influences the initial choice of post-socialist transformation strategy but the chosen policies and institutional solutions, based on a given strategy, inevitably lead to implementation problems and social struggle (VII). Such problems might be caused by policy inconsistencies, problems of sequencing of the various reform measures, contradictions and dilemmas in the relation between marketization and democratization, etc. The potentially most important problems of implementation, probably spring from the social disembeddedness of the market reforms. The market mechanism can function more or less smoothly only if it is embedded in an appropriate social structure. This is by no means the case *a priori* in the post-socialist situation. No matter how strong the denunciation of the past might be, there will be a strong element of inertia in the structure of (perceived) interests, norms and behaviour (VIII). Neither the appropriate formal institutional framework nor the appropriate informal structures (habits, attitudes, behavioural regularities) of a market economy emerge quickly and spontaneously as an effect of the efforts of marketization.

After some time the implementation problems and the social struggle around the marketization process can be expected to influence the discourse of reform and to modify the choice of strategy and policies (IX). This influence will become more pronounced as the strength of the ideological reaction against the previous system weakens. However, the change of the transformation strategies and policies will be strongly modified by the effects of the institutional isomorphism which characterizes the initial stages of the transformation process.

Anyway, the change will initiate new processes, implementation problems and social struggle and, gradually, the interests, norms and behaviour of economic agents will also change. It is the interaction of these features which might eventually eliminate the post-socialist systemic vacuum via the formation of the institutional core of the new system (X).

Below, these mechanisms of the transformation process are illustrated by means of Polish data. First, the form of collapse of socialism and the specific features of the systemic vacuum in contemporary Poland will be described. Secondly, an analysis of how the neo-liberal strategy followed by the Polish governments in the initial post-socialist transformation phase was a result of institutional isomorphism and the ideological reaction against the former system. Thirdly, we describe some of the major implementation problems and the forms of social struggle originating from the neo-liberal transformation strategy. Fourthly, we argue that the neo-liberal strategy has failed; the emergence of a deep 'financial crisis of the state' marks the end of the line and necessitates a change of strategy. Finally, the future prospects are discussed; the contradictory features and problems of the systemic vacuum can be expected to remain until the institutional core of a new system is established; certain institutional reforms are, in our opinion, essential in the process of forming this core. Of particular importance is the need for a change from the situation of 'old' forms of interest group rivalry around the demand side of the economy, which tend to block the desired supply-side changes, to a situation with 'new' forms of active participation of interest groups in the transformation of the supply side of the economy.

THE SYSTEMIC VACUUM IN POST-SOCIALIST POLAND

An understanding of the present situation in post-socialist societies requires an explanation not only of why socialism collapsed, but also of how it collapsed, because the latter exerts a fundamental influence on the prevalent social structure, and the norms and behaviour of economic agents. It is necessary to stress that the decline of socialism was in reality a lengthy process of erosion or, to put it otherwise, a protracted death-agony.

It was not only the fear that attempts at systemic change might lead to external intervention that made the opposition opt for reformist rather than anti-systemic changes; this also reflected the real state of social consciousness which never reached beyond the level of corporatist consciousness. This was the case even in Poland where the activity of the political opposition was highly visible. For decades social protest was not directed against the structure of the system. People fought for improvement in their material standard of living in the belief that the system could provide it. As late as 1980–1 the membership of Solidarity accepted slogans such as 'Socialism – yes. Distortions – no'. They behaved as employees and consumers rather than citizens. Due to the dematerialization and depersonalization of property rights nobody fought against the system, nor did anyone defend it. That there was nobody to defend the communist regime became obvious only after the Soviet leadership's abandonment of the Brezhnev doctrine. What Schumpeter thought was a threat to capitalism then actually happened to socialism. He anticipated that the disappearance of real ownership in capitalism, through the spread of forms of ownership like shares, would lead to a situation in which no one would be ready to defend capitalism (Schumpeter, 1976).

Undeniably, the breakdown of the structures of the socialist system was accompanied by tempestuous events of a revolutionary character. It is clear, however, that these events were only the final phase of disintegration and, despite the vociferous declarations of the main actors in these events, the system was not so much overthrown as left to collapse of its own accord.

Opposition forces did not have to fight for power; they were able simply to take it from representatives of the decaying regime who could no longer wield it effectively. In this final phase the façade of the system was shattered but its foundation had corroded much earlier.

The process of the 'protracted death-agony of socialism' led to a systemic vacuum. This notion contains the idea that not only did the previous system disintegrate, but the disintegration occurred in such a way that new social forces, which could have promptly created new systemic structures, failed to emerge during the process. The systemic vacuum was caused by a particular kind of 'revolution from above'; the source of dynamism was the profound crisis of socialism rather than grassroots pressure exerted by nascent social forces. This is the reason for the apparent paradox that in 1988–9, in the final phase of the disintegration of the socialist system, Solidarity was visibly weaker than in 1980–1, in terms both of its membership base and of its public support. As a result of the systemic vacuum, the social system of post-socialism lacks many pivotal elements in such areas as property rights, economic regulation, political relations and ideological consensus.

The existence of a 'systemic vacuum' does not imply that all the elements of the hitherto existing system have been destroyed. Many continue to exist such as, for example, state enterprises and branch interest groups. Also, new structures are gradually emerging. However, they are not yet established as functionally autonomous sub-systems; they have not developed (sub-)systemic features and, together, they do not constitute a system yet, because the links between them (which normally transform the economy, politics and culture into sub-systems of a connected entity) do not exist. These links consist, amongst other things, in co-evolution, mutual penetration and reciprocal adaptation of the various sub-systems. In the absence of such links the various segments of society function according to their own rules and separate logic. This leads to numerous discrepancies in the functioning of society, which are reflected in social consciousness in the form of dissonance.

Public opinion polls confirm that such dissonance is widespread in post-socialist societies, especially in people's attitudes and behaviour relating to macro- versus micro-structures in society. What individuals claim to support in their immediate environment, in relation to matters affecting them directly, is very often at odds with their general declared preferences. The majority neither perceive nor understand the connection between their own situation and structural solutions (Hausner, 1991).

The international context accounts for another important feature of the current systemic vacuum. Until now socialist societies were strongly dependent on, or rather subordinated to the USSR, forming the component parts of a wider, sub-global system. The severing of these external links enabled the transformation process to commence, but at the same time created a vacuum in the sphere of international relations. The dependence of the previously established economic links partly remains while, at the same time, the re-entry of the post-socialist countries into the international economic and political system is incomplete and in the making.

POLISH DISCOURSES OF REFORM AND STRATEGIES OF TRANSFORMATION

Taking into account Poland's international position after the collapse of the Soviet empire, a strategy whose point of reference was the broadly conceived model of highly developed capitalist society (market economy and parliamentary democracy) was an obvious choice, both ideological and pragmatically. It was all the more unavoidable considering the huge financial debt to western creditors, without whose cooperation any kind of breakthrough would have been unimaginable.

Given the systemic vacuum and the disintegration of the system, the imitation of foreign solutions became inevitable. Thus, post-socialist societies were condemned to shape their institutional structure through 'institutional isomorphism'. In the majority of these countries, including Poland, it was decided to adopt a neo-liberal strategy. This was partly due to external pressure (coercive isomorphism) and partly a result of a conscious doctrinal choice (normative isomorphism). It is quite evident that the intial strategic choice was strongly influenced by international financial institutions, and also by the fact that the authors and the advisers of 'Polish shock therapy' went to some and not other western universities. Still, we believe that the adoption of the neo-liberal model reflects, above all, an attempt to imitate well-tested paradigms (mimetic isomorphism).

The neo-liberal model of Thatcherism and Reaganomics was perceived as the most successful one in the 1980s in the West. The 'third way' was generally considered too risky or even unfeasible (Nuti, 1991). The slogan 'We do not want experiments; there is no alternative, we should simply copy what functions effectively in the West' appealed to the social mood of the initial phase of the post-socialist transformation phase. As a result, the adopted strategy included a monetarist programme of economic stabilization and a liberal doctrine of systemic transformation based on full-scale marketization.

Behind such mimetic isomorphism lay a desire to negate socialism as trenchantly as possible. Amongst various possible courses of action, the neo-liberal strategy was the most clearly opposed to socialism, which at that moment appealed to people's emotions and expectations. Society expected normality, which the majority identified with a rejection of the past and a negation of socialism. Not understanding the connection between systemic solutions and their own situation, most of society expected something better, something different, something which could bring about an abrupt turnaround in their fortunes. In a certain sense, the radicalism of the neo-liberal strategy was an answer to the social mood.

A further argument for the adoption of the liberal strategy was that it was founded on a very simple – mechanical and impersonal – vision of the market. In using the vision and phraseology of liberalism, the ruling elites wanted to strengthen the credibility of their policies and to create the conviction that the actual course of events was inevitable, that no one could change it, and that it was a consequence of the 'iron laws of the market'. At the same time they wanted in this way to speed up the educational side of their programme. The liberal vision was supposed to weaken society's opposition, and at the same time put psychological pressure on society to adapt to the new economic conditions.

The authors of the Polish stabilization programme believed that it was acceptable and desirable to enforce the hoped-for microeconomic adaptation of groups and individuals by economic coercion, resulting from restrictive monetary and fiscal policies. They also believed that should the state alternatively engage in any kind of industrial policy, it would be drawn into traditional socialist relations, which would lengthen the transformation process. They believed that if the state unilaterally abandoned the socialist relations of production, then these relations would automatically disappear, making room for human initiative and enterprise. In this sense, no policy was seen as the best policy.

IMPLEMENTATION PROBLEMS AND SOCIAL STRUGGLE

One of the general problems of implementing neo-liberal strategies is the fact that doctrinal disengagement in certain areas of the economy leads, sooner or later, to increased interference in other areas (Jessop, 1990, p. 363). This is precisely what is occurring under the conditions of post-socialism when, contrary to assumed and declared principles, the 'liberal' governments of Eastern Europe are gradually increasing the scope of their intervention into the economy, even if they officially deny it.

This paradox is caused not only by the objective situation in which post-socialist governments act (the systemic vacuum), but also by the relationships between, and the pressure exerted by, various social groups.

On the one hand, pressure is exerted by the direct beneficiaries, real or potential, of the newly created system. They force the government to become involved in such a way as to accelerate the process of primitive capitalist accumulation and the creation of a middle class. The idea of free competition is used to cover up their individual and group efforts for limiting public control over the activities of the state apparatus, thus widening the scope for arbitrary interference in the economy. In particular, this group exerts pressure on the process of privatization and aims at the recentralization of state assets, so as to appropriate them more quickly, easily and cheaply.

On the other hand, the majority of employees remain in the state-owned enterprises; they are organized along corporatist lines and put pressure on the state to intervene in the economy. In accordance with their historically determined experience, they see the state as an object of pressure from below and responsibility from above. It is perceived as a protector, an agent responsible for the preservation of their standard of living. Employees who remain within the bounds of branch corporations see no way of defending their group interests other than by enforcing, through strikes and protests, state intervention in such a way as to guarantee them their expected level of economic and social security. Branch organizations had an essential function in the allocation of resources and for social stability in the socialist system (Hausner and Wojtyna, 1992; Górniak and Jerschina, 1992). They have re-emerged recently even if their central function in the planned economy has abruptly disappeared (Hausner, 1991).

Owing to the interaction of the two forces mentioned above, the state (the government) is controlled by the new elites but is simultaneously subjected to growing pressure from below by corporatist structures, who do not find enough support within the structures of the political system and amongst governing elites. This inclines them to express their economic-corporate demands through spontaneous protest, thus destabilizing the economy.

As a result of the dual pressure, economic policy in Poland during 1990–1 was fundamentally at odds with its initial neo-liberal assumptions. The social struggle centred around the development of wages and incomes, and the ongoing process of privatization of state companies. The government gradually increased its intervention into the economy in contradiction to its monetarist aims. This was not, however, due to a conscious strategy but rather the result of forced concessions. Below, this will be illustrated with examples from the process of privatization.

From the outset, privatization was an important element in the neo-liberal strategy, meant to ensure a fundamental change in the economy's ownership structure, to curtail the state's control over the economy, and to create the structural conditions necessary to competition and improvement in efficiency. The idea of privatization did not meet with any significant opposition. However, the basic problem was always how to privatize the economy without capital and in the absence of a capital market.

In practice, the neo-liberal policy consisted in state control and financing of the privatization of the assets of state enterprises. The main road to privatization led through the transformation of state companies into joint-stock companies with the state as the sole stockholder, whose assets were subsequently sold in a supervised manner, ensuring the relative ease of acquiring a stake to control the enterprise. The transformation of state enterprises into such joint-stock companies put the privatization process beyond the control of employees and their representatives. To weaken employee opposition fiscal privileges accorded to employees of privatized enterprises were used as strong incentives. For example, large relative wage increases were made possible in such enterprises in relation to state enterprises.

Privatization through sales turned out to be very cumbersome and costly. This was used as an argument for de-bureaucratization and acceleration of privatization, which in practice meant a huge increase in the discretionary power of officials in charge of the process. Posts associated with the execution of privatization became very lucrative, both legally (wages, salaries) and illegally (bribes). A large group of people (officials, experts, entrepreneurs) made significant gains in this way, which were then used as capital, enabling them to enter more actively into the privatization game.

Another method is privatization of state companies through liquidation. In this case, many difficulties stem from problems in connection with the removal of social service establishments, in particular, company-owned apartments. The local authorities, to whom the enterprises want gratuitously to remit these institutions demand extra funds for their upkeep. Furthermore, the banks immediately refuse further credit to the companies being liquidated. As a consequence privatization through liquidation, especially of larger firms, is a particularly difficult and expensive task.

On the other hand, this form of privatization, especially when it is based on the appointment of small leasing firms, is met with great interest by employees. The motive for this interest, and often even strong pressure, is the desire to avoid the *popiwek*.[3] As a result, many decisions for liquidation are hastily made, without suitable preparation, and the numerous firms which replace the state companies may, after a short period, go bankrupt.

In addition to the theme of legal privatization, the bottom-up movement of self-enfranchisement has also intensified. Such spontaneous privatization is based on the leasing (or renting) by companies of the most valuable elements of their capital assets to partnerships or institutions with the participation of the workers of the particular company. Very often the directors of the company use social or housing funds to grant the interested workers low-interest credit, which enables them to acquire shares in the newly created enterprise. This causes a drainage of the state budget, both in the form of subsidies for companies and in the form of reduced tax fees as an effect of the transfer of ownership. The government has labelled this phenomenon 'black privatization' and has attempted to counteract it by introducing amendments to the legislation on the financing of companies.

In general the applied methods of privatization have caused a serious drain on state finances, which resulted partly from the fact that in Poland in 1991 the revenue from the privatization of state assets was many times lower than had been anticipated, despite the relatively dynamic course of privatization during that year. A full balance sheet must take into account revenue lost as well as obtained, and the former proved to be huge.

This policy was bound to provoke opposition from state employees and growing public hostility towards privatization. Social protest led to additional financial demands. Branch organizations consolidated in this way; their pressure on the government increased and, as a result of concessions given, the budget deficit further deepened.

These phenomena created unrest in government circles and the political elite, and suggestions were made for accelerating privatization. Such propositions imply the abandonment of the long-lasting attempt to appraise property value and adapt companies to privatization. The propositions involved a one-off transformation of several hundred state companies into joint-stock companies through the issuance of stock in small packages without defining its nominal value. Their 'real' value was then to be determined by the market. In practice this means the subordination of the privatization process to short-term fiscal aims.

THE FINANCIAL CRISIS OF THE STATE AND THE FAILURE OF THE NEO-LIBERAL STRATEGY

The negative phenomena linked to the emerging financial crisis of the state are so vast that they critically limit the state's ability to function properly. This breeds numerous economic, political and social effects. The critical financial situation of the state causes violent disturbances in the functioning of various institutions financed from the central or local budgets – something which is to be expected in view of the many duties carried out by public authorities (the state and local government) and the obligations to individuals and institutions; duties and obligations inherited almost intact from the socialist system. This is most spectacular in the health service (closing down of hospitals, the limitation of the range of medical services available), in the education system (the reduction of teaching time) and the judiciary (the decrease in the efficiency of the judicial system). In fact, there is no area of public life which has not suffered. The hardship that various social groups have to face is so severe that it inevitably leads to social protest, and hence to political destabilization, indirectly curtailing the state's ability to act effectively.

In addition to these short-term functional effects, the financial crisis of the state has important long-term consequences. This means that the state has entered a position where it is unable to realize any project of systemic change; it cannot overcome the state of systemic vacuum. The 'financial crisis of the state' marks a turning point tantamount to the breakdown of the neo-liberal strategy adopted at the outset of the transformation process.

The causes of the breakdown of this strategy are of course manifold. Many arguments voiced in the Polish media may therefore be correct in so far as they pertain to one of these causes. No doubt poor decisions, as a result of lack of information, incompetence and bad organization, are partly to blame. In retrospect it is easy to see the many mistakes made during the period of the Balcerowicz plan such as, for instance, the undervaluation of the zloty to the US dollar in the autumn of 1989, and the misguided 1991 budget.

To such well-known instances of 'professional malpractice' should be added the persistent and protracted neglect of all warnings concerning the fall in production. Many decision-makers confidently spurned these warnings on the grounds that the non-realized type of production was superfluous and idle, and that its elimination was desirable. This attitude indicates an ignorance of essential features of the economic fabric. The fall in production initiated a dynamic of vicious circles which is ignored when economic performance is only evaluated in terms of static efficiency.

The budget deficit is also often ascribed to external factors. Two such factors, in particular, are mentioned: the collapse of the Eastern market caused mainly by the disintegration of the USSR, and the Gulf War which for Poland meant an increase in the oil price and reduced exports, especially of weapons. There can be no doubt that these factors had a negative impact on the course and results of the stabilization programme.

Indeed, the financial problems of the post-socialist state are to a certain extent unavoidable. The transition from the command to the market economy has quite different characteristics and consequences than the reverse process (see Laski, Chapter 6 of this volume). During the formation of a socialist economy, the resources that were 'wasted' under the conditions of the 'suction of demand' can be immediately utilized, which can lead to rapid growth in production, employment and consumption, although in the long term this leads to sizeable losses resulting from the fall in efficiency and creativity. However, in the opposite case, the substitution of 'pressure of supply' by the 'suction of demand' must lead to a temporary fall in demand to a level well below production capacity, thus precipitating a temporary fall in production, consumption and employment, although as a consequence it will bring about benefits resulting from increased efficiency and creativity.

So the more resolutely and radically the socialist state assumes control over the allocation and exploitation of resources, the sooner will it secure the means necessary to the realization of its strategy and to the construction of the new system. The case of the post-socialist state is different, though: the sooner it introduces deregulation and liberalization, the more it will deprive itself of the means it needs to realize its strategy of development and to aid the formation of the new system. To some extent, therefore, the transition from the command to the market economy must entail recession and a budget deficit (the transformation deficit).

Even if the significance of the above-mentioned causes (poor decisions, external factors and transformation deficit) should not be ignored, we believe that 'the financial crisis of the state' is mainly caused by the poor progress of structural (systemic) reform. The lack of progress is not so much the result of the Balcerowicz plan itself; it is rather caused by what the programme did not contain.

According to the neo-liberal strategy western market institutions should be imitated rapidly and faithfully. State power and resources were to be used to this end, mainly through relentless economic coercion, supported by propaganda and education. It was believed that the society which brought down the communist authorities would eagerly convert to forms of organization and behaviour governed by market rules. This, however, did not happen, nor could it have happened. Market economy and political democracy can only function effectively if they are supported by a multitude of other social institutions; these must emerge from below in a process of collective learning. Marketization and democratization are processes of complex social innovation, which can be helped by external models, but which cannot take place without searching and creativity. The requirement of creativity implies the maintenance, at least temporarily, of some of the hitherto existing structures.

Full institutional isomorphism makes people abandon one form of social life in favour of another, and forces them to relinquish their past and their identity altogether. This can be accomplished only by the use of coercion; the wider the social chasm between the old and the new structures, the greater the coercion. The neo-liberal strategy envisages such an isomorphism. In order to realize the strategy, individuals and organizations were to be forced to adjust to predetermined goals primarily through the use of drastic economic coercion, and, to a lesser degree, through the reduction of the influence and functioning of all organization, whose existence was incompatible with the assumptions of the strategy. By consequence, however, the resources necessary for creative adaptation were reduced to a minimum. Society, that is individuals, groups, organizations and institutions, reacted with inertia, frustration and growing opposition. Thus, factors greatly hindering institutional change appeared, prolonging the existence of the systemic vacuum.

The neo-liberal strategy did not break down because the government failed to reach the goal of macroeconomic equilibrium by means of stabilization policy. On the contrary, this happened much sooner than was expected; yet the desired microeconomic adjustments and necessary institutional changes did not occur. In order to consistently pursue the goals of the stabilization programme it has been necessary to maintain the equilibrium, but on a still lower level, which has in turn intensified public resistance and blocked institutional change. Eventually, the 'financial crisis' emerged, making continuation of the programme impossible, regardless of who is in possession of political power.

'The financial crisis of the state' entails the loss of the state's regulatory capacity, and its ability to control events. Moreover, this is happening halfway between the riverbank left behind, on which it was still possible to regulate the economy by means of physical categories and methods typical of the command economy, and the bank whereto the country is heading, on which it will be possible to regulate the economy according to financial categories. Hence, the state can no longer use the instruments appropriate to the command economy, and at the same time it does not have at its disposal the instruments typical of a market economy, which has already partially started to emerge.

THE FORMATION OF THE CORE OF THE NEW SYSTEM

The systemic vacuum rules out the possibility of durable economic stabilization and equilibrium. Stabilization can be nothing but wavering and transient, even if supported by the most radical policies. In Poland a balanced budget and relatively stable prices were attained with the use of restrictive monetary policies in a relatively short span of time but the maintenance of these achievements over a longer period is not possible without the creation of an appropriate institutional structure in the economy.

The appearance of 'the financial crisis of the state' is a turning point. It necessitates the abandonment of the monetarist programme of economic stabilization and the liberal doctrine of systemic transformation with which it is connected. Practically, this means in Poland that the remaining elements of the Balcerowicz plan (balanced budget, stable exchange rate, interest rates higher than inflation) will have to be scrapped and inflation will have to increase significantly. The government's policy options will fall somewhere between two extremes: the renunciation of all action as a result of total loss of control over the creation and flow of money; and the exercise of full control over these processes.

Proximity to the former extreme would lead to uncontrolled hyperinflation, and in consequence to the loss of control over economic and political developments. Hyperinflation would bring about a wave of social protest, which would abolish existing forms of social organization and replace these with new ones. It is utterly impossible to predict or plan the outcome of such a process. In this event historical analogies may cease to apply, though, speaking in general terms, the emergent chaos can only lead to some sort of populist dictatorship.

On the other hand, should the government's position approach the second extreme, mechanisms characteristic of the command economy would be restored. State control over the economy would not eliminate the structural roots of inflation; on the contrary, in the long run it would reinforce it, but at the same time it would enable the state temporarily to counter its effects. By taking control over the creation and flow of money, the government would gain the means of 'buying' social consent. The government's political legitimacy would then, regardless of its ideological programme, be based on the re-emerged branch corporations of the socialist system and the corporatist mechanism of interest articulation.

The appropriate choice within these extremes would give the state some degree of control over inflation which could stop it from spiralling. Obviously, under the current conditions the attainment of such a goal must be the central tenet of any economic programme, as only this can guarantee the possibility of further market-oriented transformations. The main problem will be to find a way of directing the unavoidable inflationary wave so as to assist the restructuring process and the government's policy in this field. The possibility of a gradual and controlled overcoming of 'the financial crisis of the state', and the restoration of the state's ability to introduce innovations in the institutional sphere, depend on the efficacy of such a strategy. Without such innovations the 'systemic vacuum' will continue to exist.

Hence, the key to the solution consists in recovering not so much the state's financial room for manoeuvre as its ability to use it for stimulating growth. This latter capacity requires the formation of an institutional core of a new system. Some of the elements, which are, in our opinion, most important in this process, are presented below.

Ownership transformation plays a key role. This is essential for the evolution of social norms and economic behaviour (entrepreneurship, motivation and employee involvement in production) appropriate to a market economy. Moreover, without clear definition of property rights it would be impossible to establish effective mechanisms of articulation and negotiation of group interests, nor would it be possible to define the rules governing state intervention in the economy in a way appropriate to market conditions. The continued confusion as to the character and long-term perspectives of property rights gives a strong stimulus to recessive trends. The present state of confusion in the area of property rights should not be allowed to last too long, as this threatens complete disorganization and collapse of the economy, with the consequence that order will have to be introduced by state enforcement.

In stressing the importance of ownership transformations we have in mind not so much the commercialization of state companies, nor even the privatization of those companies, as the creation of a clearly defined structure of property rights supported by appropriate legal and financial institutions. This process cannot be carried out immediately, but must take place over many years. The point is that it should be launched, directed and constantly stimulated, thus guaranteeing an ever-increasing and a sufficient number of economic agents with well-defined property rights, capable of formulating long-term development strategies, and being able to bear the investment burden necessary for its implementation. Without this, capital accumulation would be very slow even with the best macroeconomic policies.

It is all the more necessary to generate strong and durable stimuli that would foster accumulation, given that the lack of domestic capital is one of the main obstacles to ownership transformations. In this sense one may say that a kind of 'primitive accumulation' is indispensable to the creation of a potential that would trigger off further ownership transformations and development processes in the economy. The future shape of the economic system, and also of the entire social system, will be determined by the way in which this 'primitive accumulation' is carried out and/or will occur. This process is under way, but mainly at the expense of the public sector, leading to the latter's decapitalization and disorganization, which is a major cause of the current recession and the financial crisis of the state.

The institutionalization of forms of interest articulation and negotiation characteristic of the market economy is also part of the core of the new system. Currently (1991), three bills are the object of legislative work: on trade unions, on employers' associations, and on settlement of labour disputes. The introduction of these bills will lay the foundations for a new system of interest representation. Yet it should be regarded as merely the starting point on the path to a really new system of interest representation with progress in this field depending on actual changes in economic and political relations.

The creation of formal procedures for negotiations is one of the main achievements of the Bielecki government. This developed as an effect of active participation of government representatives in handling the protests and conflicts. In this area the government has behaved in a different manner from the former government, which was prepared to negotiate only with the representatives of a central trade union body.

In the course of the many disputes and negotiations in which the Bielecki government was involved, the Ministry of Labour and Social Affairs elaborated coherent proposals for the conduct of negotiations. The proposals submitted define in detail the principles, conditions, parties and procedures of the negotiations. These interesting proposals admitted the necessity to set up a proper framework for negotiations, which is an absolute novelty in Poland and in sharp contrast with the completely implicit mechanism of previous corporatist bargaining. However, it can be anticipated that the proposals will encounter serious difficulties and may even be impossible in the short run.

Among the many barriers one should mention the attitude and the behaviour of trade unions. The organizational structure and role of Solidarity is unclear. Hence, demands articulated towards the authorities by the representatives at different levels of the union are often incoherent and even contradictory. Moreover, the relations between the central bodies of the different trade unions are so tense that one can hardly imagine their joint participation in negotiations.

The second barrier to implementation of the proposed system of negotiations is the lack of an appropriate form of representation of employers. As for the interests of the most important employers, the state enterprises, a model of their joint representation by the state enterprises' management and trade unions still prevails.

An efficient mechanism for negotiations requires stable relationships between various representative and decision-making bodies. Practice is far removed from this situation. Strong clashes between different social groups and between their formal representatives in parliament mean that the government is permanently under pressure from many sides and none of the particular representations wants to recognize the agreements reached with others.

An institutional framework for stable foreign economic relations constitutes another important factor of the foundation of the new economic system. In this area, too, a carefully considered, long-term plan is visibly lacking. Obviously, attempts are being made to incorporate the Polish economy into the international division of labour by means of economic co-operation with the countries of the EC. The attention of the post-socialist Polish governments in this area has been concentrated almost exclusively on the issue of debt reduction and diplomatic negotiations to pave the way for Poland's entry to the EC. However, there is an acute danger that a premature opening up of the Polish economy will consign Poland to the position of a mere EC subsidiary. Except for its efforts to create the conditions for currency convertibility the government has failed to take steps to create the institutional conditions for an internationally open economy as shown, for example, by the general weakness of the tariff system.

The definition of the role of the state in the economy is another area which is urgently in need of system-shaping decisions. This is a battlefield of radically incompatible ideas. In the course of work on the new constitution radical liberals came up with the proposal to prohibit the state from engaging in any kind of economic activity. Social Democrats, on the other side of the political spectrum, reject the possibility of a 'social market economy' in the absence of active state participation, and oppose such doctrinally justified discrimination against the public sector. Peasant parties promote the corporatist economic model which implies the association of all producers in chambers of commerce. No clear conception stands out from this gamut of ideas. During the periods of the Mazowiecki and Bielecki governments the liberals have been dominant in government circles, attempting to implement their ideas, and to this end using the power of the state to an ever greater degree. The strategy can aptly be termed 'state liberalism'. It is based on the assumption that while the West European institutions of capitalism were forged naturally in the process of socioeconomic development they have to be imposed by the state in post-socialist Poland. What is lacking is the realization that all West European economies, even after the neo-liberal wave of the 1980s, are mixed economies with a much more extensive role for the state than is prescribed by neo-liberal doctrine.

If one saw the political disputes around the role of the state on the purely verbal level, one might think that the main dilemma was whether there is still too much of the old system or too little of the new. In reality, however, power is the object of the struggle, and this struggle has a personal rather than an ideological character. Personal rivalry predominates over a desire to reach an agreement about the basic structure and rules of the system. The personalization of the political scene is both the cause and the effect of the persistence of the systemic vacuum.

This vicious circle is an important obstacle to the formation of a majority understood in the Gramscian sense of a 'hegemonic bloc'; that is, not just a majority within governing circles, but a majority understood as an alliance of significant social groups, whose political representatives would be capable of formulating and implementing a long-term strategy of social development, which would integrate economic, political and ideological elements. The formation of such a majority is a necessary condition if the institutional core of the new system is to be formed, i.e. if the systemic vacuum is to be overcome.

In practice this requires the formulation of an appropriate strategy of accumulation and the possibility of realizing it. A more broadly understood economic policy, and an accompanying sociopolitical project, would have to be built around such a strategy. Hence, a coalition of those groups who would consider its realization to be in their basic interests and who would constitute the sociopolitical base of the government would have to be built around such a strategy.

The greatest difficulty lies in the fact that the rivalry of interest groups still concerns the demand side of the economy; the more so, the deeper the budget deficit. Only effective negotiation can shift the focus of this rivalry to the supply side. In the present circumstances, such negotiations are made difficult not only by the complexity of the economic situation and the consequent sharpening of conflicts, but primarily by the fact that the participants and the roles played by the potential sides in the negotiations are not at all well defined.

It is obvious that the state (government; local administration) must be one side in the negotiation process. It is an open question, however, who the state should negotiate with and what form such negotiations should take. Taking into account the evolution of interest representation in Poland (Hausner, 1991), it seems that the starting point must now be the initiation by the government of negotiations with branches of industry, and with the regions suffering from the highest rates of unemployment and recession. As far as branches of industry are concerned, the negotiators should, above all, include union representatives, and, if possible, interested professional and public associations. As far as regions are concerned, local government representatives and local associations and organizations should also take part.

This line of approach follows the concept of the transition from state (socialist) corporatism to societal corporatism (Hausner, 1991). Socialist corporatism was the product of a secondary, pathological (dysfunctional) adaptation by mechanisms governing the social division of labour and interest representation to the conditions of the socialist economy. An appropriate form of societal corporatism in Poland would not be all-embracing (in the sense that it would not cover all economic agents and all spheres of their performance); it would not be based on monopoly of representation, nor would it eliminate political pluralism; it would be applied in an open way in selected key areas in order to change, rather than to maintain, the economic and political system.

NOTES

1. In this context we use the term 'post-socialism' to characterize the countries in Central and Eastern Europe which were previously dominated by command economy and communist one-party rule.
2. The model as well as this chapter in general originate from common research (together with Bob Jessop, Lancaster University) within the framework of an international research

project financed through the ACE Programme of the Commission of the European Communities: 'Negotiated Economy versus Neo-Liberalism as Institutional Framework for a Market Economy. Implications for Post-Socialism'. The first book from the project is Hausner, Jessop and Nielsen (1992).

3.   The *popiwek* is a tax on excessive payments. From 1 January, 1991, this tax was to be applied only to state enterprises. Those companies which were commercialized or partially privatized were to incur a tax of a limited amount. Companies whose property was totally or largely privatized were not subject to the tax.

REFERENCES

Campbell, J. (1992), 'Institutional Theories and the Discourse of Reform: The Influence of Foreign Actors on Domestic Political-Economic Change', in J. Hausner, B. Jessop, and K. Nielsen (eds), *Markets, Politics and the Negotiated Economy. Scandinavian and Post-Socialist Perspectives,* Aldershot: Dartmouth.

Dietz, R. (1991), 'The Role of Western Capital in the Transition to the Market – a Systems-theoretical Perspective', in L. Csaba (ed.), *Systemic Change and Stabilization in Eastern Europe*, Aldershot: Dartmouth.

DiMaggio, P.J. and W.W. Powell, (1983), 'The Iron Cage Revisited: Institutional Isomorphism and Collective Rationality in Organizational Fields', *American Sociological Review*, **48**, (2), 144–60.

Górniak, J. and J. Jerschina (1992), 'Out of Corporatism towards ... Neo-Corporatism?', in J. Hausner, B. Jessop, and K. Nielsen (eds), *Markets, Politics and the Negotiated Economy. Scandinavian and Post-Socialist Perspectives,* Aldershot: Dartmouth.

Hausner, J. (ed) (1991), *System of Interest Representation in Poland 1991*, Krakow: Academy of Economics.

Hausner, J. and A. Wojtyna, (1992), 'Trends and Perspectives in the Development of a System of Interest Representation in Post-Socialist Societies', in J. Hausner, B. Jessop, and K. Nielsen, (eds), *Markets, Politics and the Negotiated Economy. Scandinavian and Post-Socialist Perspectives*, Aldershot: Dartmouth..

Hausner, J., B. Jessop, and K. Nielsen (eds) (1992), *Markets, Politics and the Negotiated Economy. Scandinavian and Post-Socialist Perspectives*, Aldershot: Dartmouth.

Jessop, B. (1990), *State Theory. Putting Capitalist States in Their Place*, Cambridge: Polity Press.

Mayntz, R. (1988), 'Funktionelle Teilsysteme in der Theorie sozialer Differenzierung', in R. Mayntz, B. Rosewith, U. Schimank and R. Stichweh, *Differenzierung und Verselbständigung. Zur Entwicklung gesellschaftlicher Teilsysteme*, Frankfurt: Campus, pp. 11–44.

Nielsen, K. and O.K. Pedersen (1991), 'From the Mixed Economy to the Negotiated Economy. The Scandinavian Countries', in R.M. Coughlin (ed.), *Morality, Rationality and Efficiency. New Perspectives on Socio-Economics,* New York: M.E. Sharpe..

Nuti, D. (1991), 'Privatisation of Socialist Economies: General Issues and the Polish Case', in H. Bloomestein, M. Marrese, and S. Zeccini (eds), *Centrally Planned Economies in Transition,* Paris: OECD.

Platteau, J.-P. (1991), 'The Free Market is Not Readily Transferable: Reflections on the Links between Market, Social Relations, and Moral Norms', *Cahiers de la*

Faculté des Sciences Economiques et Sociales de Namur, Série Recherche **117**, 1991/8: Namur.

Schumpeter, J. (1976), *Capitalism, Socialism and Democracy*, London: Allen & Unwin.

8.   In Search of a New Economic Role for the State in the Post-Socialist Countries

Andrzej Wojtyna

The redefinition of the scope and character of the economic role of the state is probably the most important theoretical and practical question to be answered in the process of systemic transformation of the post-socialist societies. Given the omnipotence of the state in the past, which was reflected, among other things, in the lack of separation of the economic and political spheres, it is understandable that the new conventional wisdom favours a minimalist approach to the economic role of the state. At the same time, this approach is encouraged by economic philosophy prevailing in some international institutions (such as the IMF) on which Poland, as a highly indebted country, is and will be dependent. One can expect, however, that after a period of over-reaction an ideological pendulum in the post-socialist societies will swing back to allow a more unbiased and pragmatic discussion about the state's involvement in economic processes.

POSSIBLE LESSONS FROM THE WESTERN DEBATE

It has become a cliché that the speed of changes in Eastern Europe took everybody by surprise. As J.K. Galbraith (1991) even put it, 'The greatest economic failure of our time, needless perhaps to say, was in not foreseeing the recent revolutionary changes in Central Europe and the Soviet Union.' It is quite understandable therefore that the 'brand-new' policymakers from the first non-communist governments looked for Western expertise and advice. This is not to say, however, that there were no serious attempts by Polish economists before 1989 to analyse the role of the market and the state within the theoretical framework going beyond a traditional market socialism paradigm which did not assume a major shift to private ownership. Probably the most coherent and elaborated vision of the interrelation between the state and the market in the future Polish economy was offered by A. Lipowski (1988).

When looking at the economic role of the state debate in the West from the point of view of its relevance to the post-socialist societies we have to distinguish between its two strands. The first does not address explicitly the changes taking place in Eastern Europe even though both direct and indirect references were sometimes made to the traditional command economies. The second one concentrates on the post-socialist economies. Both strands are very important and complementary. At the same time, however, there is a certain division of labour between the two. The former is more theoretical and long-run oriented whereas the latter is much more practical and short-run oriented. Consequently, the former should be more helpful in designing a role for the state in the mature or target system whereas the latter should offer more guidance in the transition period. For the sake of greater clarity of presentation, this section covers only the first strand in western discussion.

The debate about the economic role of the state is by no means a recent phenomenon. Wellink (1989, p. 145) is perhaps right to say that 'The role of the government in the economy was the subject of debate long before economics evolved into an independent science.' Given such an impressive time horizon one could expect that some kind of consensus must have been reached. This has not happened, though, and the consensus is further away now than it was twenty years ago. But this is not surprising since economists have generally had an ambivalent attitude to the role of the state. As Friedman (1977, pp. 41–2) observed 'all economists are ... schizophrenic: their discipline, derived from Adam Smith, leads them to favour the market; their self-interest leads them to favour intervention'. But there must have been more important factors that led to labelling the 1980s as the age of anti-government (Heller, 1986). On the one hand there was a strong revival of conservatism in both ideology and politics which was largely due to disappointment with the performance of the welfare state. On the other hand, the contribution of new classical economics, public choice theory and new political economy (or economics of politics) shed new light on the complex character of factors on which effective economic policy may depend. Those new insights had very far-reaching, revolutionary (or perhaps counter-revolutionary) implications for both theory and policy. 'Rolling back the frontiers of the state' became one of the battle cries of Thatcherites, Reaganites and their followers in other countries.

This revival of conservatism started to lose momentum in the mid-1980s, a process, however, which has so far been more visible in economic theory rather than ideology and politics. Stiglitz (Stiglitz *et al.*, 1989, p. 20) writes that 'Today, views concerning a smaller and more limited government which were held so strongly in the early 80s are coming under question, at least within the US. Deregulation is no longer viewed as an unmitigated success.' Stiglitz's comment concerns the microeconomic aspect of the state's role.

Nevertheless, since the mid-1980s one can also observe a revival of Keynesian thinking in macroeconomics. Therefore, from the point of view of the post-socialist countries the situation is far from clear. It is fully understandable that after experimenting with planning and state ownership for almost half a century there is a strong desire for 'normality'. It was hoped that ideas of what constitutes this 'normality' could be 'imported' from the West in an unambiguous form. In reality, however, what was 'imported' was a product of one school of thought, which does not reflect the actual state of debate in western theory.

Without going deeper into the subject one can conclude that the first lesson from the western debate is that it is still too early to decide whether the age of anti-government has already reached its apogee. When we approach this problem from the long-run perspective, we must probably agree with Freeman (1989, p. 136) that 'the division of functions between states and private agents must be regarded less as the result of the rational triumph of pure economic theory and more as the outcome of an historical process involving complex social learning phenomena of individual agents and groups and the associated social and political conflicts'. He looks at the debate in terms of a 'trial and error' process of defining and redefining the boundaries of private enterprise and public intervention. Using this criterion he distinguishes two periods when the tide was clearly flowing in one direction: from 1776 to the 1870s; and from the 1870s to the 1970s (1989, p. 137). However, even if we limit the analysis of the state–market dichotomy to 'pure economic theory', we can observe some cyclicality too (see e.g. Tobin, 1985; Drucker, 1980). An alternative (and also complementary) historical approach to the role of the state is to adopt Kindleberger's concept of reversible and irreversible processes in economics (Kindleberger, 1986). Perhaps the 1990s will offer a more definite answer to whether the tendencies observed in the 1980s indicate an irregularity in the 'statist tide' or the beginning of a new cycle in this never-ending debate in which 'Conservative economists, fully as much as businessmen, have feared that the redrawing of the line in favour of the government would cause the goose to lay fewer golden eggs [and] liberals have feared that a failure to exercise public regulatory or supportive power would threaten the life of the goose' (Heilbroner, 1989).

From the point of view of the post-socialist societies an equally important and related problem is to what extent (if at all) the reassessment of the role of the state in the 1980s has led to greater convergence between major competing theories. This is of course a very complicated problem which deserves much longer treatment than is possible here. My general impression is that within each of the three main theories – mainstream (neoclassical) public choice and Marxist – there has been a very clear trend towards a much higher level of sophistication in the ways in which the economic role of the state is analysed. As a result there seems to be a better understanding of the nature of the state. Pitelis (1991) defines it in his interesting review article as 'one of the three major institutions of capitalism, the others being the price mechanism (market) and the private hierarchy (firm)'. In his view, 'The differentia specifica of the institutional form of the state vis-à-vis the market and the firm, is that the state has a "legitimate" monopoly of force.' In a somewhat similar manner Stiglitz (Stiglitz *et al.*, 1989, p. 21) argues that 'there are two distinguishing features of the State, from which most of the other differences between the State and other economic organizations follow: the State is the one organization membership of which is universal, and the State has powers of compulsion not given to other economic organizations'. Those emerging common threads in the analysis of the nature of the state may offer a good starting point for some normative considerations regarding its role in the post-socialist economies.

The greater attractiveness of the public choice theory in the post-socialist landscape lies in the fact that it overcomes one of the important weaknesses of the mainstream approach, namely its assumption that the state serves the 'common good' and reflects the 'general will'. The public choice theories adopt a more realistic view that politicians or bureaucrats act to pursue their own self-interest, and conduct economic policy in line with this self-seeking code of conduct. Given the instability of political and economic institutions, a lack of balance between the legislative and the executive branch, a strong prejudice against the state in general, but at the same time an equally strong attachment to the social safety net, the theory which offers some instruments which allow market failures to be compared with government failures in situations with conflicting group interests may prove to be useful. For societies characterized by excessive involvement of the state in the economy it may be very important that the objective of public choice is, in a sense, to reverse the burden of proof: instead of starting from the principle that any podkreslony intervention is legitimate as soon as market imperfections are recorded, they want to be sure that the imperfections of government mechanisms are not podkreslony + greater podkreslony than the market imperfections we want to remedy (Lepage, 1982, p. 84).

Another interesting outcome of recent theorizing is that several of the sources of market failures are, at least potentially, sources of public failure (see Stiglitz in Stiglitz *et al.*, 1989, pp. 45–6). This may lead to yet another interesting possibility which is 'institutional failure', the situation where transactions costs are such that private sector and podkreslony government failure coincide (Pitelis, 1991). Unfortunately, it is quite likely, given the very high transaction costs typical of the post-socialist economies, that the case of 'institutional failure' may appear something more than just a theoretical curiosity. But in general, an emphasis placed recently by both neo-

classical and public choice theories on transaction costs, imperfect information and incomplete markets increases their relevance to the post-socialist
landscape not only during the transformation process but also in efforts to
construct the target system.

So far nothing has been said about the stabilization function of the state.
Musgrave's (1959) standard work on public economics dealt with three main
areas of the economic role of the state: allocation, distribution and
stabilization. Recently, however, microeconomic, welfare economic and public
economic analysis has concentrated on the distributive, allocative and regulatory roles of the state in the economy whereas stabilization has been
relegated to macroeconomics. This could be regarded as convenient scientific
labour-sharing. However, this labour-sharing runs the risk of losing the
connections between the three most important goals of public economics
(Bös, 1989, p. 123). This division of intellectual labour may lead to a serious
policy co-ordination problem because the different types of policies are
examined using different models of the private sector. Co-ordination of the
two different economic approaches is usually done in an *ad hoc* way which
is not particularly satisfactory (Schott, 1984, p. 66).

There is a danger that this analytical separation of stabilization from
distributive, allocational and regulatory considerations may be transferred to
the post-socialist circumstances. Indeed, when we look at the implementation
of the economic programme in Poland we can fairly easily identify the first
consequences of this compartmentalization of economics. In this context
one of the most important lessons to be learnt from the western debate is that
stabilization policy should take into account not only demand management
of the economy, but also, in principle, elements of supply management
(Bruno and Sachs, 1985, p. 275). I will return to some more specific
stabilization issues in the following sections.

Probably the single most important lesson from the western debate is that
a general economic theory of the capitalist state is impossible because national
economies and nation states are too varied and because economic issues are
always influenced by non-economic factors (Jessop, 1987, p. 77). To put it
differently,

> the extent and nature of the governmental role in the economy differs greatly
> between countries, depending on the political complexion of the government in
> power (and the duration and stability of its rule), and on historical cultural
> traditions that may favour a more active role for the state ... or on the contrary
> may tend to restrict it (Bottomore, 1989, p. 38)

The differences are also due to the non-economic value judgements of
citizens at large, preferences of consumers for private and public goods and
many other factors.

This difficulty with constructing a general theory may look discouraging from the point of view of the post-socialist societies' expectations. However, it also delivers an important message on the positive side – the need for much more detailed historical analyses and for taking seriously the 'political' moment of political economy (Jessop, 1987, p. 77). In the Polish context both those recommendations for further research are very relevant. On the one hand, public debate is full of superficial views and clichés about the sources of other countries' growth and prosperity. Much too often highly developed economies are used as a frame of reference whereas there is a lot to learn from experience of the countries at a lower level of development. Therefore I am fully in agreement with Sachs's (1990) suggestion that Poland could learn enormously from the large research project aimed at comparative analysis of experience of countries at different levels of development. In my opinion, development economics is relatively little known in Poland although recent surveys (e.g. Stern, 1989) reveal that many both theoretical and empirical findings have far-reaching implications for the post-socialist economies.

On the other hand, due to over-politicization of both economy and political economy in the past there is now an understandable counter-tendency which manifests itself in attempts aimed at freeing economics from all its political content. Although some interdisciplinary projects are continued, it will probably take a few years before the economics of politics is established as an academic discipline. And needless to say, knowledge just in this area would contribute significantly to overcoming the uncertainty and risk inherent in the transformation process.

The very fact that much can be learnt from the historical experience of other countries must not mean, however, that this learning process should be only (or even mainly) backward looking. In order to assess an appropriate role to be played by the state, one has to take into account both present and future trends in the world economy. One of the most important is what Toffler calls powershift. In his view, 'the power of the state has always rested on its control of force, wealth, and knowledge. What is profoundly different today is the changed relationship among these three. The new super-symbolic system of wealth creation thrusts a wide range of information-related issues onto the political agenda' (1990, p. 321).

One of the key aspects of the powershift is the fast-growing internationalization of economic processes which has been due to enormous progress in the transfer of information. This process, together with the increasing impact of new technologies, the (alleged) transition from Fordism to post-Fordism, and the increasingly triadic nature of the world economy are four tendencies with major implications for international competitiveness and hence – as Jessop, Nielsen and Pedersen (1991) rightly see it – for reorganization of the very form of the state itself. Even though it can hardly be said that the growing pressure in Poland for implementation of industrial policy mainly reflects the awareness of the importance of those new trends, one can asume that once this policy is adopted in a systematic manner it will be easier to respond to changes in the world economy.

Having discussed some positive aspects of the economic role of the state we now move to a more normative part of the analysis.

THE ECONOMIC ROLE OF THE STATE IN THE FUTURE SYSTEM

Whenever possible, normative judgement on the role of the state should be clearly distinguished from analytical or positive statements. In practice, however, those two aspects are not easy to separate. The problem becomes even more difficult when we also take into consideration the feasibility aspect. This should be done because as North (1989, p. 107) rightly put it, there are three questions that should be addressed to deal with the issue of the economic role of the state: (1) What has been the role of the state? (2) What should be the role of the state? and (3) What is it actually feasible to expect the state to do? One can reasonably assume that an answer to the first question can be limited to positive statements. By definition, an answer to the second question is normative. However, an answer to the last question is probably impossible without mixing the two. This is basically due to the interaction of uncertainty, expectations, the programmes of political parties and social organizations, pressure groups, and many other factors.

Looking at those three questions from the present Polish perspective we can say that the link between the first two groups of problems is rather weak in the sense that the future role of the state is generally perceived only as an antithesis of its role in the past. However, when we focus our attention on the transformation process and hence on the feasibility aspect, then links with the 'inherited' role of the state are simply impossible to dispense with.

From what has been said it seems that in the Polish circumstances the most important issue which can be derived from North's three general questions is whether the economic role of the state during the transformation process can, should or must be different from its role in the future, target or mature system. My point is that this role has to be different but at the same time the short-run actions taken during the transition period should be subordinated to some long-run vision. The roles of the state in those two time horizons are both different and equally important. Neither aspect must be neglected or underestimated. Of course, this view is not shared by all Polish economists. Some of them maintain that we know where we want to get to but we do not know how. The others think that even though the vision of the target system is important, it is still too early to discuss it since we have to focus our attention on the transition process. Both those views are similar in that they overemphasize the short-run perspective.

In my view, neglecting the long-run considerations may appear to be dangerous. One potential threat is that the lack of a clear vision of the future may lead eventually to the hybrid or eclectic system which does not necessarily mean an efficient one. Another danger is that without an explicitly defined long-run target it may be very difficult, if not impossible, to mobilize social energy for reforms. An interaction of these two factors can lead to a state of 'permanent transience' – a possibility that the currently emerging type of socioeconomic environment, 'the post-communist economy in-transition' may be with us for a long time (Hirszowicz and Mailer, 1991).

An even more threatening scenario arises when we look at the present situation as a systemic vacuum – a state of unstable equilibrium which may lead to complete chaos and as a consequence to dictatorship (Hausner, 1991, p. 90). This scenario is more likely the more the 'permanent transience' of the economic realm is accompanied by that of the political realm. One has always to bear in mind that even in the developed capitalist societies market economy does not automatically entail democratic political rule.

It is easy to say that there is a great and urgent demand for knowledge about the target system. However, realism requires that this be confronted with the available supply of ideas. Any blueprint for the post-socialist societies has probably to start with addressing two general questions:

Should capitalism be the system to aim at?
If so, what brand of capitalism should be chosen?

Of course, 'capitalism' is such a catch-all category that it would be unreasonable and futile to discuss the first question separately from the second. One could also say that given what has happened in Eastern Europe and more recently in the Soviet Union, there is no other alternative to capitalism any more. As Fukuyama (1989) even put it in his famous essay, 'What we may be witnessing is not just the end of the Cold War, or the passing of a particular postwar history, but the end point of history as such.' The 'triumph of capitalism' requires some second-thoughts though.

It is true that the 1980s saw not just the collapse of communism but the revival of capitalism. But as the *Economist* (5 May, 1990) rightly observed, 'on reflection, complacency is not in order. As with a victorious country, any idea that has triumphed is usually prone to exaggerated expectations and therefore to producing disappointment. Anyway, beating an opponent as arthritic and flabby as communism hardly constitutes a true test'. This scepticism about whether the present state of capitalism conveys an unambiguous message to the post-socialist societies is shared by other economists. Rohatyn (1990), for example, thinks that experience with free markets and a deregulated economy is far from being a success.

The point is, however, that very often 'the advice now being offered the Central and Eastern European states proceeds from a view of the so-called capitalist or free-enterprise economies that bears no relation to their reality.... What is offered is an ideological construct that exists all but entirely in the minds and notably in the hopes of the donor' (Galbraith, 1990). A similar view is expressed by Stiglitz (1989, p. 57) 'Socialism as an economic doctrine ... is now dead. What I fear, however, is that the inadequacies of the doctrines of the right will only gradually become apparent.' One can say that it is up to the post-socialist countries to decide whether they are willing to accept this ideological construct instead of a more realistic vision. This is true, however, only under the assumption that no institutional pressure is exerted upon those countries. This assumption may be unjustified if a given country cannot overcome a crisis and restructure without substantial foreign aid, and is even more the case with a highly indebted country. In such a situation, when aid can come only from the advanced capitalist countries and international lending institutions (such as the IMF) the way to qualify for such support may be by demonstrating a commitment to the free-market model (Pollin and Cockburn, 1991). Even though one has to be careful not to go too far with this kind of interpretation in order to avoid the trap of the conspiracy theory of history, there is obviously some merit in this argument. And as the Polish experience reveals, the charge that the government is carrying out a policy imposed by the IMF may be used as a convenient tool in the political game.

Adopting the free-market ideological construct as a frame of reference for the future economic system in post-socialism effectively eliminates other potential options from the discussion. At the same time, glorification of existing capitalism weakens a tendency towards a search for its further improvement. And both East and West the task should be the same: to seek and find the system that combines the best in market-motivated and socially motivated action (Galbraith, 1990).

Those who favour a view that adopting a market mechanism will solve all the problems of transformation to capitalism seem to forget that markets are systems of co-ordination but are not social orders in themselves (Heilbroner, 1990). Even if we focus only on the economic realm we can observe that historically markets have been only one of the three overarching ideal types of decision-making and co-ordinating – the other two being communities and states (Arts, 1991). Therefore the main task for the post-socialist societies is to choose not a single ideal type but an optimal combination of all three.

This choice becomes much more complicated when the aspect of economic justice is additionally taken into account. This leads inevitably to the 'third way' considerations.

It is perhaps understandable that recently the 'third way' has not received a good press in the post-socialist countries which are deeply disappointed with the previous experiments with reform socialism. This allergy to searching for more unorthodox solutions was well expressed by Vaclav Klaus, a Czechoslovak minister of finance, when he said that 'the third way is the fastest road to the Third World' (Nuti, 1990). However, one has to distinguish between a third way still within the socialist economy (where state ownership prevails) and that already within the capitalist economy. Most economists now oppose what Kornai (1990a) calls associative co-ordination (various patterns of co-ordination based on self-governance, free association, reciprocity, altruism and mutual voluntary adjustment). But sooner or later discussion about the third way will reappear (Kolodko, 1990). In the Polish circumstances this may result from the fact that the labour self-management tradition is fairly strong. Once the links between Solidarity and the government are broken, one can expect much more opposition at the micro level against purely market-oriented forms of privatization.

In the meantime, as some economists think, the post-socialist countries may be losing a historical chance to build a system superior to the existing capitalism. As Lutz (1991), for example, sees it, 'the judgement holding the transformation to capitalism as progressive generally fails to see or appreciate the lack of democracy characterizing its major institutions, the investor-owned business corporation'. In his view, to the extent that the option of the emergence of economic democracy is ignored or bypassed in the post-socialist countries, 'civilization may be wasting a unique and precious opportunity for real progress'. So far 'progress' has meant dismantling welfare state institutions and moving to raw capitalism rather than discovering new forms of economic democracy or other unconventional solutions.

From what has been said it follows that the post-socialist countries are not willing to spend too much time discussing their own, original contribution to the future system. They seem to prefer an 'imported recipe' strategy. But then the already mentioned question arises: which of the existing capitalisms should be chosen? The choice is not an easy one since there are many varieties of capitalism and, ironically, the contrasts between them are going to be easier to appreciate now that they are no longer lumped together as non-communism (*Economist*, 1990).

The first step could be to address the question of whether the post-socialist countries should use the highly developed economies or the newly industrialized countries as a basic frame of reference. But even if this choice could be agreed upon the next step appears: is the Anglo-Saxon version of capitalism more appropriate than the German or the Japanese variant? Or alternatively: is the Far East model more suitable than that of Latin America? To be able to make a decision at this stage would probably mean to many people the end of controversy. But searching for a target system requires going beyond clichés prevailing in a society. For an average person the Asian 'dragons' or 'tigers' are a highly homogenous group of countries. But a closer look at, for example, South Korea and Taiwan reveals that the role of the government differs. The Taiwan government has been supportive rather than interventionist, whereas the Korean government has been collaborative and even coercive in relations with the private sector (Park, 1990).

Going further down this decision-making process leads us close to Landes's (1990) conclusion that 'the transition to modernity is necessary a case-by-case process. Many try but few are chosen.' This is not to say that there is not much to be learnt from other countries' experience. It means, however, that each post-socialist country is doomed to follow its own, specific route, no matter whether we call it the third way or not. This requires, among many other things, selecting an appropriate, tailor-made economic role for the state.

Given the importance of the vision of the system to be achieved for the successful process of transformation it is perhaps surprising to find not only that there is no ready-made and detailed blueprint available yet of the post-transformation system but even more so that there is not much discussion about it. In my opinion, discussion in Poland about the target system was much more lively in the 1980s under reform socialism than it is now. This is probably true for Hungary too. One could also expect that although J. Kornai's (1990b) recent book is devoted mainly to the transformation process itself, more will be said about the future system in general and about the economic role of the state in particular.

Many (if not most) statements about the future system in Poland are fairly general, even vague. This level of generality allows the economist, politician or party involved in the debate to remain noncommittal. As a result we have a set of political slogans to which almost everybody would subscribe: 'Return to Europe and to normality'; 'Only a market economy' etc. This uniformity of views (or, better, lack of views) regarding the future system is in sharp contrast with the heated discussion about current policies.

The short-term bias and vagueness of the discussion is partly due to the fact that the official economic programme launched by the government in October 1989 (the so called Balcerowicz programme) is rather economical with details about the future system. It starts with the statement that 'The Polish economy requires fundamental changes to set up a market system akin to the systems found in industrially developed countries' (*Program gospodarczy*, 1989). In Part IV, devoted to systemic changes, both instruments and objectives are also formulated in a general way with the emphasis on the transformation process. One could perhaps expect then that programmes of political parties should offer a clear vision of the future economic system particularly now, when the campaign for the first free parliamentary election has just started. Unfortunately, this is not the case. The most important economic issues in the campaign seem to be corruption scandals and the social costs of prolonging the recession. Criticizing the Balcerowicz programme without offering an equally logically consistent and viable alternative has become a dominant feature of political life in pre-election time.

There are of course significant differences between major political parties regarding the economic role of the state. This is reflected in different specific charges raised against the Balcerowicz programme. The peasant parties criticize a liberal import policy and the lack of an active price-support mechanism. The Social-Democratic party (together with the OPZZ trade union) raises the issue of the collapse of the state sector and calls for an active industrial policy. The Centre Alliance opts for a less restrictive demand policy and for replacing a progressive tax on the wage bills of state enterprises exceeding a permitted limit with a tax on excess price increases. On the other hand, the Liberal-Democratic Congress (of which the prime minister J.K. Bielecki is a member) criticizes Balcerowicz for not being liberal enough with tariff and tax policies. The common feature of all those criticisms is their preoccupation with short-run, policy-oriented matters. In practice, only the Democratic-Social movement criticizes the government for their lack of a long-term economic programme. Perhaps the post-election landscape with hopefully a more clear and stable political situation will eventually bring a serious, long-run oriented economic debate.

ECONOMIC FUNCTIONS OF THE STATE DURING TRANSITION

Neoclassical economists tend to assume that the pace of human adjustments to new situations is swift and basically unproblematic. This assumption was therefore also applied to the process of systemic changes in Eastern Europe – it was hoped that capitalism could be fairly effortlessly achieved. In reality, however, as the experience of post-socialist countries has already shown, adjustments have been slow and costly (or friction has been high). Etzioni (1991) analysed different forms of friction (human factors, capital, infrastructure, labour mobility, values and external factors) and concluded that a list of the factors that slow down transition in post-communist societies was familiar from other, less developed economies. His analysis confirms the view that transformation will last much longer than was expected in the euphoric months of 1989–90.

This perspective of a continuing (if not never-ending) transition period makes it necessary to emphasize the economic role of the state during the transformation. One can say that the longer and more difficult the transition period, the stronger the impact of the state's transitory functions on their shape in the 'mature' system. This is due to inertial forces which are particularly strong when there are not many corrective feedbacks coming from confrontation with the features of the target system because these are partly vague and inconsistent and partly non-existent. In such a situation there is a real threat that a highly eclectic, hybrid system, reflecting current political and economic compromises, will emerge. This course of events would confirm Heilbroner's (1990) opinion that 'we are likely to have a spectrum of such outcomes, none of which will be quite what the architects of Not Socialism hoped for'.

Even though one can assume that the transition period has its own logic, it still remains unclear what is actually meant by the 'transition' itself. An attempt to approach this definitional problem explicity was made by Hirszowicz and Mailer (1991). Their classification scheme is based on two major dimensions: (a) assumptions about the nature of government control over the economy; and (b) the dominating sector in the economy. Taking into account the possible combinations of these two dimensions, they regard a 'transitional' post-communist society as a society in which the state exercises control over the economy only through 'enabling', often indirect, mechanisms while the public sector organizations still dominate the economy.

Although I find this classification of possible cases quite useful, I disagree with the definition of transitional post-communist society unless one fully abstracts from real-world processes. In my view, the post-communist case should be characterized by a specific mix of 'enforcing' and 'enabling' mechanisms and not the latter mechanism alone. This leads us to the concept of meta-intervention or meta-functions of the state which I find relevant here.

By meta-intervention I mean a deliberate action taken by the state in order to change significantly the scope of its intervention in the economy (or, in other words, to change the 'intervention regime'). Whereas it is quite natural to think of the state shifting to a regime involving more intervention (war economy, command economy) it is much less obvious to conceive of the opposite situation. In history, however, we have seen examples of the latter case of meta-intervention. As Polanyi showed, *laissez-faire* in Britain was created by the state itself. More recently, Thatcherism and Reaganomics were the attempts to reduce the role of the state considerably.

An important characteristic of meta-intervention is that it entails a high level of uncertainty. This point is emphasized by Altman (1989), although in a slightly different context, when he says that

Government can be used to smash economic orders and to create radically new ones, and there appear to be no substantive claims one can make a priori about the character of the new orders. They may achieve the kind of economic break-throughs which Marxism postulates but they may also stifle economic productivity. They may increase economic inequality or they may decrease it. They may create entirely new patterns in the distribution of economic power, or they may reconstitute old patterns.

I think this quotation illustrates pretty well the scale of the 'pioneering' role taken on by the state when it decides to meta-intervene.

The concept of meta-intervention is somewhat similar to what Jessop, Nielsen and Pedersen (1991) call strategic capacity. In their view, 'strategic capacity is nothing more (but also nothing less) than the ability to formulate and implement strategies' and 'can also be a property of societal systems (such as the economic or political system)'. As for the strategic capacity of the state they argue that it depends on 'its ability to project its power beyond its boundaries through linking up with the micro-physics of power in economy and society'.

Trying to apply the concept of meta-intervention (or strategic capacity) to the Polish circumstances, one can start with using it while defining a transition period in post-socialist societies. I think, therefore, that one of the useful definitions of the transition period is to see it as a period in which meta-intervention plays a much more important role than the traditional economic functions of the state.

Even though the future economic role of the state in Poland remains 'qualitatively' undefined, the direction of changes in 'quantitative terms' is fairly clear: it is rolling back the frontiers of the state. This process should lead to the free economy, whatever this may mean.

Performing meta-functions requires, however, a strong state. If we agree that a good balance between legislative and executive branches is one of its important characteristics, then it is obvious that this criterion has so far been very far from being met in the Polish situation. The president elected in a free election (but with powers defined in the 'communist' constitution), the parliament with the higher house elected in a free election and the lower one being a result of a 'contract' signed during the Round Table negotiations in April 1989, and the government which does not reflect a balance of political power are theoretically the three major actors in the process of systemic changes.

In practice, however, the government and not any political party or social movement is the author of economic change now being implemented (Kolarska-Bobiñska, 1991). One could also say, though, that in Britain under Thatcher the new strategy was implemented by the government. This analogy is false, however, because in mature democracies (unlike in Poland) government is the creation of a political party or coalition of parties which has a more or less definite economic and social policy, and is supported by particular interests (Bottomore, 1989, p. 37). A similar point is made by Jessop (1987, p. 77): 'In general, state intervention reflects the balance among all polical forces.... This helps to explain the incoherence of economic policies and the difficulties of rational economic planning.' Jessop's point is very relevant, although perverse, to the Polish case where state intervention does not reflect the balance among political forces and economic policies are coherent or even, as more and more observers see them, 'over-coherent'.

The decisive role played during transition by the government and the state bureaucracy is due not only to the lack of the parliament's full legitimacy. Another argument stressed by the government is the necessary speed of the transformation process. The legislative procedures may be slowing down this process and hence the tension between legalism and effectiveness arises (cf. Kolarska-Bobińska, 1991). This tension has recently been reflected in the conflict between parliament and government over granting the latter special powers to govern by decree.

Probably the most important factor behind this key role played by the executive branch in the transition period lies in the origin of the Polish (and not only Polish) revolution which has been basically the revolution from above. One of the main characteristics of the revolution from above is that it is particularly concerned with economic changes, as Czarnota and Krygier (1991) observe. These authors analyse the circumstances in which the economic and political programmes were born and come to the conclusion that 'the major difference between them was the degree of social acceptance, or at least the degree to which they figured in social consciousness. While the political programme was widely accepted, the economic one did not exist in social consciousness. From the point of view of knowledge of economic policy alternatives, one can speak of a hole in social awareness.' As a consequence, 'people voted for a photograph with Walesa, not a political – and certainly not an economic – programme. The electorate had no idea of the Balcerowicz plan'.

The 'hole' in social consciousness has had its counter-part in the lack of social support for the economic programme. The only consistent promoter of the reform is the state administration supported by the active part of public opinion, chiefly journalists and intellectuals who are guided by ideological arguments (Mokrzycki, 1991). This is due to the absence of social groups whose interests would be directly linked with the new system. The emerging class of small businessmen is still too weak to play a leading role whereas most other groups have been adversely affected by the costs of transformation. This lack of social groups directly and immediately gaining from the implementation of the new system has contributed probably more than any other accompanying factor to the 'executive branch bias'.

Both the prime minister J.K. Bielecki and the deputy prime minister L. Balcerowicz are aware of this peculiar situation in which liberal policies have to coexist with strong meta-intervention. J.K. Bielecki, one of the leaders of the Liberal-Democratic Congress, argued nevertheless that recent East German experience indicated that the classic leave-it-to-the-market approach was 'inherently flawed' in relation to the needs of the post-communist countries with their 'fragile, even non-existent market controls'. Instead, he argued, governments themselves have to manage the transition to a market economy 'by creating the legislative and administrative machinery that underpins the market and which is taken for granted in the West' (Robinson, 1991). He made a similar point more explicitly at a recent International Liberal Congress where he said that the specific difficulty of the Polish situation is that liberal goals have to be achieved with illiberal measures (Mokrzycki, 1991). Similarly, Balcerowicz said: 'in our conditions the state is responsible for the construction of the new economic system' (Kolarska-Bobiñska, 1991).

I would argue, however, that this awareness of the consequences resulting from the interaction of intervention and meta-intervention is a fairly new phenomenon. Otherwise one of the important aspects of meta-intervention probably wouldn't have been neglected. By this I mean an important feature of the transformation process, namely that while creating a new social and economic system the state is still the owner of most enterprises. Therefore I fully agree with Kornai's (1990b, p. 82) view on the role of the state during the transition period: 'its apparatus is obliged to handle the wealth it was entrusted with carefully until a new owner appears who can guarantee a safer and more efficient guardianship'. Neglecting this important meta-function by treating the state-owned enterprises largely as nobody's property and at the same time expecting them to behave as the market-oriented firms has contributed significantly to prolonging the recession which is now probably impossible to overcome without goverment intervention (unless after a further and much deeper fall in production). Thus consistently refraining from performing meta-functions (or confusing them with functions) may now force the government to take on much more interventionist measures, such as industrial policy, which otherwise perhaps wouldn't be necessary.

CONCLUDING REMARKS

As I have tried to show, designing an optimal economic role for the state in post-socialist society is a very complex and multi-dimensional task. This difficulty reflects uncertainty inherent in the actual process of transformation on the one hand and controversies in western theory of the state on the other. Probably one should not expect much change in the near future. I share Heertje's (1989, p. 2) scepticism that 'Even if economic theory in the coming years proves able to develop a suitable interpretation of an optimal economic role of the state, it does not follow that such a concept will have any other significance for actual economic and social policy than simply being a wellfounded frame of reference'.

Neverthless I think it is worthwhile to sketch one's own version of the economic role of the modern state no matter how subjective, normative and incomplete it may or perhaps has to be. In my view this would be the state which:

1. tries to co-ordinate optimally short- vs. long-run, macro- vs. micro-economic, and external vs. domestic functions which means among other things that:
    (a) it takes into account both positive and negative consequences of its economic policies for the world economy and resulting feedbacks;
    (b) it avoids to using instruments of stabilization policy which could adversely affect investment and hence growth processes in the future;
    (c) whenever unavoidable it influences in a selective manner different industries in order to encourage their necessary restructuring;
2. is capable of meta-intervention, of imposing self-limits on its involvement in the economy;
3. defines the scope of its action using case-by-case cost and benefit analysis and not by subordinating its activities to the objectives of the state bureaucracy;
4. is able to reduce its role if it appears that performing a given function has become inefficient (even though it was highly efficient in the past);
5. does not subordinate its economic policy to the short-run political goals determined for example by the electoral cycle;
6. is in a position to resist pressure groups while formulating and implementing economic policy;
7. does not treat dismantling the welfare state as the only or the most rational method of stimulating the economy; it tries to achieve this by improvement in the wage-bargaining process;
8. is capable of providing conditions in which public expenditures support the private sector rather than crowd it out;
9. attaches much importance to the credibility of its policies and to the role of the expectations of economic agents;

10. whenever possible, gives priority to transparent policy rules over discretionary actions;
11. does not favour a particular form of ownership on ideological grounds;
12. takes the best advantage of the present state of economic knowledge irrespective of ideological preferences of the ruling party.

REFERENCES

Altman, A. (1989), 'Power, Politics and Economics', in: Samuels (1989).

Arts, W. (1991), 'Community, Market and State: Their Potentials for Achieving Economic Justice', paper presented at the IAREP/SASE Conference, Stockholm, 16-19 June.

Bös, D. (1989), 'Comment', in: Stiglitz *et al.* (1989).

Bottomore, T. (1989), 'Economic Systems, Government, and Group Interests', in: Samuels (1989).

Bruno, M. and J.D. Sachs (1985), *Economics of Worldwide Stagflation*, Oxford: Basil Blackwell.

Czarnota, A. and M. Krygier (1991), 'Legal and State Traditions, Civil Society and the Revolution from above: Prospects for the Rule of Law after Communism', paper presented at the joint meeting of Law and Society Association and Research Committee on the Sociology of Law of the International Sociological Association, Amsterdam, 26–29 June.

Drucker, P.F. (1980), 'Toward the Next Economics', in *Public Interest, Special Issue, The Crisis in Economic Theory*, 4–18.

The Economist (1990) 'In triumph, in flux', 5 May, 1–24.

Etzioni, A. (1991), 'A Socio-Economic Perspective on Friction', paper presented at the IAREP/SASE Conference, Stockholm, 16–19 June.

Freeman, C. (1989), 'Comment', in Stiglitz *et al.* (1989).

Friedman, M. (1977), *From Galbraith to Economic Feedom*, London: Institute of Economic Affairs.

Fukuyama, F. (1989), 'The End of History', *National Interest*, Summer, 3–18.

Galbraith, J.K. (1990), 'The Rush to Capitalism', *New York Review of Books*, 25 October.

Galbraith, J.K. (1991), 'Political Change, Military Power: the Failed Economic Response', paper presented at the IAREP/SASE Conference, Stockholm, 16–19 June.

Hausner, J. (ed.) (1991), *In Systemic Vacuum? Dilemmas of the Transformation Process*, Cracow: Academy of Economics.

Heertje, A. (1989), 'Introduction' in Stiglitz *et al.* (1989).

Heilbroner, R. (1989), 'The Triumph of Capitalism', *The New Yorker*, January 23, 98–109.

Heilbroner, R. (1990), 'After Communism', *The New Yorker*, 10 September, 91–100.

Heller, W.W. (1986), 'Activist Government: Key to Growth', *Challenge*, March–April, 4–10.

Hirszowicz, M. and A. Mailer (1991), 'The Post-communist Business Enterprise in Transition: Developing a Framework for Institutional and Strategic Choice', paper presented at the IAREP/SASE Conference, Stockholm, 16–19 June.

Jessop, R. (1987), 'Economic Theory of the State', in *The New Palgrave*, Vol. II, London: Macmillan.

Jessop, B., K. Nielson and O.K. Pedersen (1991), 'Structural Competitiveness and Strategic Capacities: Rethinking State and International Capital', paper presented at the IAREP/SASE Conference, Stockholm, 16–19 June.

Kindleberger, C.P. (1986), 'Reversible and Irreversible Processes in Economics', *Challenge*, September–October, 4–10.

Kolarska-Bobiñska, L. (1991), 'The Role of the State in the Transition Period', paper presented at the joint meeting of Law and Society Association and Research Committee on the Sociology of Law of the International Sociological Association, Amsterdam, 26–9 June.

Kolodko, G.W. (1990), 'W poszukiwaniu strategii lat 90', *Zycie Gospodarcze*, **11**.

Kornai, J. (1990a), 'The Affinity Between Ownership Forms and Coordination Mechanisms: The Common Experience of Reform in Socialist Countries', *Journal of Economic Perspectives*, **3**, 131–47.

Kornai, J. (1990b), *The Road to a Free Economy*, New York: Norton.

Landes, D.S. (1990), 'Why Are We so Rich and They So Poor?', *American Economic Review*, **2**, 1–13.

Lepage, H. (1982), *Tomorrow Capitalism*, La Salle: Open Court.

Lipowski, A. (1988), *Mechanism rynkowy w polskiej gospodarce*, Warsaw: PWN.

Lutz, M.A. (1991), 'Eastern European Economic Reforms and Progressiveness', paper presented at he IAREP/SASE Conference, Stockholm, 16–19 June.

Mokrzycki, E. (1991), 'The Social Limits of East European Economic Reforms', paper presented at the IAREP/SASE Conference, Stockholm, 16–19 June.

Musgrave, Richard Abel (1959), *The Theory of Public Finance: A Study in Political Economy*, New York: McGraw Hill.

North, D.C. (1989), 'Comment', in Stiglitz *et al.* (1989).

Nuti, D.M. (1990), 'Tertium non datur?', *Zycie Gospodarcze*, **44**.

Park, Y.C. (1990), 'Development Lessons from Asia: The Role of Government in South Korea and Taiwan', *American Economic Review*, **2**, 118–21.

Pitelis, C. (1991), 'The Nature of the Capitalist State', paper presented at the conference in Vienna, 15–17 July.

Pollin, R. and A. Cockburn (1991), 'The World, the Free Market and the Left', *The Nation*, 25 February, 224–36.

Program gospodarczy rzadu (1989), Warsaw.

Robinson, A. (1991), 'The Prereqisities of Prosperity. Survey on Poland', *Financial Times*, 3 May.

Rohatyn, F. (1990), 'Becoming What They Think We Are', *The New York Review of Books*, 12 April.

Sachs, I. (1990), 'Wielka transformacja', *Zycie Gospodarcze*, **34**.

Samuels, W.J. (ed.) (1989), *Fundamentals of the Economic Role of Government*, New York: Greenwood Press.

Schott, K. (1984), *Policy, Power and Order*, New Haven, CT: Yale University Press.

Stern, N. (1989), 'The Economics of Development: A Survey', *Economic Journal*, September, 597–685.

Stiglitz, J.E., M. Perlman, D.C. North, D. Bös, C. Freeman, A.H.E.M. Wellink, I. MacGregor, J.-J. Laffont (1989), *The Economic Role of the State*, Oxford: Basil Blackwell.

Tobin, J. (1985), 'Cycles in Macroeconomic Theory', *Indian Economic Review*, **1**, 1–24.

Toffler, A. (1990), *Powershift*, New York, Bantam Books.
Wellink, A.H.E.M. (1989), 'Comment', in Stiglitz *et al.* (1989).

9. Need Satisfaction as a Measure of Human Welfare

Len Doyal and Ian Gough

BACKGROUND AND PURPOSES

The purpose of this chapter is to outline an operational concept of 'human need' which can be used as a criterion to evaluate the welfare outcomes of different socioeconomic structures and policies. The importance of this concept is commonly accepted for the moral justification of welfare provision. Yet there is wide disagreement about what human needs actually are and how they should be measured both within and across cultures. Debates also rage about the links, if any, between the existence of recognized needs and the right to their satisfaction. The concept of need is found in two distinct sets of literature – philosophy and social science. However, these two discourses rarely come into contact. One of the goals of our book, *A Theory of Human Need* (Doyal and Gough, 1991) is to remedy this through attempting to develop a concept of need which is grounded in both. It purports to show why individuals have a right to high levels of need satisfaction and what this entails as regards substantive empirical indicators. Here we will summarize some of our general arguments.

Need, Preference and Welfare Economics

First, we must confront the claims of orthodox economists who argue that there is no need for 'need'. This position is based on two fundamental principles. The first is the subjective concept of interests: the premiss that individuals (or, frequently, households) are the only authorities on the correctness of their interests or, more narrowly, their wants. Following from this, the second is the principle of private sovereignty: that what is to be produced, how it is to be produced and how it is to be distributed should be determined by the private consumption and work preferences of individuals (Penz, 1986, pp. 55, 40). While numerous criticisms have been made over the last century, these principles still form the normative basis for the inattention paid to the concept of need by neoclassical economics.

A variety of approaches have been adopted to translate the first principle into an operational method of evaluating well-being. Early theories relied on utilitarian thinking and the contributions of objects to an assumed equal capacity for subjective pleasure or happiness. Later this was modified to assess desire fulfilment as indicated by choice expressed in market situations. From here it is but a short step to the direct equation of well-being with opulence or the real income of people as measured by the vector of commodities they consume (Sen, 1985, ch. 3; 1987, pp. 5–17). In this way it is claimed that subjective want satisfaction can be measured scientifically and thus be used to evaluate states of affairs or policies. Despite the differences between these approaches they all have in common the implicit rejection of an objective and universal notion of need.

Yet there are so many inconsistencies within the principles of want satisfaction and consumer sovereignty, and so many problems in measuring want satisfaction, that welfare economics cannot do without some criterion of welfare external to the subjective preferences of individuals. Let us briefly rehearse each of these issues in turn.

The idea that individuals are the sole authority in judging the correctness of their wants is severely compromised once we admit limits to people's knowledge and rationality. 'Wants based on ignorance are epistemically irrational' and there are further limits to practical rationality concerning future events and ulterior preferences (Penz, 1986, p. 63, ch. 5; cf: Sen, 1970). 'Evaluation circularity' poses another serious problem. If wants are shaped by the institutions and processes of production and distribution which meet those wants, then they cannot provide an independent standpoint with which to evaluate the functioning of those institutions and processes. 'What is being evaluated determines, in part, the criterion by which it is being evaluated' (Penz, 1986, p. 87). The shaping of wants can be direct, as in much modern advertising, but much more pervasive is the indirect influence of socialization and past patterns of demand (Penz, 1986, ch. 6).

If, for the moment, we set aside these weaknesses, there are also problems in comparing the want satisfaction of people with different want structures and in ranking levels of want satisfaction as higher or lower. As Sen graphically illustrates, utilitarian traditions of welfare measurement which equate welfare with desire fulfilment ignore all the ways that people lower their desires and reconcile themselves to fate:

> Our mental reactions to what we actually get and what we can sensibly expect to get may frequently involve compromises with a harsh reality. The destitute thrown into beggary, the vulnerable landless labourer precariously surviving at the edge of subsistence, the overworked domestic servant working round the clock, the subdued and subjugated housewife reconciled to her role and her fate, all tend to come to terms with their respective predicaments. The deprivations

are suppressed and muffled in the necessity of endurance in uneventful survival (Sen, 1985, pp. 21–2).

Conversely, it is inadmissible to equate the state of a person with the extent of his or her possessions, as do 'opulence' interpretations of welfare (Sen, 1985, p. 23). According to either interpretation, welfare economics lacks an objective basis for comparing people's welfare.

Penz draws two conclusions from this catalogue of problems and inconsistencies. First, 'want satisfaction is a principle that cannot be made measurable without additional normative judgements that are neither contained in nor entailed by the preference principle'. Secondly, were such external normative judgements to be drawn up:

> their insertion into the want satisfaction principle subverts the principle's fundamentally open-ended and subjective character. Yet not to insert them leaves it open to the problems of ignorance and irrationality, of the evaluation circularity, and of non-comparability. This dilemma quintessentially reflects the short-comings of the want satisfaction principle and of the sovereignty conceptions that are based on it. (Penz, 1986, pp. 132, 136).

Penz argues that the best candidate for these 'additional normative judgements' is some conception of human need. For Sen, whose contribution to this position is of the greatest importance, it is the allied conception of human capabilities.

Direct Measures of Well-being

What then of the alternative approach: direct measures of human well-being? The post-war period has witnessed expanding research utilizing concepts such as the 'level of living', 'social indicators', the 'basic needs approach' and 'human development'. Drewnowski and others associated with the UN Research Institute of Social Development pioneered the concept of 'level of living' – direct measures of need satisfaction in various areas of life. This was subsequently theorized by other social scientists mainly in the Nordic countries (Erikson and Uusitalo, 1987). Allardt (1973) for example broadened the approach from material level of living to embrace those aspects of life usually the subject of the personal and political realms. In this way he distinguished three fundamental dimensions of objective well-being 'having', 'loving' and 'being', while retaining the contrast with subjective well-being.

This body of work has informed comparative research on welfare outcomes, but almost entirely focused on the Third World. Examples include Hicks (1982), Ram (1985), and Stewart (1985, chs 4, 5). Frequently this research uses the Physical Quality of Life index or its separate components (life expectancy, infant mortality and literacy) as measures of need satisfaction. Unsurprisingly perhaps, since it reveals high aggregate levels of need satisfaction, this approach is seen to hold little relevance for developed societies, despite the contributions of such research as the Scandinavian level of living surveys.

For various reasons the movement for social indicators and human development focused on human need appears to have run into the sand in the 1980s. In the First World the social indicators approach was weakened by the rise of neo-liberalism, especially in the English-speaking world. The basic needs strategy fell foul of IMF-led policies of 'structural adjustment' in the Third World. But well before this time the conceptual foundations were weakened by a series of theoretical critiques. The basic needs approach, it was argued by some, incorporated arbitrary postulates about human nature (in particular western cultural values) and about social change (in particular a uniform, linear model of development). Either the very idea of a universal approach was rejected, or the theoretical possibility of universal needs was granted, but their concrete assessment was perceived as beyond reach due to the cultural and political bias of concepts and evidence (e.g. Rist, 1980; Galtung, 1980).

More generally, the idea of an objective, non-monetary concept of welfare succumbed to the dominant relativist standpoint in social methodology and social action, one which has been given succour by the intellectual environment of postmodernism. Some time ago, Winch set the stage for much that has followed through arguing: 'Reality is not what gives language sense. What is real and what is unreal shows itself in the sense that language has' (Winch, 1974, p. 82). The result has been either scepticism that common human needs exist or a belief that they are so mediated by time and culture as to have only an abstract universality. Indeed, in recent years the idea of common human needs has been criticized and denounced from all quarters (Doyal and Gough, 1991, ch. 1). Thus the rejection of the idea of universal human needs is remarkably pervasive. The decline and fall of the basic needs/social indicator/human development movements has been due first and foremost to the lack of a unifying conceptual framework with which to resist the new relativism.

A THEORY OF HUMAN NEED

In our book, we attempt to confront and refute this pervasive critique of the idea of human need. Our theory draws on much previous work in a wide variety of disciplines including political philosophy (Plant *et al.*, 1980),

Braybrooke, 1987; Thompson, 1987), ethics (Gewirth, 1978; and Wiggens, 1985) and Sen's work (1984, 1985, 1987) at the interface of welfare economics, development economics and philosophy.

The Grammar of Need

To begin with, some conceptual clarification is necessary, since need is such a ubiquitous word in the English language. And while it may not be literally translatable into other languages, 'need' is correlatable to other linguistic ways of prioritizing preferences and imputing necessity of various sorts to them. Let us distinguish three common usages of the noun and verb 'need'. First, it can refer to a 'drive' or motivational force, such as the need to sleep or eat. Maslow (1954) interprets the term thus in his famous hierarchy of needs. This meaning draws our attention to the biological aspects of human activity over which we have no choice. But over a far broader spectrum of action biology constrains rather than determines human choice.

Secondly, 'need' is used to refer to any necessary means to a given end. For example, to say 'I need a new hi-fi' implies that I have the goal of a better quality of reproduced music. It is this protean use of the word (and its equivalents in other languages) that in part explains the widespread view that needs are essentially relative. In this purely instrumental sense 'to need' and 'to want' amount to the same thing. The truth behind this is that all needs statements conform to the relational structure 'A needs in order to Y'. We shall wish to refer at times to the means necessary to attain specific ends, but when doing so shall qualify the word need in some way, or use the term 'need satisfier'.

Thirdly, the question is, therefore, whether or not there is some Y which can be said to be in the interest of everyone to achieve, whatever the culture. Generally, speaking the answer is clearly yes. Universality *is* often imputed to some aims and not to others. The imputation rests upon the belief that if needs are not satisfied then serious *harm* of some specified and objective kind will result. Not to try to satisfy needs will thus be seen to be against the objective interests of the individuals concerned and viewed as abnormal or unnatural. When goals are described as 'wants' rather than needs, it is precisely because they are not believed to be linked to human interests in this sense.

But what counts as serious harm? Unless we can identify some universalizable characteristics, any conception of need which is linked to its avoidance must be hopelessly relative. Our approach equates serious harm with fundamental impairment in the pursuit of one's vision of the good. We go on to link this to an individual's success in social *participation*. Whatever our goals they must always be achieved on the basis of past, present or future interaction

Figure 9.1 The needs theory in outline

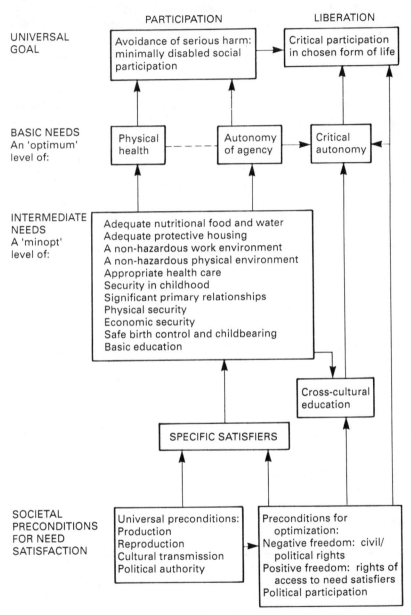

Source: Doyal and Gough (1991).

with others. We build a self-conception of our own personal capacities through learning from others. Thus objective basic needs are, at the very least, those universalizable preconditions which optimize sustained participation in one's form of life. At the most, they are those universal preconditions which optimize critical participation in one's form of life – which permit one morally to choose it through having the opportunity to choose otherwise.

If there are preconditions for social participation which apply to everyone in the same way then universal needs can be said to exist. Needs can thus be distinguished from wants – our subjective desires for objects or situations. To repeat a hackneyed example, a diabetic may want sugar, but she needs insulin. She needs insulin even if she does not know of its existence, indeed if she lived at a time before its discovery. She needs it ultimately because without it her social participation will become more and more impaired. It is this strong link between need and harm so defined that provides the possibility of identifying common human needs in a cross cultural way.

Figure 9.1 provides a diagrammatic representation of the stages of our theory. Let us now discuss the remaining stages in turn.

Basic Needs

We identify *physical health and autonomy* as the universal prerequisites for successful social participation. Let us look at each in turn. The bottom line, so to speak, of physical health is survival. To act and participate we need to be at least alive, so survival chances are an important indicator here. However, much more than this is required for social participation to be minimally impaired. We must also enjoy a modicum of good physical health. At this point we encounter the first relativist counterattack: what health consists of is disputed and regarded by some as having no objective meaning.

We reject this and argue for a negative conceptualization of health as the absence of specific diseases, where disease is defined according to the bio-medical model. This provides, we claim, the best available understanding, and cross-cultural taxonomy of, diseases. For example, it is unclear what it would mean to deny that cholera both exists and is treatable in terms which are laid down by the biomedical model. Not only do the international agencies of health care accept this in their epidemiological studies and policies for primary health care, it is also endorsed by critics of the model as well. For they too base their criticisms of, say, an over-emphasis on cure rather than prevention on the same epidemiological evidence. Health status defined in these terms is best operationalized via measures of mortality patterns and disability. 'Disability', according to the WHO, is any restriction on a person's ability to perform an activity in the manner or within the range considered normal for a human being. It is distinguished from 'handicap' which is an explicitly social notion referring to limits on a person's ability to fulfil a social role. Reliable and comprehensive studies of disability are available for a few advanced countries.

Yet physical health alone is insufficient to tap impairments to successful social participation. Autonomy of agency – the capacity to initiate an action through the formulation of aims and beliefs – is the definitive attribute of human beings. To be sure, individual actions, along with their actual identification as actions of a specific type, will vary across different cultures. Yet the fact remains that individuals will be unable personally to succeed within their culture unless they have the capacity to do the many things which, for them, this must entail. Impaired autonomy is tantamount to individual harm and concerns a deficit of three attributes: *mental health, cognitive skills and opportunities to engage in social participation*. We further argue that each component of autonomy can and should be assessed in a cross-cultural way.

The concept, even the very existence, of mental health has of course aroused fierce debate and criticism. We follow the work of Edwards (1982) and Boorse (1982) among others in defining mental illness as an 'extreme and prolonged inability to deal in a rational way with one's environment'. Yet problems remain in operationalizing this concept, due to the frequent lack of a specific aetiology and the reliance in diagnosis on a syndrome of symptoms. Moreover these symptoms are known to vary across cultures. For example, 'depression' is signalled more commonly by feelings of guilt and/ or suicide in Western cultures than in some non-western cultures, and less commonly by certain somatic symptoms. However, cross-cultural research has identified within this variation a common core of symptoms which appear to be universal (anxiety, lack of energy, difficulty in concentration, etc.) and which in all cultures incapacitate a person's confidence and competence to participate in social life. Increasingly, there is an acceptance that the social dysfunction associated with mental illness can be identified across cultures, despite particular variations in how such illness is conceptualized.

The second component of autonomy of agency comprises the cognitive skills necessary for social participation. These include a person's understanding of the rules of his culture and his ability to reason about them and interpret them. At one level these require culturally specific measures of skills. But underlying this variation are universal cognitive skills (language use) or near universal skills (literacy, numeracy, basic science, etc.). Direct measures of the absence of such skills provide a good indicator of blocks to autonomy stemming from this source.

Opportunities to participate in significant social roles constitute the third component of autonomy of agency. Parallel to Braybrooke (1987) we identify four social roles common to all human societies which we label production, reproduction, cultural transmission and political authority. To be deprived of the opportunity to participate in all of these, let alone any of them, is a serious restriction on personal autonomy. This restriction can of course stem from many different factors, including cultural rules (e.g. the exclusion of women, or untouchables, from certain roles), economic circumstances (e.g. unemployment or poverty) or role stress stemming from conflicting demands (e.g. the 'dual burden' of women).

We contend, therefore, that universal, objective basic needs exist, can be identified and their satisfaction monitored. Levels of need satisfaction can then be compared with an optimum yardstick. The latter should be interpreted, not as the abstract notion in economic theory, but as 'the best feasible level' within that culture. We shall return shortly to what this means in practice.

Thus far we have specified the general preconditions for successful participation in any social form of life. But some forms of life are extremely oppressive to their members, and all existing forms harm some of their members. Successful participation in a cruel or exploitative system is hardly a recipe for objective welfare. An 'internal' notion of autonomy such as this would also impart a static or functional bias to the concept of need which flies in the face of past historical progress. Beyond the goal of successful participation lies the goal of critical participation in a social life form which is, as far as possible, of one's own choosing. Similarly, beyond autonomy of agency lies critical autonomy – the ability to situate, criticize and if necessary challenge the rules and practices of the culture one is born into, or currently lives in. Critical autonomy entails the same levels of physical and mental health as autonomy of agency but with extra increments of cognitive skills and social opportunities. In particular, these will include, we argue, certain knowledge of other cultures and of a world language through which this can accessed. A further prerequisite is political freedom, an issue which is returned to below.

Table 9.1 draws together the components of basic needs that we have identified, and suggests some indicators for charting their levels of satisfaction.

Intermediate Needs

If this much is agreed, many problems still remain in charting need satisfaction in practice. To resolve them, we must face another set of issues concerning the operationalization of our theory of human need.

Basic needs can be met in numerous different ways. Common needs do not imply uniform satisfiers. There is an almost infinite variety of goods, services, activities and relationships which, to a greater or lesser extent, meet basic needs. These are illustrated at the fourth level in Figure 9.1. It is this open-endedness which has led many researchers who accept the theo-

Table 9.1   Suggested indicators of basic need-satisfaction

Basic need components	Suggested indicators
Physical health Survival chances	α Life expectancy at various ages (including disaggregated and distributional measures) α Age-specific mortality rates, especially infant and under-5 mortality rates
Physical ill-health	β Prevalence of disabilities, according to severity β Prevalence of children suffering from developmental deficiencies, according to severity β Prevalence of people suffering from serious pain β Morbidity rates for various disease categories
Autonomy Mental Disorder	β Prevalence of severe psychotic, depressive and other mental illness
Cognitive deprivation	χ Lack of culturally relevant knowledges α Illiteracy β Lack of attainment in mathematics, science and other near-universal basic skills β Absence of skill in world language
Opportunities for economic activity	β Unemployment, and other measures of exclusion from significant social roles β Lack of 'free time', after accounting for productive and reproductive activities.

α Reasonably reliable universal or near-universal data
β Data for few countries only, but where there is a clear idea of operationalization
χ More speculative suggestions for indicators

Source: Doyal and Gough (1991).

Table 9.2   Suggested indicators of intermediate need-satisfaction

Universal satisfier characteristics	Social indicators
1 Food and water	
Appropriate nutritional intake	α Calorie consumption below FAO/WHO requirements
	β Other nutrients consumption below requirements
	α % lacking access to adequate safe water
	α % suffering malnutrition/deficiency diseases*
	α % low birthweight babies*
	β % overweight/obese*
2 Housing	
Adequate shelter	β % homeless
	β % in structures that do not protect against normal weather
Adequate basic services	α % lacking safe sanitation facilities
Adequate space per person	β % living above specified ratio of persons per room
3 Work	
Non-hazardous work environment	β Incidence of specified hazards
	χ Incidence of job tasks undermining emotional/cognitive autonomy
	α Deaths/injuries from work accidents*
	α Deaths/illness from work-related diseases*
4 Physical environment	
Non-hazardous environments	β % experiencing concentrations of pollutants > specified levels: air, water, land, radiation, noise
5 Health care	
Provision of appropriate care	α Doctors/nurses/hospital beds per population < specified levesls
Access to appropriate care	α % without access to community health services
	α % not fully immunized against specified diseases

Universal satisfier characteristics	Social indicators
6 Childhood needs	
Security in childhood	χ % of children abandoned, abused, neglected
Child development	χ % lacking stimulation, positive feed-back, responsibility
7 Support groups	
Presence of significant others	χ % without close, confiding relationship
Primary support group	β % with no/very low social contacts
	χ % with nobody to call on when in need
8 Economic security	
Economic security	α % in aboslute poverty
	χ % in relative poverty (participation standard)
	β % with poor protection against speci-fied contingencies
9 Physical security	
A safe citizenry	α Homicide rates
	β Crime victim rates
A safe state	β Victime of state violence
	α War victims
10 Education	
Access to cultural skills	α Lack of primary/secondary education
	α Years of formal study < specified level
	β Lack of specified qualifications
Access to cross-cultural knowledge	α Lack of higher education
11 Birth control and childbearing	
Safe birth control	α Lack of access to safe contraception and abortion
Safe childbearing	α Maternal mortality rate[*]

α Reasonably reliable universal or near-universal data
β Data for few countries only, but where a clear idea of operationalization
χ More speculative suggestions for indicators
* Indicator of health or autonomy related to a particular universal satisfier characteristic

Source: Doyal and Gough (1991).

retical possibility of universal needs to argue that their objective assessment is beyond our reach. How is relativism of this second sort to be rebutted?

To do so we follow Sen (1984, 1985, 1987) and distinguish between commodities, their characteristics, the 'capabilities' or 'functionings' which they make possible and the final subjective mental states which their consumption generates:

Commodities → characteristics → capabilities → mental states.

His model implies two alternative measures of well-being to the two identified in orthodox welfare economics: wealth (commodities) and utility (subjective end states). The first – his notion of capabilities – is very close to our basic needs; indeed we believe that our theory systematizes his concept and makes it directly operational. Can his (and Lancaster's, 1966) second concept of characteristics furnish a bridge between these universal 'capabilities' and socially specific 'commodities'?

This can be done through stipulating all characteristics – 'satisfier characteristics' – which have the property of contributing to the satisfaction of basic needs in one or more cultural settings. Let us next take as a subset of this set those satisfier characteristics which apply in all cultures. These 'universal satisfier characteristics' thus refer to those properties of goods, services, activities and relationships which enhance physical health and autonomy everywhere. For example, provision of energy and/or protein is (or should be) a common property of foodstuffs, protection from the elements is (or should be) a common property of dwellings, and so on. Such characteristics are from now on referred to as 'intermediate needs'.

These intermediate needs are grouped into eleven categories in Figure 9.1. Like all taxonomies these groupings are in one sense arbitrary. The crucial thing is that all the characteristics gathered under these headings are universally and positively associated with one or more of the components of physical health and autonomy, according to the best available natural and social scientific knowledge. Nine of these categories apply to all people, and one refers to the specific needs of children. The other refers to the specific needs of women for safe birth control and childbearing – reflecting the one salient biological difference within the human species. We reason that each of these eleven groups of characteristics is essential to protect the health and autonomy of people, and thus to enable them to participate to the maximum extent in their social form of life, whatever that is. Table 9.2 shows for each of these categories some of the components for which reasonably generalizable evidence exists, and suggests cross-cultural indicators of these.

The level of intermediate need satisfaction corresponding to the optimum level of basic need satisfaction we shall call the 'minimum optimorum' or 'minopt' for short. Following Warr (1987, ch. 1) we argue that a particular level of satisfaction of each intermediate need (e.g. housing) is required if health and autonomy are to be optimized, but that beyond this point no further inputs will improve the 'output' of basic need satisfaction. For example, the available evidence suggests that dwellings harm physical health, mental health and cognitive development if they offer insufficient protection against weather, pests and disease-carrying vectors, if they are not supplied with clean water and effective sanitation, and if they are overcrowded. Certain levels of these characteristics must be present if basic need satisfaction is not to suffer. But no further improvements in space, amenities, fittings and so forth will enhance the need satisfaction (as opposed to the want satisfaction) of its inhabitants.

In general then, we have argued that universal human needs exist, that sets of basic and intermediate needs can be identified and that degrees of need satisfaction can be charted using indicators which can be validated cross-culturally (in theory, if not always in practice). In this way substantive need satisfaction can provide a generalizable index of welfare outcomes with which to compare the socioeconomic structures and policies of different nation states. The measures are necessarily multiple and diverse. All attempts so far to provide a unitary index of human development have been flawed, and any search for such a replacement for GNP per head is likely to be doomed to failure (but see UNDP, 1990, 1991).

Societal Preconditions for Optimizing Need Satisfaction

But the task cannot stop here. Even if this argument is accepted we still face the reality of a million and one disagreements over which strategies, satisfiers and policies best achieve the goal of improving need satisfaction. In practice there will be three kinds of dispute: first, over the effectiveness of particular technologies (e.g. what particular diets best contribute to good nutrition); secondly, over which social arrangements will optimize need satisfaction (e.g. what is the form of income maintenance policy); and thirdly, over priorities in an inevitable situation of resource constraints (e.g. should the needs of the elderly take precedence over the needs of young children). In the face of disagreements of this sort, the goal of optimizing need satisfaction faces severe problems of moral and political indeterminacy.

The only solution is that the *substantive* theory of need outlined above must be complemented by a *procedural* theory which sets out the framework wherein such disputes can be resolved in the most rational way possible. We draw upon the works of Habermas and Rawls to sketch out certain communicational and constitutional preconditions for optimizing need satisfaction in practice. Habermas outlines a theory of communicational competence in the resolution of debates (Habermas, 1970; cf. Roderick, 1986) about need satisfaction which underlines the importance for rational outcomes of the best available understanding and of truly democratic debate. With modifications to his three principles, we argue that Rawls identifies the constitutional framework which will potentially optimize the competence of citizens to engage in such debate (Rawls, 1972). To do so, for example, they must enjoy the right codified in law to both negative and positive freedom.

Negative freedoms entail many standard civil and political rights, the enjoyment of which can be charted through various measures developed by political scientists and illustrated in Table 9.3. Positive freedoms entail rights to optimum need satisfaction, as defined and operationalized above. However, it is more difficult to specify and monitor the social preconditions for such need satisfaction because the potential gap between *de facto* and *de jure*

Table 9.3   Suggested indicators of societal preconditions for optimization

Societal preconditions	Examples of social indicators
Respect for civil/political rights	α Index of respect for UN rights
Political participation	α Index of representative democracy
	β Voting rates
	χ Indices of citizen influence within polity
Material bases for rights to need-satisfaction:	
Production of satisfiers	χ Value of production of 'basics' per head
Distribution of satisfiers	β Real income of lowest percentile groups (as proportion of best-achieving country at each stage of development)
Need transformation	χ Ratio of need satisfaction to consumption of basics
	α Sex ratio of population
Material reproduction	α Non-renewable energy consumption per head
	β Greenhouse gas emissions per head
	α Total fertility rate

α Reasonably reliable universal or near-universal data
β Data for few countries only, but where a clear idea of operationalization
χ More speculative suggestions for indicators

Source: Doyal and Gough (1991).

rights is so much greater. The fact that socioeconomic rights entail substantial claims on resources means that a poverty stricken country with the most comprehensive bill of social rights cannot deliver on these.

To operationalize socioeconomic rights we utilize a cross-cultural model of production developed by Stewart (1985, ch. 2). This enables us to distinguish four features of material production systems which affect levels of need satisfaction:

1. Production – the total quantity, composition and quality of need satisfiers.
2. Distribution – the pattern of distribution of these satisfiers among households.
3. Need transformation – the effectiveness with which these satisfiers are transformed into individual need satisfactions, together with the direct impact of production processes and the environment on need satisfactions.
4. Material reproduction – the rate of depletion/accumulation of capital goods, the natural resource base and human resources.

Again indicators of each stage can be suggested, as illustrated in Table 9.3. Together with the measures of human rights and political democracy, they chart the extent to which the social preconditions for optimum need satisfaction obtain in given nations, or groups of nations. However, unlike Rawls, we argue that rights to need satisfaction have parity with the more traditional liberal rights.

Global Dilemmas

The huge variations today in the material capacity of the First and Third Worlds to meet needs raises one last issue which any theory of human need must tackle. Are rights to need satisfaction to be limited to members of specific nation states, or should they be cast more broadly? We have already indicated in brief our moral argument that the right to need satisfaction cannot be limited to members of the same culture or political system. Strangers in other cultural and political systems have an equal right to need satisfaction and to need satisfaction at optimal, not just basic, levels. A theory of human need cannot stop at national boundaries and national welfare states – we must, with Myrdal (1960), go 'beyond the welfare state' to consider human welfare on a world scale.

This moral argument generates further issues in operationalizing and measuring need satisfaction over space and time. In particular, how are we to evaluate social policies and practices which benefit human well-being in the First World, but which are either at the expense of, or cannot be generalized to, the Third World? Further difficulties are raised once we recognize the rights of future generations to need satisfaction. Although these problems cannot be accorded the attention they merit in this chapter, some brief observations are in order.

The issue of measuring success in meeting needs in the context of gross global inequality is tackled by identifying 'best performers' among low- and middle-income nations which can act as a standard for other countries in their income group. We identify Costa Rica, for example, as a middle-income country with exceptionally good levels of substantive need satisfaction. It is the world's poorest country to have approximated western levels of welfare across a wide range of need indicators. Costa Rica therefore provides a constrained optimum standard with which the performance of other middle-income nations can be compared.

The problems of defining optimum levels of need satisfaction over time and between generations are still more difficult to resolve. However, certain well established threats to economic sustainability over time can be monitored via indicators such as use of unrenewable resources per capita, even if there is not yet a set of agreed standards by which they can be evaluated (see Table 9.3).

NEED SATISFACTION AS A MEASURE OF HUMAN WELFARE

The upshot of all this is three sets of indicators to chart basic need satisfaction, intermediate need satisfaction and the presence/absence of societal preconditions for optimal need satisfaction. It is these which we propose as cross-cultural indicators of welfare outcomes. They provide external and independent standards with which to evaluate the performance of very different social, economic and political systems. They thus permit objective human welfare to be assessed independent of the cultural values of any single social grouping.

Tables 9.4 and 9.5 draw together some of the national data available on a global scale, aggregated for groups of countries in the three worlds. The Third World is subdivided into low- and middle-income nations, following World Bank definitions, with China and India – the Jupiter and Saturn of the world system – separately identified. These tables are concerned only with national averages: they can of course be disaggregated to present information for sub-groups in the population. We shall not extend this chapter any further by offering a commentary on the results (see Doyal and Gough, 1991, chs 12, 13).

Of course, there is little that is new in these tables. The information is readily available from international agencies and other publications (see

Table 9.4   Substantive need-satisfaction in the three worlds

	Third World				Second World	First World	World
	China	India	Other low income	Medium income			
1 Pop., 1986 (m)	1 054	781	663	1 230	396	742	4 885
2 GNP/head, 1986	300	290	242	1 330	(2 059)	12 964	2 780
3 GDP/head ppp, 1980	–	573	(760)	(2 594)	–	9 699	(3 879)
Survival health							
4 Life expectancy, 1986	69	57	50	61	72	75	64
5 Infant MR, 1985	36	105	119	66	23	9	61
6 Under-5 MR, 1985	50	158	193	108	27	12	94
7 Low birth weight (%)	6	30	24	12	6	6	14
Autonomy							
8 Literacy, 1985 (%)	69	43	46	73	(c.100)	(c.100)	70
Intermediate needs							
Water/nutrition							
9 Safe water, 1983 (%)	–	54	33	59	(c.100)	(c.100)	–
10 Calories, 1982	111	96	92	110	132	130	111
Housing							
11 Overcrowding, 1970s (%)	–	–	–	(61)	13	2	–
Health services							
12 Pop/phys., 1981	1.7	3.7	11.6	5.1	0.34	0.55	3.8
13 Access, 1980–3 (%)	–	–	49	(57)	(c.100)	(c.100)	–
Security							
14 War dead, 1945–85 (%)	0.2	0.1	1.0	0.4	0.0	0.0	0.3
15 Homicide, 1987	–	–	–	(8.3)	1.9	3.8	(4.6)
16 Poverty, 1977–84(%)	–	48	(55)	(33)	–	–	–
Education							
17 Adults: sec. ed.(%)	16	14	(9)	10	42	30	16
18 Adults: post-sec. ed. (%)	1.0	2.5	(1.4)	4.8	(8.9)	11.7	3.7
19 Students: sec. ed (%)	39	35	23	47	92	93	51
20 Students: post-sec. ed. (%)	–	–	3	14	20	39	19
Reproduction							
21 Contraception, 1985 (%)	77	35	21	50	——66——		50
22 Maternal MR, 1980–7	44	340	510	130	——10——		250

Source: Doyal and Gough (1991).

Table 9.5   Societal preconditions for optimal need-satisfaction in the three worlds

	Third World				Second World	First World	World
	China	India	Other low income	Medium income			
Civil/political							
1 Human rights, 1984	23	60	(38)	56	24	91	50
2 Democracy, 1985	0	3.0	0.7	1.8	0.3	4.0	1.7
Material							
3 Basics output, 1975	⎯⎯⎯0.4⎯⎯⎯			[0.6]	0.8	1.6	3.4
4 Income of poorest 20% c. 1980	–	201	(189)	(582)	–	3 113	(1 353)
Sustainability							
5 Energy consumption 1985	532	208	88	767	4 661	4 952	1 498
6 Carbon emissions, 1987	0.36	0.29	–	(1.82)	2.47	3.00	–

Source: Doyal and Gough (1991).

especially UNDP, 1990, 1991). By this stage it may reasonably be asked what we have achieved that is new. For the purposes of this paper there are three things we wish to highlight. First and most important is precisely the fact that the indicators used in these tables have been derived from, and validated by, an appeal to an explicitly universal and generalizable theory of human need. In the absence of this, the idea and measurement of 'human development', 'social growth', 'quality of life', 'human well-being' and associated concepts are vulnerable to the raids and reconstructions of relativists with the dangers we have outlined.

Secondly, and related to this, the indicators are intended to be explicitly cross-cultural (whether or not the actual indicators one is forced to use always live up to this ideal). The same measures can be used to compare the nations and regions of the world: North and South, West and East. They can also be used to compare the levels of welfare of peoples with different belief systems and ideologies: communist and capitalist, Catholic and Confucian. Thirdly, the theory can select from the mass of social indicators those which are valid measures of human need from those which are not. Furthermore, it can identify the many gaps in present social reporting. Valid and comparative indicators are lacking in many areas; for example, morbidity rates and the prevalence of disability, syndromes of mental illness, the extent of child neglect, abuse and ill treatment, the presence or absence of primary support groups and economic insecurity.

In short, universal and objective human needs are knowable and at any point in time there is a body of best knowledge about what they are and how best to meet them. Such knowledge is dynamic and open-ended. It is not reducible to subjective preferences best understood by sovereign individuals, nor static essences best understood by planners or party officials.

REFERENCES

Allardt, E. (1973), *About Dimensions of Welfare*, Helsinki: Research Group for Comparative Sociology.

Boorse, C. (1982) 'What a Theory of Mental Health Should Be', in R.E. Edwards (ed.), *Psychiatry and Ethics*, Buffalo, NY: Prometheus Books.

Braybrooke, D. (1987), *Meeting Needs*, Princeton, NJ: Princeton University Press.

Doyal, L. and I. Gough (1991), *A Theory of Human Need*, London: Macmillan.

Edwards, R.E. (1982), 'Mental Health as Rational Autonomy', in R.E. Edwards (ed.), *Psychiatry and Ethics*, Buffalo, NY: Prometheus Books.

Erikson, R. and H. Uusitalo (1987), 'The Scandinavian Approach to Welfare Research', in R. Erikson *et al.* (eds), *The Scandinavian Model*, London: M.E. Sharpe.

Galtung, J. (1980), 'The Basic Needs Approach', in K. Lederer (ed.), *Human Needs*, Cambridge, MA: Oelgeschlager, Gunn & Hain.

Gewirth, A. (1978), *Reason and Morality*, Chicago: University of Chicago Press.

Habermas, J. (1970), *Towards a Rational Society*, Boston: Beacon Press.

Hicks, N. (1982), 'Sector Priorities in Meeting Basic Needs: Some Statistical Evidence', *World Development*, **10**, (6), 489–99.

Lancaster, K. (1966), 'A New Approach to Consumer Theory', *Journal of Political Economy*, **74**, 132–57.

Maslow, A. (1954), *Motivation and Personality*, 2nd edn, New York: Harper & Row.

Myrdal, G. (1960) *Beyond the Welfare State*, New Haven: Yale University Press.

Nagel, T. (1978), *The Possibility of Altruism*, Princeton, NJ: Princeton University Press.

Penz, P. (1986), *Consumer Sovereignty and Human Interests*, Cambridge: Cambridge University Press.

Plant, R., H. Lesser and P. Taylor-Gooby (1980), *Political Philosophy and Social Welfare*, London: Routledge.

Pogge, T. (1989), *Realizing Rawls*, Ithaca, NY: Cornell University Press.

Ram, R. (1985) 'The Role of Real Income Level and Income Distribution in the Fulfilment of Basic Needs', *World Development*, **13**, (5) 580–94.

Rawls, J. (1972), *A Theory of Justice*, Oxford: Oxford University Press.

Rawls, J. (1982), 'The Basic Liberties and Their Priority', in S. McMurrin (ed.), *The Tanner Lectures on Human Value, III*, Salt Lake City: University of Utah Press.

Rist, G. (1980) 'Basic Questions about Basic Human Needs', in K. Lederer (ed.), *Human Needs*, Cambridge, MA: Oelgeschlager, Gunn & Hain.

Roderick, R. (1986), *Habermas and the Foundations of Critical Theory*, London: Macmillan.

Sen, A. (1970), *Collective Choice and Social Welfare*, San Francisco: Holden & Day.

Sen, A. (1984), *Resources, Values and Development*, Oxford: Basil Blackwell.

Sen, A. (1985), *Commodities and Capabilities*, Amsterdam: Elsevier.

Sen, A. (1987) *The Standard of Living: the Tanner Lectures*, ed. G. Hawthorn, Cambridge: Cambridge University Press.

Stewart, F. (1985), *Planning to Meet Basic Needs*, London: Macmillan.

Thompson, G. (1987), *Needs*, London: Routledge.

UNDP (United Nations Development Program) (1990, 1991), *Human Development Reports*, Oxford: Oxford Univesity Press.

Warr, P. (1987), *Work, Unemployment and Mental Health*, Oxford: Clarendon Press.

Wiggens, D. (1985), 'Claims of Need', in T. Honderich (ed.), *Morality and Objectivity*, London: Routledge.

Winch, P. (1974), 'Understanding a Primitive Society', in B.Wilson (ed.), *Rationality*, Oxford: Blackwell.

PART FOUR

European Economic Convergence or
Divergence?

Part 4 an Ecumenical Convergence in
Dogmatics

10. Patterns of Trade and the Integration of Eastern Europe into the European Community

Paolo Guerrieri

The integration of the East European countries into the world economy will have far-reaching economic effects on Europe, and on the European Community in particular. In this respect, trade relations are going to play a key role. A widespread view is that trade integration will be dealt with by the market, provided that economic liberalization is fully implemented. This is to say that the freeing of trade in Eastern and Western Europe together with microeconomic reforms in the East will ensure a smooth trade integration of East European economies into world and European markets. While these arguments are partially true, the problems facing Europe as it approaches trade integration of the East are more difficult and complex. The present chapter focuses on these problems.

First, the evolution of the trade performance and specialization of Eastern Europe[1] over the last two decades is examined by using an original data base and sectoral taxonomy for trade flows (sections 1 and 2). The aim is also to provide empirical evidence for technological levels and innovative capabilities of eastern countries. Patterns of technological activities and trade is also examined with reference to the EC countries (section 3). The results of this analysis are used to assess the effects of trade integration of Eastern Europe into the European economy (section 4). The final section provides some concluding remarks on these findings.

1. TRADE AND TECHNOLOGICAL PERFORMANCE OF EASTERN EUROPE

In this section the trade performance of the East European countries over the last two decades is analysed using a variety of indicators. To this end, an original data base and sectoral taxonomy are used.

As is well known, the trade flows data of former Council for Mutual Economic Assistance (CMEA) countries should be used with great caution when assessing their trade performance and specialization, as both patterns and volume of trade were greatly distorted by the central planned strategy followed by these countries in the period considered here (1970–89). The data of Eastern Europe's exchanges with OECD and non-OECD market economies, however, may offer useful insights into both the past trade performances and future trade patterns of the East, to the extent that they are adequately disaggregated and classified. This chapter therefore uses the 400 product groups of Servizi Informativi per l'Estero (SIE) World Trade data base,[2] and classifies them into nine broad categories according to an *ad hoc* taxonomy. The first three product groups comprise all primary commodities (food products and agricultural raw materials, fuels, other raw materials). The other six groups, which are related to industrial products, are defined by readapting and extending Pavitt's taxonomy (Pavitt, 1984, 1988), which equates the industrial system not so much with a simple list of sectors, as with a structure with its own internal hierarchy, characterized by a complex technological interdependence between its various components. Thus, the following six groups of industrial sectors are considered here: (1) science-based, comprising industries such as fine chemicals, electronic components, telecommunications and aerospace, which are characterized by innovative activities directly linked to high R&D expenditures; (2) specialized suppliers, which include most producers of investment goods in mechanical and instrument engineering, such as the machinery for specialized industries (i.e. machine tools), and involve a high diversification of supply, high economies of scope, relatively medium to small companies; (3) scale-intensive (automobiles, certain consumer electronics and consumer durables), covering typical oligopolistic large firm industries, with high capital intensity, wide economies of scale and learning, and significant in-house production engineering activities; (4) primary resource-intensive sectors in which access to abundant raw materials strongly influences production localization choices and countries' trade advantages (such as petroleum refineries, non-ferrous metal basic industries, manufacturing of pulp and paper); (5) supplier-dominated sectors, which encompass the more traditional consumer and non-consumer goods industries; they are net purchasers of process innovations and innovative intermediate inputs from other sectors and are sensitive to price competition, but are also influenced by 'non-price factors' such as product design and quality (includes textiles, clothing, wood and furniture, leather and shoes, ceramics, the simplest metal products); (6) the food industries, comprising all of the main components of this branch and considered separately here because of their particular features.

In this respect, the sectoral classification adopted here is consistent with recent works on technological change and international trade theory,[3] which point out that the processes of technological accumulation tend to assume varying sectoral features, in terms of differences in technological opportunities, cumulativeness and appropriability conditions (Levin, 1984; Scherer, 1986; Dosi, *et al.*, 1990a).

The trade performance of Eastern Europe is the first issue to be addressed. For this purpose, the market shares in world trade and the standardized trade balances of the East have been computed either for total commodities or for each group of commodities under consideration.[4] Figures in Tables 10.1 and 10.3 provide clear evidence of a substantial loss of international competitiveness by Eastern Europe, which is distributed over the entire period considered here. Eastern Europe's share in world exports experienced a sharp decline from 1970 to 1989 (from 1.51 per cent to 0.93 per cent) and their manufactured exports suffered an equal loss in market share (–34 per cent), over the 1980s in particular.

Many factors may be used to account for this poor trade performance by Eastern Europe. Most of them may be related to the central planning mechanism of resource allocation prevailing in these countries in the period considered.[5] In this respect, a major role was played by the 'technology factor', which negatively affected the competitive position of Eastern Europe over the last two decades (Poznanski, 1987). The argument that technology is the main factor determining the trade performance and international competitiveness of a country has been supported by a number of empirical studies over the eighties.[6] This is also confirmed by the present study of the evolu-

*Table 10.1   Eastern Europe's shares in world exports**

	1970	1976	1979	1982	1985	1987	1989
Total trade	1.51	1.38	1.29	1.06	1.09	1.03	0.93
Total manufactures	1.49	1.50	1.44	1.20	1.18	1.03	0.96
Agricultural products	2.22	1.52	1.18	1.03	1.12	1.23	1.19
Fuels	1.28	0.89	0.62	0.40	0.54	0.62	0.54
Other raw materials	0.97	1.15	1.30	1.73	2.01	1.68	1.37
Food industries	2.78	2.25	1.80	1.21	1.47	1.54	1.61
Traditional products	2.00	2.17	1.95	1.70	1.57	1.55	1.34
Resource-intensive products	1.36	2.06	2.30	2.05	2.37	2.06	1.76
Scale-intensive products	1.41	1.30	1.31	1.15	1.08	0.94	0.92
Specialized supplier products	1.08	1.05	1.08	0.92	0.79	0.69	0.65
Science-based products	0.60	0.61	0.53	0.39	0.31	0.31	0.26

* Ratio of Eastern Europe export to world export in each product group; percentage shares in values

Source: Servizi Informativi per l'Estero World Trade Data Base.

Table 10.2   Trade balance of Eastern Europe*

	1970	1976	1979	1982	1985	1987	1989
Total trade	−0.089	−0.405	−0.200	0.062	0.146	0.119	0.090
Agricultural products	−0.065	−1.489	−1.743	−0.896	−0.485	−0.039	−0.118
Fuels	1.122	0.849	0.578	0.340	0.296	0.452	0.431
Other raw materials	−0.333	−1.589	−1.002	−0.357	−0.031	0.082	0.281
Food industries	1.209	0.741	0.270	−0.194	0.440	0.456	0.824
Traditional products	0.694	0.607	0.800	0.727	0.633	0.776	0.596
Resource-intensive products	−0.028	0.630	1.090	1.196	1.530	1.256	1.098
Scale-intensive products	−0.101	−0.636	−0.374	0.103	0.150	0.117	0.118
Specialized supplier products	−1.684	−2.561	−2.010	−0.991	−1.105	−1.369	−1.188
Science-based products	−0.911	−1.072	−0.616	−0.344	−0.348	−0.323	−0.373

*Standardized trade balance expressed as percentage of total trade in single product groups

Source: Servizi Informativi per l'Estero World Trade Data Base.

tion of trade performance of Eastern Europe in various sectoral groups which have been characterized by rather different patterns.

Within manufacturing, the most negative results have been in specialized-supplier and science-based sectors. In mechanical engineering (specialized suppliers), i.e. machine tools, Eastern Europe's share in world exports remained relatively stable up to the late 1970s, but afterwards it showed a severe decrease (from 1.08 per cent in 1979 to 0.65 per cent in 1989), inaugurating a long-term negative trend (Table 10.1). A sharp decline also affected the Eastern exports of R&D-intensive products (science based), such as fine chemicals, electronics and telecommunications, in which their share dropped by 50 per cent during the 1980s (Table 10.1).

It should be kept in mind that Eastern Europe had placed a high priority on capital-good industries such as mechanical engineering (specialized suppliers) and on R&D-intensive sectors such as electronics; both were considered a major engine of technological change in the system of production (Poznanski, 1987). In fact mechanical engineering has a notable capacity for product innovation that enters most sectors of scale-intensive and supplier-dominated groups as capital inputs (Rosenberg, 1976); in addition, the product innovations of R&D-intensive sectors generate broad spillover effects on the whole economic system, and a large number of other industries heavily rely on them as capital or intermediate inputs (Chesnais, 1986).

During the 1970s the East European countries had been massively importing western technologies and capital goods in order to stimulate technological change and strengthen their weak technological capability. The evidence reported here shows that this did not result in any improvements in the technological performance and competitiveness of Eastern Europe's productions and exports. Furthermore, the sharp decline of the competitive position of Eastern Europe in mechanical engineering and in science-based sectors indicates the failure of these countries to deal with the information and communication technology revolution the last decade.

Standardized trade balances of Eastern Europe both in specialized supplier and science-based sectors are less negative. Trade deficits increased until the late 1970s, yet they had substantially decreased over the 1980s (Tables 10.2 and 10.4). This improvement should be attributed, however, to the fact that since the late 1970s most of the East European countries have been forced by debt crisis to stop their ambitious growth plans. The East European countries took similar drastic adjustment policies to face that crisis. As a consequence, imports were cut back, particularly in investment goods, and there has been a shift in export structure. These both aimed at improving trade balance, which did in fact improve, but at the cost of further deterioration in the trade performance of Eastern Europe.

Evidence of this derives from the figures in Table 10.4, which illustrates the export composition of Eastern Europe. It shows that both resource-intensive sectors (e.g. petroleum refineries and coal products) and traditional sectors (e.g. textiles, clothing and footwear) increased their shares in the total export of Eastern Europe over the 1980s. Furthermore, Eastern Europe's share in world exports of resource-intensive products substantially increased over the period 1970–85, from 1.36 per cent to 2.3 per cent; it subsequently declined to 1.76 per cent in 1989, but registered an overall net increase over the entire period considered here (Table 10.1). Within resource-intensive products, the highest gain of Eastern Europe was in the group of petroleum products and related materials. It should be noted that during the first half of the 1980s the lower price of oil imported from the Soviet Union had been favouring Eastern Europe's exports of petroleum products toward OECD countries (Seurot, 1987). One could add that since the early 1980s the exports of petroleum products strongly supported the volume of Eastern Europe's exports toward OECD countries.

With regard to export of traditional products, whose share in total exports of the East has also increased (Table 10.4), Eastern Europe experienced a declining share in world exports (Tables 10.1 and 10.3), but substantial positive trade balances throughout the period considered here (Tables 10.2 and 10.4). In this case, however, there is a sharp contrast between Eastern Europe's performance and that of Asian countries, which are net exporters of traditional goods. The Asian NICs and NECs both registered substantial increases in their shares of world exports of traditional goods over the period 1970–89; yet the Asian NICs sharply exceeded the performances of the others (Table 10.7). Furthermore, Eastern Europe's exports have also been

Table 10.3　Shares in world exports and trade balance of Eastern Europe in trade with OECD countries and non-OECD countries

	Shares in world exports towards					
	OECD countries			non-OECD countries		
	1970	1979	1989	1970	1979	1989
Total trade	1.62	1.47	1.04	1.19	0.83	0.58
Agricultural products	2.71	1.49	1.41	0.5	0.4	0.58
Fuels	1.37	0.63	0.52	0.6	0.51	0.65
Other raw materials	0.85	1.25	1.15	2.59	1.74	2.42
Food industries	3.12	2.3	1.83	1.47	0.49	0.87
Traditional products	2.19	2.23	1.57	1.35	0.94	0.5
Resource-intensive products	1.42	2.73	2.06	1.23	0.73	0.62
Scale-intensive products	1.37	1.34	0.93	1.59	1.28	0.91
Specialized supplier products	1.08	1.28	0.74	1.07	0.82	0.46
Science-based products	0.51	0.56	0.28	0.9	0.52	0.23

	Trade balance in trade with					
	OECD countries			non-OECD countries		
	1970	1979	1989	1970	1979	1989
Total trade	−0.089	−0.196	0.044	−0.001	−0.004	0.046
Agricultural products	0.635	−1.288	−0.045	−0.699	−0.456	−0.073
Fuels	1.109	0.513	0.346	0.013	0.064	0.085
Other raw materials	0.102	−0.115	0.250	−0.435	−0.887	0.031
Food industries	1.378	0.669	0.677	−0.169	−0.399	0.146
Traditional products	0.710	0.822	0.585	−0.016	−0.021	0.012
Resource-intensive products	−0.062	1.175	1.123	0.034	−0.085	−0.025
Scale-intensive products	−0.406	−0.640	0.001	0.304	0.267	0.116
Specialized supplier products	−1.945	−2.234	−1.221	0.261	0.224	0.033
Science-based products	−1.072	−0.717	−0.393	0.160	0.101	0.020

Source: Servizi Informativi per l'Estero World Trade Data Base.

falling behind those of the Asian NICs in all other manufacturing groups, with the exception of the resource-intensive category (Tables 10.6 to 10.8). The widest gap between export performances of the East and Asian NICs was in R&D-intensive sectors (science-based) and in specialized suppliers, which are the two manufacturing groups with the highest technological content. This suggests that the positive performance of the Asian NICs should be attributed not only to a lower factor cost, such as cheaper labour,

Table 10.4 *Eastern European trade: product composition and specialization*

| | Product composition* | | | | | | Index of revealed comparative advantages (I) | | |
| | Exports | | | Imports | | | | | |
	1970–73	1979–82	1986–89	1970–73	1979–82	1986–89	1970–73	1979–82	1986–89
Agricultural products	13.8	6.9	7.2	13.7	16.0	9.1	140	94	119
Fuels	6.0	6.1	4.2	0.6	0.7	1.3	81	35	61
Other raw materials	1.6	2.2	1.9	2.0	3.2	1.9	66	121	161
Food industries	13.3	7.6	8.7	7.4	8.1	5.9	179	126	159
Traditional products	21.5	21.3	24.6	13.2	11.7	14.4	139	158	149
Resource-intensive products	8.5	18.5	15.3	7.2	7.8	6.7	96	197	192
Scale-intensive products	22.6	23.9	24.8	23.6	24.3	24.4	90	107	96
Specialized supplier products	7.7	7.8	6.8	20.5	17.2	21.8	71	87	68
Science-based products	3.7	4.4	5.0	8.7	8.3	12.0	39	40	30
Residuals	1.4	1.4	1.5	3.2	2.6	2.5	43	60	45

* Percentage values
(I) the index is the ratio of the share of Eastern Europe in world exports of a given product group to the share of Eastern Europe in total world exports (percentages)

Source: Servizi Informativi per l'Estero World Trade Data Base.

but also to more rapid technological modernization (Guerrieri, 1991; Noland, 1990); and that the competitive gap suffered by Eastern Europe significantly widened with respect to both OECD countries and other developing countries over the past two decades.

2. INTERNATIONAL TRADE SPECIALIZATION OF THE EAST EUROPEAN COUNTRIES

Trade specialization patterns in the East European countries in the period considered above (1970–89) provide further insight into their trade perform-ance. The patterns of specialization are measured by two indicators: (1) the well-known index of revealed comparative advantage;[7] (2) a measure of the contribution to the trade balance of the various product groups in considera-tion (ICTB).[8] A positive value of the latter indicates a comparative advan-tage in a given product group, whereas a negative value is as sign of com-parative disadvantage. Both indicators have been calculated with regard to either the nine-product group classification or a more traditional one com-prising 25 commodity classes.

Figure 10.1   Patterns of trade specialization of Eastern Europe*

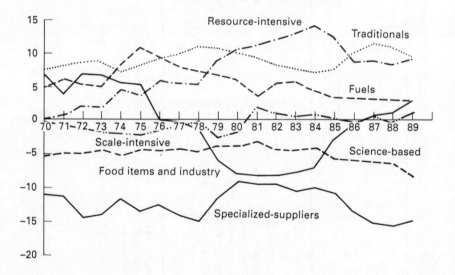

* Indicator of comparative advantages (>0) or disadvantages (<0)

The specialization pattern of the East European countries is complex and reflects the evolution of their competitiveness in world markets. By the end of the 1980s Eastern Europe appeared to hold a sound comparative advantage in traditional goods (textiles, apparel, footwear, paper products); fuels and related materials; and resource-intensive sectors (basic metals and petroleum products) (Figure 10.1, Table 10.5). In the latter, the specialization of Eastern Europe increased sharply over the 1980s, confirming the shift in its export composition noted above. The main contribution to this increase was made by petroleum products during the 1970s, and by the basic metals during the 1980s. These overall trends in the patterns of East European specialization are also confirmed by the evolution of the index of revealed comparative advantages (Table 10.4). Thus, it is quite evident that over the

Table 10.5   *Eastern Europe: specialization in trade with the world and the EC 12 (revealed comparative advantage index)**

	to world			to EC 12		
	1970–72	1977–79	1986–88	1970–72	1977–79	1986–88
Foodstuffs	1.01	0.06	0.85	0.83	–0.14	0.89
Agricultural products	3.11	–3.36	–1.53	8.67	2.12	1.71
Agricultural raw materials	–4.14	–2.47	–0.70	0.86	1.02	0.62
Fuels	5.44	7.24	2.66	5.86	8.23	4.75
Other raw materials	–0.12	–1.01	0.14	1.29	0.72	0.82
Food industries	5.65	3.14	3.71	9.04	6.18	4.10
Beverages	0.32	0.23	–0.08	0.06	–0.05	–0.34
Tobacco	–0.18	–0.13	–0.18	–0.11	–0.14	–0.14
Textile, apparel, leather, footwear	1.93	4.94	3.36	1.88	6.17	5.39
Wood, furniture, paper products	2.86	3.18	4.82	7.16	6.16	7.69
Chemicals, drugs, rubber products	–4.88	–5.15	–6.51	–8.64	–12.06	–11.88
Petroleum refineries, coal products	2.92	7.01	8.27	1.89	6.32	8.33
Pottery, glass, building materials	0.99	0.95	1.58	0.28	0.14	0.85
Basic metal industries	1.61	1.05	5.71	–0.84	0.03	3.99
Metal products	–0.66	–0.67	–0.32	–1.32	–1.63	–0.38
Industrial machinery	–6.84	–7.52	–9.32	–11.40	–11.99	–11.76
Turbines and mech. components	–4.39	–5.10	–5.24	–6.38	–7.02	–6.23
Office and computing machinery	–0.77	–0.38	–1.02	–1.18	–0.61	–1.26
Telecomm., electronical goods	–0.54	–0.47	–1.71	–0.95	–0.45	–1.46
Electrical apparatus and materials	–1.35	–1.18	–1.11	–2.04	–1.61	–1.10
Motor vehicles	0.06	0.32	–0.42	–1.68	–0.23	–0.04
Ships, railroad equipment, aircraft	0.32	1.50	–0.16	–1.18	0.69	–0.85
Professional, optical phot. goods	–1.08	–1.14	–2.12	–1.81	–1.61	–2.63
Other manufacturing	1.23	0.85	–0.13	1.10	0.81	–0.30
Residuals	–2.51	–1.88	–0.54	–1.40	–1.03	–0.77

* Index of revealed comparative advantages (>0) and disadvantages (<0)

Source: Servizi Informativi per l'Estero World Trade Data Base.

1980s the increase of East European exports toward world markets took place together with a deterioration of its export structure. The strong points of East European specialization continued to be and/or shifted toward those sectors which have been at the core of the de-localization processes of advanced countries toward the newly industrialized countries: energy-intensive intermediate industries (resource-intensive) and labour-intensive products in traditional industries.

In food items and industry there were sharp fluctuations in the comparative advantage of Eastern Europe over the period considered here, reaching positive values in the late 1980s, following a period of decline. The index of revealed comparative advantages also confirms a significant specialization of Eastern Europe in food items and industry by the late 1980s.

Comparative disadvantages of the East are to be seen in most of the manufactures product groups with the exception of traditional and resource-intensive ones. Specifically, in specialized suppliers (such as agricultural machinery and machinery for specialized industries) and in science-based (such as electronics components, telecommunications, data processing units), the East was and continues to be strongly dependent on foreign suppliers.[9] This confirms the increasing difficulties of Eastern Europe in dealing with innovative activities stemming from the microelectronics revolution.

As illustrated in Figure 10.2 the specialization pattern of Eastern Europe in its trade with the EC is quite similar to that described above with respect to world trade since the Community accounts for a large share of total trade in Eastern Europe; however, it should be pointed out, as argued in greater detail in the following sections, that the absolute values of indicators of Eastern Europe's comparative advantage in traditional goods and food items are substantially higher in its trade with the EC than with the world at large (Table 10.5).

Additional insights into the trade specialization of Eastern Europe may be gained from a more disaggregated analysis of individual eastern countries. Figures 10.3, 10.4 and 10.5 show the evolution over the past two decades (1970-89) of the indicator of contributions to trade balance for three major East European countries, Czechoslovakia, Hungary and Poland. This highlights both the country-specific nature of trade specialization patterns and some common sectoral features.

By the late 1980s the comparative advantages of Czechoslovakia were mostly concentrated in manufacturing, traditional goods being the strongest area of specialization. There was also a significant increase in the values of the indicator of contributions to trade balance for both the resource-intensive groups and food items over the 1980s. In scale-intensive industries (especially chemicals and iron-steel) Czechoslovakia maintained a relatively sound comparative advantage over the last decade, though it registered a sharp

Figure 10.2   *Patterns of trade specialization of Eastern Europe in trade with the EC**

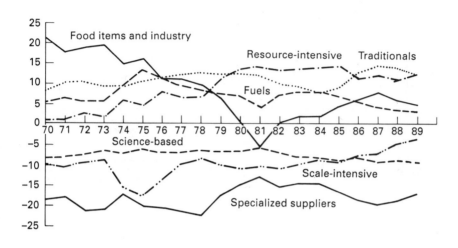

* Indicator of comparative advantages (>0) or disadvantages (<0)

Figure 10.3   *Patterns of trade specialization of Czechoslovakia*

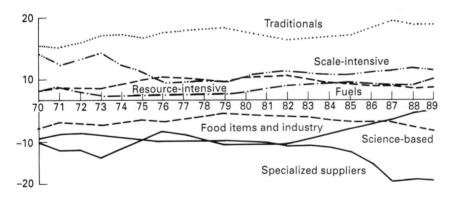

Figure 10.4   Patterns of trade specialization of Hungary

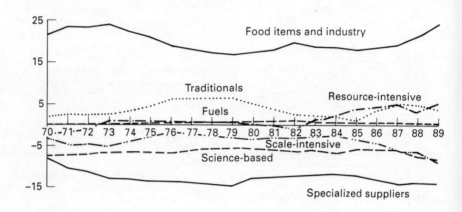

Figure 10.5   Patterns of trade specialization of Poland

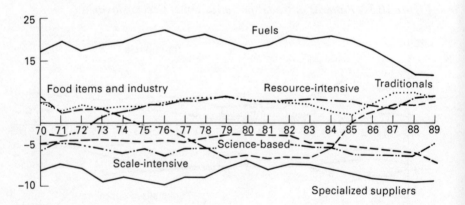

decrease in the specialization indicator compared to the early 1970s. It should be stressed, however, that of the three eastern countries, only Czechoslovakia has a positive specialization in scale-intensive sectors.

Hungary shows a rather different specialization pattern, distinguished by strength in agricultural products and food industries. Within this group, the food industry has been increasing its relative share throughout the past two decades. Agricultural products have also continued to provide highly positive contributions to the trade balance over the 1980s. As in all East European industries, there has been an increasing comparative advantage of the Hungarian industry in resource-intensive sectors throughout the 1980s. While Hungary's specialization is rather weak in traditional goods, its remarkable growth since the mid-1980s should be stressed.

The specialization pattern of Poland lies somewhere between the two considered above. By the late 1980s there were highly comparative advantages in raw materials, especially in fuels, as well as significant positive values for the specialization measure in various industrial product groups. Over the course of the past decade Polish industry continued to hold the comparative advantages either in resource-intensive products, which it acquired in the mid-1970s, or in traditional goods, though in the latter it went through a negative cyclical phase in the early 1980s. In food items, after a disappointing period of decreasing competitiveness from the mid-1970s to the early 1980s, Poland improved its trade performance, particularly since the mid-1980s, as shown by the increasingly positive values of the indicator of contribution to trade balance by food industries and, to a lesser extent, by agricultural products.

In addition to this country-specific nature of specialization, the trade patterns of the three major eastern economies have common sectoral features. All present increasingly high comparative disadvantages in specialized supplier and science-based sectors, especially over the 1980s. As has already been indicated above, this stems from the sharp deterioration of the technological capability of the East over the past decade.

To sum up, the present analysis seems to suggest that Eastern Europe's competitiveness severely deteriorated over the last two decades. The technological factor seems to have played a crucial role in determining this poor trade performance. The specialization pattern clearly indicates the backwardness of Eastern Europe's trade structure and technological capability. The Asian NICs have out-performed Eastern Europe in many industries, not only in traditional and resource-intensive product groups but also in other more technologically sophisticated sectors.

Clearly, deep microeconomic reforms are needed to restructure and reconvert Eastern Europe's domestic supply, because of the poor competitiveness of its industrial system. In this respect, trade liberalization and integration of the East into the world economy will play a key role. From this perspective, western countries, in general, and the European Community in particular may facilitate this process considerably, not only by providing financial and technical aid, but also by moving towards a free trade relationship with eastern countries (Pinder, 1991).

The preceding analysis of trade performance and specialization of eastern countries may be used to make inferences about how the trade pattern will evolve following economic liberalization in the East. It is true that the inward-looking centrally planned strategy pursued by the East has led to significant misallocations of resources among sectors, which market reforms should correct in the medium to long term. It is also true, however, that the current structure of production of eastern countries will continue to influence their trade flows and specialization in the near future. As recent innovation theory suggests, technology is cumulative in its development and technological capability evolves gradually along a rather stable long-run path.[10] Thus, the current trade and production structure of the East may be used, albeit with great caution, to assess the future trade patterns of the East European countries.

First, it must be pointed out that the liberalization of trade in the East and the official dismantling of CMEA trading arrangement will increase the aggregate trade volumes of Eastern Europe, and will result in a substantial geographic reorientation of their trade flows toward Western Europe, in general, and the EC in particular (Collins and Rodrik, 1990). This has already been observed in the past two years.

With regard to commodity composition, the present analysis has shown that Eastern Europe's comparative advantages in manufacturing lie in resource-intensive and labour-intensive traditional products. As a consequence, these countries are likely to expand their manufactures exports in sectors such as textile, clothing, footwear and other product groups in which cost of labour is more important than technology.[11] The future competitiveness of Eastern Europe's heavy industry is less clear, because the adoption of market criteria and western environmental standards in the East could have a negative impact on its supply capacity and exports. In addition, net exports of Eastern Europe are likely to increase in agricultural products because its supply is already competitive (as we have shown in the cases of Hungary and Poland) and is going to become larger and more efficient. As for imports, manufactured capital goods and technological inputs associated with (both specialized supplier and science based groups) will be at the core of Eastern European purchases on foreign markets.

As already noted, the expansion of trade flows of Eastern Europe will have major effects on West European economies and on the European Community in particular. This will be the focus of the next sections, the first of which examines the trade patterns of the EC countries.

3. TRADE PERFORMANCE AND SPECIALIZATION OF THE EC COUNTRIES

Over the last two decades the trade performance of the European Community (EC) has shown elements of strength and weakness distributed across sectors and member countries. The market shares of EC countries as a group with respect to world exports registered a slight decrease from the early 1970s to the late 1980s (–1.5 per cent), with greater losses (-4.7 per cent) if manufactures' exports are taken into account (Table 10.6). This decrease, however, occurred almost entirely within the first half of the 1980s, and losses have been partly reabsorbed in the more recent years. Trends in the Community's trade balance appear more satisfactory, with high deficits throughout the 1970s and slight surpluses over the 1980s.

This general evolution in European competitiveness, however, has been sharply differentiated with respect both to the various sectoral groups and the performances of its individual member states. The competitive position of the EC in specialized-supplier sectors (mechanical engineering) was very strong in the past and maintained high levels in the 1980s. After decreasing during the first half of the 1980s, market shares substantially increased in the later years, while standardized trade balances maintained highly positive values (see Tables 10.8 and 10.10). This was the result of the positive performance of Germany, which had maintained a highly competitive position, especially in terms of trade surpluses, and of Italy, the only European country which increased both its world market shares and its positive trade balances despite the upsurge of Japan in these sectors during the 1980s. In contrast, the competitiveness of France and especially of the United Kingdom deteriorated sharply.

The EC competitive position has also remained solid in scale-intensive industries, despite a slight decrease in market shares (see Tables 10.8 and 10.10). Again, this may be attributed to the highly differentiated performance of the major EC countries. Germany, in particular, continued to be highly competitive in these sectors, as demonstrated by its increase in market shares following a drop in the early 1980s and by a recent net gain in what had already been a high surplus. The new member countries, Spain, Greece and Portugal, also improved their competitive positions during much of the period considered here. The United Kingdom and Italy, on the other hand, clearly deteriorated, registering considerable increases in their trade deficits in scale-intensive industries during the 1980s.

Table 10.6   Shares of selected countries and areas (I)*

	Total world trade						
	1970–73	1976–79	1979–82	1982–85	1986–87	1988–89	1970–89
United States	13.67	11.76	11.91	11.85	10.50	11.92	–1.75
Canada	5.35	3.93	3.70	4.49	4.16	4.10	–1.25
Japan	7.19	7.54	7.60	9.15	10.31	9.89	2.70
EC (12)	41.36	38.77	36.82	35.62	40.44	39.91	–1.45
Germany (Fed. Rep.)	12.27	11.47	10.43	10.15	12.52	12.14	–0.14
France	6.49	6.28	5.88	5.43	6.14	6.12	–0.37
United Kingdom	6.48	5.65	5.83	5.57	5.32	5.45	–1.03
Italy	4.61	4.51	4.40	4.33	5.02	4.91	0.30
Other EC countries	10.01	9.33	8.63	8.33	9.35	9.10	–0.91
Greece, Portugal, Spain	1.50	1.54	1.66	1.82	2.11	2.20	0.69
EFTA	6.75	6.25	5.97	5.98	6.72	6.67	–0.09
Asian NICs	2.34	3.47	4.16	5.55	6.89	6.62	4.28
Other Asian countries	2.72	3.35	3.66	3.96	3.43	3.76	1.04

	Total manufactures						
	1970–73	1976–79	1979–82	1982–85	1986–87	1988–89	1970–89
United States	13.52	12.23	12.68	12.33	10.32	11.27	–2.25
Canada	5.06	3.81	3.61	4.34	3.96	3.88	–1.18
Japan	9.01	10.16	10.45	12.09	12.35	11.62	2.61
EC (12)	48.63	48.47	46.15	42.40	44.54	43.95	–4.68
Germany (Fed. Rep.)	15.02	14.91	13.68	12.75	14.45	13.91	–1.11
France	7.43	7.85	7.49	6.58	6.71	6.59	–0.85
United Kingdom	7.76	6.96	6.69	5.71	5.38	5.77	–1.99
Italy	5.58	5.83	5.85	5.59	5.89	5.64	0.06
Other EC countries	11.26	11.11	10.41	9.61	9.88	9.72	–1.54
Greece, Portugal, Spain	1.59	1.82	2.03	2.17	2.25	2.33	0.74
EFTA	8.12	7.87	7.38	6.98	7.49	7.19	–0.93
Asian NICs	2.53	4.24	5.24	6.83	7.78	7.51	4.97
Other Asian countries	1.54	1.96	2.16	2.44	2.52	3.11	1.57

	Agricultural products						
	1970–73	1976–79	1979–82	1982–85	1986–87	1988–89	1970–89
United States	22.04	24.90	25.78	24.01	15.75	19.12	–2.92
Canada	5.54	4.48	4.94	5.74	4.42	4.58	–0.97
Japan	0.73	0.41	0.35	0.42	0.48	0.48	–0.25
EC (12)	21.15	20.76	20.85	21.19	26.86	26.47	5.32
Germany (Fed. Rep.)	1.88	1.74	1.66	1.76	2.35	2.40	0.51
France	5.65	5.19	5.68	6.03	7.20	7.55	1.90
United Kingdom	1.46	1.67	1.97	2.06	2.64	2.03	0.57
Italy	2.21	2.08	1.80	1.69	1.97	1.85	–0.36
Other EC countries	7.70	7.88	7.52	7.41	9.48	9.33	1.64
Greece, Portugal, Spain	2.27	2.20	2.24	2.25	3.22	3.33	1.06
EFTA	1.90	1.73	1.68	1.78	2.26	2.15	0.25
Asian NICs	2.37	3.24	3.26	3.55	4.31	3.27	0.90
Other Asian countries	10.08	9.80	9.18	8.65	9.20	9.08	–1.00

* Ratio of national to world exports; percentage shares in values.

Source: Servizi Informativi per l'Estero World Trade Data Base.

Table 10.7   *Shares of selected countries and areas* (II)*

	Food industry						
	1970–73	1976–79	1979–82	1982–85	1986–87	1988–89	1970–89
United States	8.68	9.25	9.89	9.47	8.45	9.95	1.27
Canada	2.82	2.05	2.15	2.51	2.37	2.13	−0.69
Japan	1.63	1.18	1.25	1.20	0.96	0.86	−0.77
EC (12)	44.82	49.79	49.99	49.88	54.95	55.98	11.16
Germany (Fed. Rep.)	4.79	7.51	8.17	8.27	9.30	9.31	4.52
France	9.18	9.70	9.83	9.34	10.35	11.24	2.06
United Kingdom	4.96	5.21	5.22	4.95	5.16	5.36	0.39
Italy	2.72	3.09	3.53	3.63	3.94	4.03	1.31
Other EC countries	19.82	21.38	20.53	20.76	23.13	22.93	3.11
Greece, Portugal, Spain	3.36	2.91	2.71	2.92	3.08	3.12	−0.24
EFTA	3.97	3.53	3.34	3.30	3.36	3.02	−0.96
Asian NICs	1.75	2.30	2.48	2.94	3.33	3.08	1.32
Other Asian countries	3.77	6.03	6.21	7.05	4.92	5.33	1.56

	Traditional sectors						
	1970–73	1976–79	1979–82	1982–85	1986–87	1988–89	1970–89
United States	6.86	6.61	6.78	6.01	4.51	5.37	−1.49
Canada	3.23	2.62	2.37	2.72	2.48	2.45	−0.79
Japan	8.15	5.65	5.54	5.92	4.46	3.92	−4.24
EC (12)	50.39	48.85	46.31	42.98	43.25	42.48	−7.90
Germany (Fed. Rep.)	11.88	11.53	10.64	10.11	10.86	10.57	−1.32
France	7.16	6.40	6.06	5.46	5.33	5.21	−1.95
United Kingdom	8.14	7.65	6.53	4.85	3.96	4.50	−3.64
Italy	8.64	9.79	10.34	10.46	10.67	9.98	1.34
Other EC countries	11.78	10.37	9.38	8.62	8.79	8.76	−3.03
Greece, Portugal, Spain	2.80	3.10	3.37	3.50	3.64	3.47	0.68
EFTA	8.34	8.45	8.27	7.60	7.54	7.02	−1.33
Asian NICs	7.02	10.58	12.17	15.01	16.57	14.00	6.98
Other Asian countries	3.33	4.05	4.57	5.35	6.14	7.64	4.31

	Resource-intensive sectors						
	1970–73	1976–79	1979–82	1982–85	1986–87	1988–89	1970–89
United States	8.50	6.70	7.91	7.44	7.38	8.58	0.08
Canada	12.07	8.36	7.28	7.46	8.52	9.47	−2.61
Japan	1.61	1.87	1.83	1.95	2.53	2.58	0.97
EC (12)	32.22	35.98	36.36	34.14	34.54	33.35	1.13
Germany (Fed. Rep.)	6.77	7.25	6.97	6.48	8.01	8.31	1.54
France	3.72	4.50	4.70	3.99	4.06	4.21	0.49
United Kingdom	5.29	4.86	5.12	4.59	4.47	4.25	−1.05
Italy	3.96	4.50	4.32	3.82	3.60	3.25	−0.71
Other EC countries	11.17	13.40	13.31	12.62	11.57	10.44	−0.73
Greece, Portugal, Spain	1.32	1.47	1.96	2.64	2.84	2.91	1.59
EFTA	12.69	10.73	9.47	9.31	11.59	12.27	−0.42
Asian NICs	1.89	3.29	4.17	5.04	4.45	4.39	2.50
Other Asian countries	2.44	2.81	2.49	2.44	2.23	2.33	−0.11

* Ratio of national to world exports; percentage shares in values.

Source: Servizi Informativi per l'Estero World Trade Data Base.

Table 10.8   Shares of selected countries and areas (III)*

	Scale-intensive sectors						
	1970–73	1976–79	1979–82	1982–85	1986–87	1988–89	1970–89
United States	12.77	11.30	11.01	10.35	8.76	9.59	–3.18
Canada	5.95	4.76	4.52	6.31	5.73	5.14	–0.82
Japan	15.43	17.96	18.62	20.47	19.28	16.71	1.28
EC (12)	51.69	50.33	48.44	43.41	46.72	47.44	–4.25
Germany (Fed. Rep.)	18.00	17.38	16.84	15.57	17.51	17.11	–0.90
France	8.67	9.20	8.89	7.43	7.69	7.49	–1.18
United Kingdom	7.35	6.16	5.83	4.96	5.23	5.76	–1.59
Italy	4.98	5.01	4.82	4.30	4.31	4.33	–0.65
Other EC countries	11.51	10.91	10.08	9.03	9.82	10.33	–1.18
Greece, Portugal, Spain	1.18	1.67	1.98	2.11	2.15	2.43	1.25
EFTA	6.76	6.94	6.45	6.21	6.49	6.25	–0.51
Asian NICs	1.24	2.57	3.69	5.11	5.31	5.52	4.28
Other Asian countries	0.44	0.41	0.50	0.62	0.70	1.09	0.65

	Specialized-supplier sectors						
	1970–73	1976–79	1979–82	1982–85	1986–87	1988–89	1970–89
United States	20.28	18.33	18.51	16.80	11.17	12.66	–7.62
Canada	2.07	1.91	2.06	2.17	1.73	1.95	–0.12
Japan	6.99	9.82	11.88	14.77	15.32	15.71	8.72
EC (12)	57.20	54.93	50.66	47.43	51.45	49.85	–7.35
Germany (Fed. Rep.)	25.14	23.65	20.21	18.96	22.07	20.81	–4.33
France	7.18	7.80	7.05	6.32	5.93	5.68	–1.50
United Kingdom	10.06	8.26	8.06	6.97	6.41	6.28	–3.78
Italy	6.92	6.87	7.42	7.75	8.76	8.67	1.75
Other EC countries	7.11	7.23	6.63	6.24	6.96	6.93	–0.18
Greece, Portugal, Spain	0.79	1.12	1.31	1.20	1.34	1.48	0.69
EFTA	9.20	9.69	9.83	9.76	11.02	10.30	1.09
Asian NICs	1.09	1.41	2.05	3.23	3.73	3.91	2.82
Other Asian countries	0.29	0.43	0.53	0.72	0.93	1.30	1.00

	Science-based sectors						
	1970–73	1976–79	1979–82	1982–85	1986–87	1988–89	1970–89
United States	27.13	22.74	23.84	24.18	20.49	20.10	–7.03
Canada	4.25	2.39	2.23	2.44	2.25	2.55	–1.70
Japan	8.47	10.64	11.18	13.77	16.17	16.44	7.97
EC (12)	46.40	46.93	43.90	39.53	39.23	37.79	–8.61
Germany (Fed. Rep.)	16.58	16.26	14.42	12.92	13.45	12.36	–4.22
France	6.98	8.46	7.86	7.05	6.99	6.69	–0.30
United Kingdom	10.11	9.39	9.56	8.24	6.95	7.47	–2.64
Italy	4.39	3.98	3.79	3.62	3.63	3.35	–1.04
Other EC countries	7.87	8.18	7.48	6.84	7.26	6.85	–1.03
Greece, Portugal, Spain	0.48	0.66	0.81	0.88	0.96	1.09	0.60
EFTA	9.14	7.87	6.62	5.85	6.41	6.03	–3.12
Other Asian countries	0.31	1.01	1.40	1.77	2.00	2.50	2.19

* Ratio of national to world exports; percentage shares in values.

Source: Servizi Informativi per l'Estero World Trade Data Base.

In traditional products, there was a notable decrease in the EC trade balance and market share, mostly to the advantage of the newly industrialized Asian countries (Tables 10.7, 10.9). This may be attributed to significant deterioration in competitiveness in the United Kingdom, France, and, to a lesser extent, in Germany. Italy and the group of the newer EC member states (Spain, Greece and Portugal), however, did not follow this trend, as they had strengthened their competitive position in traditional industries during the 1970s and were able to maintain their advantage during the last decade, though with some difficulty in recent years.

Finally, in science-based sectors EC countries registered a highly negative performance (Tables 10.8, 10.10). The EC competitive position, which was relatively strong in the early 1970s, experienced a net deterioration in the 1980s. EC standardized trade balance maintained positive and high values by the late 1970s but sharply declined in the 1980s. This negative performance affected all EC countries, including Germany. It should be underlined that this negative performance is attributable almost entirely to the significant deterioration of the EC competitive position in all electronic sectors of the science-based group. In fact, in data-processing systems, electronic office equipment and electronic components, EC countries registered significant reductions in their market shares and increasing trade deficits to the advantage primarily of Japan and, to a lesser extent, of Asian NICs (Guerrieri, 1991; Guerrieri and Milana, 1990). In the other sectors of the science-based group, on the other hand, European industries maintained or strengthened their competitiveness.[12]

Among the non-manufactured products, EC countries strongly increased their shares in world exports of agricultural products and in the food industry (Tables 10.6, 10.7), mainly thanks to the strong protectionist attitude of their Common Agricultural Policy (CAP).

These trends in the competitive position of the EC are reflected in its patterns of specialization over the period considered here. European specialization patterns are analysed according to the same indicators used in the preceding sections of this chapter: (1) the indicator of relative contributions to a country's trade balance (ICTB) of the various groups of sectors in consideration (Figure 10.6); (2) and the index of revealed comparative advantages (Table 10.11).

European industry maintained sound comparative advantages in many chemical and mechanical sectors of specialized-supplier and scale-intensive groups. EC specialization increased in chemicals and pharmaceuticals, rubber products, basic metals and mechanical engineering, such as machine tools and machinery for specialized industries (Guerrieri and Milana, 1990); the latter, it must be recalled, are vital investment goods for many manufacturing industries. Foodstuffs and the food industry constitute a special case:

Table 10.9 *Trade balance of selected areas and countries* (I)*

Total trade

	1970	1973	1976	1979	1982	1985	1987	1989
United States	0.92	0.15	-0.98	-2.89	-2.78	-8.59	-7.67	-5.11
Japan	0.15	-0.26	0.30	-0.47	0.49	2.69	3.56	2.39
EC (12)	-2.89	-2.14	-3.38	-2.68	-2.47	-0.87	0.05	-1.18
Germany	1.52	2.45	1.58	0.91	1.26	1.44	2.85	2.55
France	-0.41	-0.26	-0.95	-0.58	-1.36	-0.57	-0.62	-0.62
United Kingdom	-0.84	-1.58	-1.10	-0.79	-0.15	-0.45	-1.00	-1.60
Italy	-0.60	-1.06	-0.64	-0.21	-0.61	-0.53	-0.24	-0.32
Greece, Portugal, Spain	-1.49	-1.41	-1.61	-1.06	-1.31	-0.74	-1.10	-1.49
Other EC countries	-1.06	-0.28	-0.67	-0.95	-0.32	-0.02	0.16	0.31
EFTA	-1.34	-0.85	-0.90	-0.61	-0.36	-0.03	-0.35	-0.30
Asian NICS	-0.92	-0.54	-0.31	-0.50	-0.39	0.57	1.02	-1.19

Agricultural products

	1970	1973	1976	1979	1982	1985	1987	1989
United States	10.90	20.60	19.61	14.80	15.96	8.16	4.89	9.83
Japan	-16.57	-17.57	-16.86	-17.38	-15.30	-15.72	-16.40	-18.29
EC (12)	-31.05	-25.76	-24.59	-24.64	-20.71	-19.21	-18.16	-14.79
Germany	-11.74	-10.04	-9.95	-9.95	-8.65	-8.61	-9.29	-7.44
France	-1.77	-0.15	-0.61	-0.97	-0.07	1.20	1.22	1.96
United Kingdom	-9.06	-6.45	-5.92	-4.49	-3.45	-3.24	-3.18	-2.98
Italy	-5.58	-6.22	-5.11	-5.54	-4.80	-5.44	-5.62	-5.56
Greece, Portugal, Spain	-0.90	-1.62	-1.97	-1.64	-2.45	-1.75	-1.39	-1.34
Other EC countries	-2.00	-1.28	-1.02	-2.05	-1.30	-1.37	0.10	0.58
EFTA	-3.46	-2.78	-2.68	-2.96	-2.98	-2.50	-2.96	-2.47
Asian NICs	-2.11	-2.76	-2.98	-3.08	-3.43	-3.59	-2.98	-5.29

Food Industry

	1970	1973	1976	1979	1982	1985	1987	1989
United States	-7.56	-4.79	-2.52	-1.71	-0.94	-5.14	-2.53	0.37
Japan	-2.53	-5.13	-5.35	-5.03	-4.30	-4.63	-6.19	-8.62
EC (12)	-8.30	-6.78	-1.34	1.12	4.85	4.95	4.42	5.52
Germany	-7.89	-6.38	-5.07	-3.12	-1.56	-1.37	-1.48	-1.29
France	1.05	2.54	1.91	1.90	2.22	1.95	2.20	3.02
United Kingdom	-9.43	-7.88	-5.13	-4.55	-3.27	-3.31	-3.28	-3.22
Italy	-3.68	-5.40	-3.92	-3.09	-2.82	-3.32	-4.01	-3.54
Greece, Portugal, Spain	1.09	0.31	0.70	0.79	0.56	0.75	-0.38	-1.14
Other EC countries	10.56	10.03	10.18	9.18	9.72	10.26	11.37	11.70
EFTA	-1.63	-1.62	-1.46	-1.18	-0.66	-0.72	-1.23	-1.40
Asian NICs	-0.93	-0.52	-0.56	-1.01	-1.43	-0.87	-0.47	-2.25

Traditional sectors

	1970	1973	1976	1979	1982	1985	1987	1989
United States	-8.47	-7.56	-5.66	-6.99	-8.98	-19.07	-15.52	-13.71
Japan	6.62	1.39	3.05	0.75	2.48	2.04	-0.60	-2.82
EC (12)	7.26	2.78	1.94	0.82	3.20	4.77	0.60	-0.11
Germany	0.83	-0.30	-0.35	-1.68	-0.16	0.45	-0.46	-0.13
France	1.21	0.77	-0.88	-1.27	-1.56	-1.00	-2.03	-1.84
United Kingdom	0.66	-1.18	-0.45	-1.53	-2.24	-2.59	-2.94	-3.25
Italy	5.51	3.94	5.38	7.13	7.16	7.12	6.45	5.97
Greece, Portugal, Spain	0.73	1.25	1.51	1.82	1.84	2.08	1.39	0.58
Other EC countries	-1.68	-1.70	-3.26	-3.65	-1.82	-1.28	-1.80	-1.45
EFTA	-1.66	-0.82	-1.17	-1.18	-1.01	-1.13	-2.12	-1.92
Asian NICs	2.21	4.65	6.88	6.57	8.24	9.81	10.27	5.19

* standardized trade balances expressed as percentage of total world trade in each single product group

Source: Servizi Informativi per l'Estero.

Table 10.10   Trade balance of selected areas and countries (II)*

Resource-intensive sectors

	1970	1973	1976	1979	1982	1985	1987	1989
United States	-6.73	-10.77	-10.83	-9.42	-7.94	-12.39	-10.02	-8.30
Japan	-5.67	-6.13	-5.72	-6.07	-6.01	-5.88	-7.15	-8.97
EC (12)	-19.02	-12.87	-11.15	-8.95	-9.58	-10.37	-11.16	-11.84
Germany	-7.25	-6.78	-6.77	-6.62	-5.38	-5.60	-4.03	-3.78
France	-2.88	-2.72	-2.32	-1.34	-2.95	-2.34	-3.47	-3.28
United Kingdom	-6.01	-3.82	-3.37	-2.38	-1.82	-2.27	-2.40	-2.75
Italy	-1.43	-0.19	-0.38	0.35	-0.89	-2.56	-2.98	-3.27
Greece, Portugal, Spain	-0.90	-0.40	-0.29	-0.19	0.24	0.96	0.41	0.03
Other EC countries	-0.54	1.03	1.98	1.24	1.23	1.45	1.30	1.22
EFTA	3.13	3.15	1.65	0.22	0.84	2.24	5.00	5.01
Asian NICs	-0.58	-0.23	0.11	-0.05	0.76	0.88	-1.30	-2.28

Scale-intensive sectors

	1970	1973	1976	1979	1982	1985	1987	1989
United States	-1.36	-3.39	-1.47	-3.09	-5.50	-13.84	-11.93	-8.65
Japan	11.31	13.72	16.93	13.91	17.80	18.67	15.30	12.64
EC (12)	15.21	15.32	14.18	13.53	11.75	10.86	8.77	6.51
Germany	9.41	11.05	9.42	9.25	9.52	8.31	9.36	8.35
France	2.89	2.46	2.58	3.61	1.58	1.89	1.21	0.66
United Kingdom	4.25	1.55	1.80	0.37	-0.27	-0.43	-0.62	-1.35
Italy	0.23	0.35	0.93	0.53	0.30	0.01	-0.75	-1.26
Greece, Portugal, Spain	-2.24	-1.41	-1.54	-0.74	-0.53	0.05	-1.15	-1.62
Other EC countries	0.68	1.33	0.99	0.51	1.15	1.03	0.73	1.72
EFTA	-2.55	-1.95	-1.35	-0.47	-0.36	-0.13	-1.06	-1.70
Asian NICs	-1.55	-1.09	-0.61	-0.65	0.25	1.00	0.81	-0.80

222

Specialized-supplier sectors

	1970	1973	1976	1979	1982	1985	1987	1989
United States	14.36	10.84	14.21	7.59	9.01	-2.25	-4.96	-1.76
Japan	3.24	4.99	6.46	8.53	10.69	13.80	12.71	13.10
EC (12)	18.02	19.12	22.48	21.70	19.15	17.60	15.37	12.47
Germany	16.57	20.10	17.92	16.04	13.18	12.82	14.34	12.91
France	-0.42	-0.44	1.27	1.43	0.45	0.55	-0.92	-1.29
United Kingdom	4.78	2.78	2.95	2.65	2.56	1.02	0.54	-0.31
Italy	2.87	1.96	3.09	4.12	4.44	4.81	4.72	4.70
Greece, Portugal, Spain	-3.08	-3.60	-2.30	-1.55	-1.57	-1.04	-2.44	-3.00
Other EC countries	-2.71	-1.69	-0.46	-0.99	0.09	-0.57	-0.87	-0.54
EFTA	-0.26	0.70	1.40	2.49	2.22	2.18	1.82	1.87
Asian NICs	-2.67	-2.90	-2.77	-3.70	-3.03	-2.07	-3.18	-5.13

Science-based sectors

	1970	1973	1976	1979	1982	1985	1987	1989
United States	19.37	13.98	13.75	10.88	10.84	3.70	1.36	2.12
Japan	3.16	4.59	6.05	6.91	7.90	10.80	12.36	12.04
EC (12)	5.40	5.29	8.27	5.65	5.09	2.71	0.38	-1.50
Germany	8.14	8.99	7.49	5.27	4.37	3.28	3.71	2.64
France	-0.70	-0.70	0.98	1.00	0.78	0.86	0.14	0.12
United Kingdom	3.99	2.67	2.76	1.86	1.75	0.46	-0.17	-0.36
Italy	-0.12	-0.72	-0.08	-0.43	-0.33	-0.60	-1.15	-1.19
Greece, Portugal, Spain	-2.87	-3.30	-2.52	-1.56	-1.49	-1.16	-1.83	-2.20
Other EC countries	-3.14	-1.65	-0.36	-0.50	0.00	-0.13	-0.32	-0.50
EFTA	0.51	0.69	0.53	0.21	-0.08	-0.26	-0.24	-0.48
Asian NICs	-2.14	-2.31	-1.52	-2.09	-1.57	-0.01	0.36	-1.11

* standardized trade balances expressed as percentage of total world trade in each single product group

Source: Servizi Informativi per l'Estero.

Figure 10.6   Patterns of trade specialization of the EC 12*

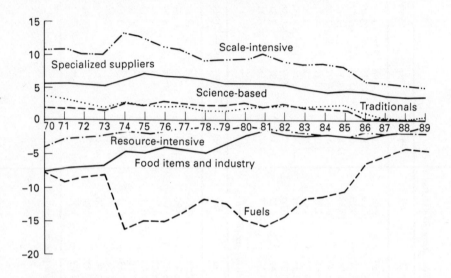

* Indicator of comparative advantages (>0) or disadvantages (<0)

they increased their positive contribution to EC trade balance, as already noted, thanks to a highly protectionist Community agricultural policy.

In contrast to these areas of relative strength, EC specialization patterns reveal a declining trend in traditional sectors, and above all in the science-based industries, particularly in microelectronics and in the 'information technology' area. This weakness, as explained below, must not be underestimated, as electronic products represent vital inputs in the manufacturing restructuring currently under way in all major countries. These overall trends, however, mask the sharp differences that have characterized the trade patterns of individual EC countries.

Germany retained its position of competitive strength, maintaining a market share (at 12.1 per cent in 1989) which is double that of any other EC economy. Germany's share increased in the late 1980s largely thanks to gains on the European internal market at the expense of its EC partners, reabsorbing the losses suffered in the first half of the 1980s. This positive German performance may be attributed to a relatively stable pattern of specialization, the strong points of which have always been scale-intensive industries (especially automobiles, chemicals and pharmaceuticals) and specialized suppliers (particularly industrial machinery and mechanical components)(Figure

Table 10.11   Index of revealed comparative advantages of the EC countries, 1987–89

	Exports*					
	EC (12)	Germany	France	United Kingdom	Italy	Greece Portugal Spain	Other EC countries
Agricultural products	66	19	120	44	38	152	102
Fuels	22	6	3	103	1	3	24
Other raw materials	42	25	37	47	30	106	54
Food industries	138	76	176	98	80	144	250
Traditional products	107	87	86	78	208	165	95
Resource-intensive products	84	66	67	81	69	133	119
Scale-intensive products	117	140	124	102	87	106	109
Specialized-supplier products	126	174	95	118	176	65	75
Science-based products	96	105	112	134	70	47	76

	Imports†					
	EC (12)	Germany	France	United Kingdom	Italy	Greece Portugal Spain	Other EC countries
Agricultural products	104	109	84	79	137	137	100
Fuels	98	83	107	59	139	159	91
Other raw materials	98	115	73	94	93	94	104
Food industries	126	112	125	131	149	111	133
Traditional products	104	114	108	110	75	71	117
Resource-intensive products	108	123	107	100	116	77	104
Scale-intensive products	97	89	98	99	99	106	99
Specialized-supplier products	88	79	99	90	77	114	84
Science-based products	96	100	100	112	89	88	83

* Ratio of the share of single countries in world exports of a given product group to the share of the same countries in total world exports (percentages)
† Ratio of the share of single countries in world imports of a given product group to the share of the same countries in total world imports (percentages)

Source: Servizi Informativi per l'Estero World Trade Data Base.

10.7, Table 10.11). The evolution of the competitive position of German industry is thus one of renewed strength with respect to its EC partners. If other more industrialized countries, such as Japan, are also considered, however, the German specialization appears much less strong because of the relatively poor performance of German exports in those science-based products of key importance for 'primary' innovation such as electronics.

Figure 10.7   Patterns of trade specialization of Germany*

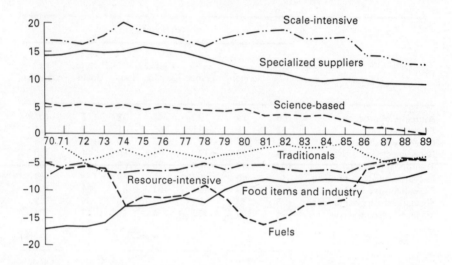

* Indicator of comparative advantages (>0) or disadvantages (<0)

The United Kingdom, on the other hand, has had a distinctly negative trade performance. The deterioration in competitiveness that has characterized the position of British industry on international markets over the last two decades is clearly reflected in its decidedly unfavourable specialization pattern in the same period (Figure 10.8, Table 10.11). Comparative advantage indicators registered considerable decreases in all four groups of industrial products, while there were increases only in agricultural products and foodstuffs, and especially in the energy sector (fuels). A slight reversal in trends in the last few years has not modified these overall negative results of the UK trade performance.

The French economy, unlike the German one, is characterized by generally low levels of trade specialization, though there have been significant qualitative and quantitative changes in the structure of its comparative advantages over the last two decades (Figure 10.9, Table 10.11). High R&D-intensity industries (science based) have emerged as new strong points, while there has been a relative despecialization in the traditional sectors. At the same time, recent years have seen a weak specialization position of France in specialized-supplier sectors, as in the early seventies. These changes are still at work and have not yet yielded the expected results, in terms of replacing

Figure 10.8   Patterns of trade specialization of the United Kingdom*

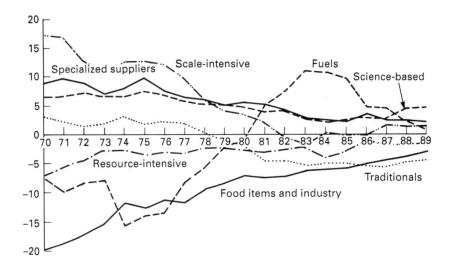

* Indicator of comparative advantages (>0) or disadvantages (<0)

old comparative advantages with the new ones, thus mostly accounting for the overall negative trade performance of French industry in the last decade.

Italy distinguishes its position in the EC by the increasing heterogeneity of its specialization pattern with respect to other advanced members (Figure 10.10, Table 10.11). The trade performance of Italian industry has been decidedly positive over the last two decades and is attributable not only to the strong competitive position of Italian firms in traditional industries but also to the strengthening of specialization and competitiveness in the sectors of mechanical engineering (specialized suppliers), such as industrial machinery (machine tools). This was the result of the process of extensive restructuring in Italian industry beginning in the mid-1970s, based largely on application and diffusion of mostly imported technology, which also allowed some so-called mature sectors to be revitalized. In the case of Italy, this external acquisition of technological input, however, also resulted in increased deficits and despecialization in many science-based sectors and in some scale-intensive product groups (such as chemicals) with negative implications for the future position of Italian industry in world economy (Guerrieri and Milana, 1990).

Figure 10.9   Patterns of trade specialization of France*

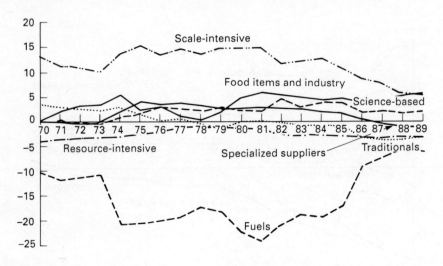

* Indicator of comparative advantages (>0) or disadvantages (<0)

The new EC member countries (Spain, Portugal and Greece), like Italy, also maintained trade specialization patterns mainly based on traditional products and sectors, such as textiles, clothing, footwear and so on (Figure 10.11, Table 10.11). Agricultural products and food industries, the other strong points of the specialization of this group of countries by the early 1970s, suffered a decreasing trend during the entire period considered here. Resource-intensive sectors, and to a lesser extent scale-intensive ones, have emerged over the 1980s as new sources of comparative advantage, especially in the case of Spain. Finally, the high external dependence of these countries on specialized-supplier and science-based goods has been confirmed over the last decade.

4. TRADE INTEGRATION OF THE EAST AND THE ROLE OF THE COMMUNITY

The evidence reported in the preceding section is indicative of complex trends in trade patterns of the EC, which cannnot be unequivocally interpreted. There are two points, however, which should be stressed.

Figure 10.10 Patterns of trade specialization of Italy*

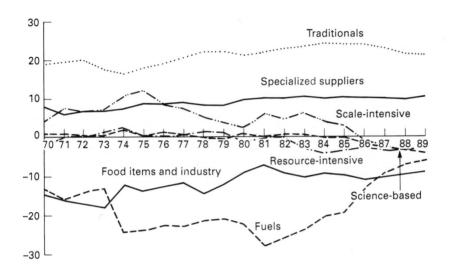

* Indicator of comparative advantages (>0) or disadvantages (<0)

The first is the severe loss of competitiveness experienced in the last decade by the EC countries as a group in science-based sectors, and especially in microelectronics and information technologies. In almost every sector of the latter group the trade data clearly demonstrate that European industries are substantially weaker than Japanese and US industries. As the diffusion of microelectronics and information technologies affects the entire industrial system and is transforming all industrial sectors, competitiveness in this area is going to play a key role in the future growth path of all advanced countries.

The EC move toward the 1992 Single Market in an attempt to remove remaining barriers to trade and competition, was also aimed at regaining competitiveness in these high-tech sectors. But a larger and competitive European market will not be sufficient to ensure European firms higher competitive standards in the electronics and related sectors. Other active common policies for industry and technology are also needed. To be implemented they require a clear set of strategies, which, however, is still lacking.

The second point pertains to the growing heterogeneity and differences within the EC. The present analysis has shown that EC countries have been characterized by significantly different patterns of specialization and competitiveness. Rich countries in the north of the Community rely on speciali-

*Figure 10.11   Patterns of trade specialization of Greece, Portugal and
            Spain**

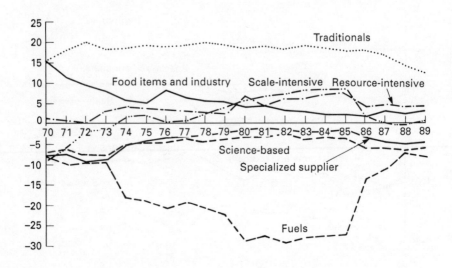

* Indicator of comparative advantages (>0) or disadvantages (<0)

zation patterns characterized by technologically advanced sectors, whereas
in the countries in the south of the Community labour-intensive traditional
sectors still constitute the key sources of competitive advantage. These differences are bound to be of particular importance once the European internal
market is completed. In fact, the Single Market and economic and monetary
union will exacerbate these differences. To facilitate intra-Community adjustments, therefore, a stronger emphasis should be put on structural policies
and the redistribution programme of the Community than is currently the
case (Jacquemin and Sapir, 1991).

Furthermore, the heterogeneity of trade patterns within the Community is
of great importance to the prospective trade integration of the eastern countries
into European economy.

While considering the specialization patterns of the West and East European countries together (Tables 10.4, 10.5 and 10.11), it is quite evident that
the imports and exports of Eastern Europe could have asymmetrical effects
on member countries of the EC, in terms of net costs and benefits associated
with trade flows. With respect to imports, the rich northern members of the
EC, and Germany in particular, holding sound comparative advantages in

specialized suppliers and, to a lesser extent, in science-based sectors, are likely to be major beneficiaries of the new markets in Eastern Europe. In contrast, the growth of exports of manufactured traditional goods and agricultural products of the East will have the most negative impact on the poorer southern members of the EC (Spain, Portugal and Greece), given their specialization which is distinguished by the same product groups. For France and Italy the effects are less clear-cut. France could benefit by the eastern imports in scale-intensive and science-based, and Italy could gain in specialized suppliers; nevertheless, both countries may yet be penalized by the exports of the East – food items in the case of France and traditional goods in the case of Italy.

Although the figures indicated above could provide only preliminary insights into the future trade patterns of East–West integration, it seems likely that the East–EC exchanges will take the form of inter-industry trade and will thus be akin to the existing North–South trade pattern within the EC and to the EC–South flows. This would imply that East–EC trade could produce serious income distribution effects and, consequently, deep adjustment problems within the Community. As is well known, income distribution is of crucial importance in the actual politics of trade policy. Thus, to liberalize its import, the EC has some hard decisions to take, which are connected with the effects, within and outside the Community, of future integration of the eastern region into European economy. This will clearly have important implications for the Community's economic policy towards the East.

In this regard, it may be noted that the Community (its individual member states and the institution as a whole) has in fact responded quickly to the new challenges from the East. Over the last two years substantial multilateral and bilateral initiatives have been carried out according to different approaches depending on the recipient country. On one hand, the Community has launched its own policies to support reconstruction in the East, financed directly by the EC budget and individual member states; on the other hand, the Community has signed trade and co-operation agreements with many eastern countries aimed at eliminating trade barriers and facilitating access for eastern countries to the Community markets (Pinder, 1991). In addition, with regard to Czechoslovakia, Hungary and Poland, given their progress toward democracy and a market economy, new Association agreements were signed at the end of 1991. Based on Article 238 of the EC Treaty, these agreements provide for gradual integration of eastern countries through increasing co-operation in such areas as trade relations, technical assistance, finance and the environment, and joint projects involving infrastructures, cultural and political relations. As regards trade relations in particular, the agreements aim at setting up a free trade area in non-agricultural products (and a lowering of protectionist barriers in raw materials and agricultural products), which should be realized not later than six years on the part of the EC, and ten years on the part of the three eastern countries. Thus, important steps should be taken in the elimination of barriers to EC trade with the East in the near future, especially in a variety of sectors (so-called sensitive sectors), such as textiles, the iron and steel industry, and agriculture. The latter, as has been indicated, holds the greatest potential for most of the East European countries.

Guaranteeing eastern countries free access to Community markets in these products is the most effective way of (1) smoothing their balance of payments constraints; (2) stimulating the restructuring of their systems of production; (3) favouring direct investment of western firms in the East. Clearly the intensity and rapidity with which the EC countries move towards a greater openness in trade in the sensitive sectors will constitute a key test of the credibility of EC commitment to co-operation with the East. If this test is to be passed, account must be taken of the unequal distribution within the Community of the costs and benefits associated with East integration, as previously assessed.

It is desirable that the EC absorb these effects without shifting the major impact on to poor southern EC members, exacerbating their adjustment costs connected with the completion of the Single European Market and thus widening the economic disparities which already exist within the EC. One option could be exercised by reinforcing European protectionism towards the developing countries in the South. Such a policy would be extremely negative, however, either for reasons of social equity or because the economic development of many Third World countries, such as the Mediterranean ones (which requires more openness rather than new barriers in the EC markets) should be considered a security issue for Europe at this point.

Actually, in order to open the Community market to the East, steps should be taken by the EC to implement structural policies and a redistribution programme. These could be used to favour trade adjustment within the Community, first of the southern members (Jacquemin and Sapir, 1991), thus providing a fairer distribution of the net benefits stemming from the East integration. But the risk is that divergent national interests within the Community could hinder further liberalization of the EC markets, as early alarming signals have already shown. This would lead to extremely negative outcomes because the openness of the Community market, together with adequate financial and technical assistance, constitutes, as already noted, a necessary condition for recovery in Eastern Europe. Finally, it should be recalled that the growth in trade volume of Eastern Europe will depend largely on the evolution of overall macroeconomic conditions. Slow growth in the EC region will increase the likelihood that adjustment policies in the transition phase will become defensive and protectionist; in contrast, sustained EC growth will increase the likelihood that trade integration will enhance the openness and efficient industrial specialization of European countries and, hence, reinforce future economic growth. In this respect, the EC macroeconomic policy will also play a very important role.

5. CONCLUDING REMARKS

This study has focused on the issue of East–West European trade integration through an analysis of the trade and technological performances of Eastern Europe and the EC countries over the last two decades.

As regards East European countries, our findings suggest that their competitiveness severely deteriorated over the last two decades. The technological factor seems to have played a crucial role in determining the poor trade performance of Eastern Europe. The East's longstanding technological lag behind the major OECD countries has in fact expanded in this period. The specialization pattern clearly indicates the backwardness of Eastern Europe's trade structure and technological capability, generally reflecting its failure to adopt advanced technologies imported from the West because of a highly inefficient system of intra- and inter-sector diffusion of these technologies. The NICs have outperformed Eastern Europe in many industries, not only in traditional and resource-intensive product groups but also in other more technologically sophisticated sectors.

The main factor determining the poor technological development of Eastern Europe has been its centrally planned mechanism of resource allocation. Characterized by state monopoly of trade, administered prices and non-convertible currencies, it isolated domestic firms from external competition, depriving them of any substantial incentives to innovation, such as cost reductions and product quality improvements. Wide microeconomic reforms, therefore, are needed to restructure and reconvert the domestic supply of Eastern Europe because of the poor competitiveness of its industrial system. In this respect, trade liberalization will play a key role. Western countries, and particularly the EC, may be of particular assistance to eastern countries, not only by providing financial and technical aid, but also by moving toward a free trade relationship with the East. In order to liberalize its imports, however, the EC has some hard decisions to make, which must take account of the effects of future integration of the East region into world economy. These problems are associated with the trade patterns of the EC countries.

EC trade performance and specialization over the past two decades has shown elements of strength and weakness distributed across sectors and member states. Two points, however, have been stressed. The first is the severe loss of competitiveness registered over the past decade by the EC countries as a whole in highly R&D-intensive sectors, and especially in microelectronics and information technologies. The second point relates to the growing heterogeneity and differences characterizing patterns of specialization and competitiveness within the EC. Rich countries in the North of the Community rely on specialization patterns characterized by technologically advanced sectors, whereas in the countries in the South labour-intensive traditional sectors still constitute key sources of competitive advantage. These national differences increased rather than diminished in the last decade and are bound to be of particular importance in the phase of deepening the European integration process.

A larger and competitive European market will not be sufficient to solve the two kinds of problems discussed above. More active common policies are needed, both for industry and technology and for structural adjustments of southern EC countries. Such active Community policy is also needed with relation to the effects of the trade integration of Eastern Europe. Although increased trade will provide economic gains to both sides in the long run, there seems to be a real possibility that in the short to medium term the pattern of specialization of the East will cause problems in intra-European trade. Eastern Europe imports and exports may create a fundamental asymmetry within the EC, exacerbating existing disparities. Steps should be taken by the EC to implement structural policies to favour trade adjustment within the Community and to provide adequate financial and technical assistance for recovery in Eastern Europe.

To sum up, the key point which emerges from the analysis presented here is that trade integration of the East will create problems which are unlikely to be resolved automatically by the market. The openness of Eastern Europe will be important in itself, but will not be sufficient to resolve the problems associated with it. In order to address these issues, the Community must act quickly and provide a clear set of unitary strategies. This effort is still lacking.

NOTES

1. Reference to Eastern Europe in this chapter includes the following countries: Bulgaria, Czechoslovakia, Hungary, Poland, Romania and the former East Germany.
2. For further information on the Servizi Informativi per l'Estero World Trade data base see Guerrieri and Milana (1990) and Guerrieri (1991). It should be noted that the exports and imports of Eastern Europe in the present analysis do not include intra-CMEA trade flows.
3. Surveys of the recent literature on innovation and technological change are in Scherer (1986), Dosi *et al.* (1988).
4. The standardized trade balance or the indicator of relative competitive position (IRCP) highlights the international distribution over time of trade surpluses and deficits among countries in each group of products. Trade surpluses and deficits are standardized by total world trade in the same group of products (CEPII 1983, 1989). The evolution of

trade balance distribution reveals competitiveness patterns of various countries in a certain group of products. For each country (j) the indicator is given by:

$$\text{IRCP} = \frac{xi - mi}{WTi}$$

xi = total exports of country (j) in the product group (i)
mi = total imports of country (j) in the product group (i)
WTi = total world trade in the product group (i).

5. A classical analysis of the major shortcomings of a planned economy is in Kornai (1982, 1985).
6. For such empirical evidence see, among others, Soete (1987); Fagerberg (1988); Dosi, *et al.* (1990a); Amendola *et al.* (1992).
7. This is the ratio of the share of individual countries in world exports (imports) of a given product group to the share of the same country in total world exports (imports).
8. The indicator of the contribution to trade balance (ICTB) of a country (j) with respect to a given group of products (i) is the following:

$$\text{ICTBi} = \frac{(Xi - Mi)}{(X + M)/2} * 100 - \frac{(X - M)}{(X + M)/2} * \frac{(Xi + Mi)}{(X + M)} * 100$$

Xi = total exports of country (j) in the product group (i), Mi = total imports of country (j) in the product group (i), X = total exports of country (j), M= total imports of country (j). The sum of the indicators with respect to the various product groups (i) in which the total trade of a country is disaggregated, equals to zero (see CEPII, 1983).

9. It should be noted that most of these sectors constitute the strong point of specialization of Eastern Europe in intra-CMEA trade, and especially in trade with the Soviet Union (see Drabek, 1989). This essentially dual trade specialization structure provides further evidence of the poor competitiveness of Eastern Europe in technologically complex sectors.
10. See Cantwell (1989); Dosi *et al.*(1990a); Pavitt (1988)
11. For similar results on the impact of Eastern Europe see Collins and Rodrik (1991); Landesman and Szekely (1991). In contrast, a recent report of the CEPR (1990) suggests that the Eastern European comparative advantage will be in high-tech goods rather than in labour-intensive ones. CEPR's conclusions, however, are not based on trade data but on statistics on the composition of the Eastern European workforce, which present various problems of interpretation.
12. The sectoral indicators reveal a positive evolution and a maintenance of the competitive position of European industry in many science-based (R&D-intensity) product groups over the 1980s, such as chemicals-pharmaceuticals, electrical machinery, engineering instruments and, more recently, aerospace, see Guerrieri and Milana (1990), Guerrieri (1991).

REFERENCES

Amendola, G., P. Guerrieri and P.C. Padoan, (1992), 'International Patterns of Technological Accumulation and Trade', *Journal of International Comparative Economics.*

Cantwell, J.A. (1989), *Technological Innovations and Multinational Corporations,* Oxford: Basil Blackwell.

Centre d'Etudes Prospectives et d'Information Internationales (1983), *Economie mondiale: la montée des tensions*, Paris: Economica.

Centre d'Etudes Prospectives et d'Information Internationales (1989), *Commerce international: la fin des avantages acquis*, Paris: Economica.

Centre for Economic Policy Research (1990), *Monitoring Eastern Europe: The Impact of Eastern Europe*, London: CEPR Annual Report.

Chesnais, F., (1986), 'Science, Technology and Competitiveness', *OECD STI Review*, **1**, 85–129.

Collins, S.M. and D. Rodrik (1991), *Eastern Europe and the Soviet Union in the World Economy*, Washington, DC: Institute for International Economics.

Dosi, G., C. Freeman, R. Nelson, G. Silverberg and L. Soete (1988), *Technical Change and Economic Theory*, London: Frances Pinter.

Dosi, G., K. Pavitt and L. Soete (1990), *The Economics of Technical Change and International Trade*, Brighton: Wheatsheaf.

Drabek, Z. (1989), 'CMEA: the Primitive Socialist Integration and its Prospects', in D. Greenaway, T. Hyclak and R. Thornton (eds), *Economic Aspects of Regional Trading Arrangements*, New York: New York University Press.

Fagerberg, I. (1988), 'International Competitiveness', *The Economic Journal*, **98**, (391), 355–74.

Guerrieri, P. (1991), 'Technology and International Trade Performance of the Most Advanced Countries', (BRIE Working Papers) Berkeley: University of California.

Guerrieri, P. and C. Milana (1990), *L'Italia e il commercio mondiale*, Bologna: Il Mulino.

Jacquemin, A. and A. Sapir (1991), 'The Internal and External Opening Up of the Single Community Market: Efficiency Gains, Adjustment Costs and New Community Instruments' *International Spectator*, **26**, (3), July–September, 29–48.

Kornai, J. (1982), *The Economics of Shortage*, Amsterdam: North Holland.

Kornai, J. (1985), *Contradictions and Dilemmas*, New York: Corvina.

Landesman, M. and I. Szekely (1991), 'Industrial Restructuring and the Reorientation of Trade in Czechoslovakia, Hungary and Poland', *CEPR Discussion Paper*, **546**, April.

Levin, R. (1984), *Survey Research on R and D Appropriability and Technological Opportunity*, New Haven: Yale University Press.

Noland, M. (1970), *Pacific Basin Developing Countries: Prospects for the Future*, Washington, DC: Institute for International Economics.

Pavitt, K. (1984), 'Sectoral Patterns of Technical Change: Towards a Taxonomy and a Theory', *Research Policy*, **13**, 343–73.

Pavitt, K. (1988), 'International Patterns of Technical Accumulation', in N. Hood and J.E. Vahlne (eds), *Strategies in Global Competition*, London: Croom Helm.

Pinder, J. (1991), *The European Community and Eastern Europe*, London: Frances Pinter.

Poznanski, K. (1987), *Technology, Competition, & the Soviet Bloc*, Berkeley: University of California, Institute of International Studies.

Rosenberg, N. (1976), *Perspectives on Technology*, Cambridge: Cambridge University Press.

Scherer, F.M. (1986), *Innovation and Growth: Schumpeterian Perspectives*, Cambridge MA: MIT Press.

Seurot, F. (1987), *Le Commerce Est–Ouest*, Paris: Economica.

Soete, L. (1987), 'The Impact of Technological Innovation on International Trade Patterns: The Evidence Reconsidered', *Research Policy*, **16**, 101–30.

11. Core–Periphery Inequalities in European Integration, East and West*

Andrew Tylecote

CORE AND PERIPHERIES, OLD AND NEW

There are various criteria of economic development by which nation states and regions within them may be ranked, or categorized as 'core', 'periphery' or 'semi-periphery'. GNP per head presumably reflects the level of development, but it reflects an economy's dynamism only with a considerable lag. Recent rates of growth of GNP or GDP, per head or otherwise, are helpful, but can they be extrapolated? (Tables 11.1 and 11.2 and Figures 11.1, 11.2, 11.3 and 11.4.)

Factors which are likely to force deflationary action and thus lead to slower growth in future include:

1. a large balance of payments deficit on current (and long term capital) account;
2. a large foreign debt;
3. higher inflation than competitors. (This will cause the more severe problems, the further economic integration proceeds – see below).

By the same token, a country with a strong balance of payments and net foreign assets position, and low inflation, can expect to sustain and even increase its growth rate in future. (Tables 11.3–11.7).

Looking further below the surface, a country's ability to supply its own and foreign markets in future depends upon its accumulation of the necessary capital, of which the most important is intangible: the individual and collective knowledge and expertise generated largely by training and R&D expenditure, and (imperfectly) reflected by patenting. Fagerberg (1988) and Soete (1981) have shown the link, at a sectoral level, between patenting performance – presumably an indicator of rate of product innovation – and trade performance. Patel and Pavitt, (1988, 1991) have shown the relative worsening of British patenting performance, and the improvement of German, during the post-war period. Stout (1977, 1979) has examined, and largely established, the effect of (poor) non-price competitiveness on UK trade performance. (See also Panic, 1976). More recently Greenhalgh (1990) has shown the linkage between innovation and trade performance in the UK context. (Tables 11.8–11.15 show the position in terms of different indicators of technological performance and their determinants.)

There is a causal sequence which can be simplified to:

High spend on R&D and training → High patenting rate → High innovation rate → Current account surplus and faster GNP growth → Revaluation and high demand → Low inflation and unemployment and high GNP growth.

A low spend on R&D and training in due course leads to high inflation and unemployment and low GNP growth. If revaluation or devaluation is ruled out the effect on demand is all the larger, but that on inflation is less, as deteriorating price competitiveness increases the pressure on wage- and price-setters. (For a fuller argument on inflation see below.)

The tables and figures referred to allow us, on the basis of the above reasoning, to make some definite, and some more tentative, categorizations of economies. On the basis alike of income levels, balance of payments, unemployment, inflation and the various indicators of 'technological dynamism', (West) Germany and Switzerland emerge as a clear-cut core – the former rising to join the latter. (West) Germany shows so much dynamism and now enjoys such an advantageous central position that its difficulties in absorbing East Germany should count for little in the long run. A number of other countries have less clear-cut claims to core status.

The Scandinavian countries have very high incomes but Denmark and Norway have relatively low R&D and patenting rates – though low R&D may be excused by the small size of their firms (see table 11.15). (On the tendency of small firms to carry out 'informal' unrecorded R&D see Kleinknecht *et al.* (1991).) Denmark has a high foreign debt, Norway a remote geographical position. Sweden has a high rate of R&D and patenting but a tendency to channel this into process not product innovation (see Edquist and Lundvall, 1991); it is, for all that, technologically the strongest of the Nordic economies. To judge by its GDP growth rates and the rapid improvement in its patenting position, Finland has shown the most dynamism of any European economy over the last twenty years and seems to be moving quickly to join the core. (Its commitment to Soviet markets has recently become a disadvantage, reflected in its balance of payments, but may in another few years turn into a big advantage.)

The Netherlands' rates of R&D and patenting have been high but have been tending to decline. Its heavy dependence on Philips now looks like a serious weakness. Belgium's rate of R&D and patenting have been rising but its heavy dependence on foreign multinationals is a weakness (Table 11.14). France's R&D intensity and patenting rates have lagged obstinately behind Germany's although it has been closing the gap on training; it remains weak in high-technology industries and the higher-tech areas of medium-tech industries (see Patel and Pavitt in Freeman *et al.*, 1991). Italy is really (at least) two countries, with the rich and dynamic north burdened by a poor south whose influence extends to the central government and bureaucracy. A high inflation rate points to structural weaknesses, as does low R&D intensity and patenting rates, partly excused by the small size of most firms – which are, typically, successful competitors in relatively low-tech industries (see Guerrieri and Milano, 1990). Austria's economic performance throughout the post-war period has been remarkable and its location, together with language and culture, encourages its inclusion in supplier networks centred on south Germany. There is no evidence, however, that it is capable of significant technological dynamism on its own account.

There is one more country which has some claim to core status but is steadily losing it. The UK still has a relatively high market share in high-tech sectors but has been losing ground in most – disastrously in electronics; there and elsewhere much native-owned industry has been taken over by foreign multinationals (MNCs). The data on R&D, patenting, inflation and balance of payments speak for themselves. Much controversy surrounds the net foreign assets position, which improved dramatically in the early 1980s thanks to North Sea oil (and gas). Coutts and Godley (1990) argue plausibly that the large 'balancing item' on the balance of payments is mostly composed of unrecorded capital inflows, and (from this) that the North Sea windfall is already spent, with net foreign assets already around zero.

There is an established periphery of market economies in south and west Europe: Ireland, Spain, Portugal and Greece. The first two are much more advanced than the others, with relatively high incomes and technology: Ireland's strength in high-technology sectors is not self-generated, but due to MNC investment in electronics, taking advantage of its English language and high education standards as well as its welcoming attitude. Its net asset position (Table 11.3) is, however, alarming, and it has paid dearly in higher unemployment for its recent improvement in balance of payments and inflation. Spain has developed a broad range of manufacturing industry for its (substantial) home market, and has at least one region, Catalunya, of real industrial dynamism. Greece, on the most recent figures, is even poorer than Portugal and has a dire net asset position and current account deficit, and high inflation. The four countries' peripheral status, with the gradations indicated, is clearly reflected by their R&D and patenting performance, and (in the case of Greece and Spain) their proportion of scientists and technicians among the workforce.

The ex-command economies of Central and Eastern Europe are much more difficult to categorize with the indicators used so far. Partly this is due to unavailability or inaccuracy of data (as with GNP data), partly because what we do know is conflicting. For example, the proportion of scientists and technicians in the workforce in Czechoslovakia and Hungary (let alone East Germany) is higher than West Germany's. On the other hand, the command economy was very wasteful of technological resources and efforts, as of other things, and it will be extremely difficult to teach those who are accustomed to its routines and relationships to operate effectively in a market economy. (See for example Kaldor, in Freeman *et al.*, 1991, pp. 348–64).

We have also to bear in mind that at least two of these countries are in the process of subdivision and that the interesting figures would be those for units for which they are largely unavailable. In Yugoslavia clearly Slovenia is by far the most advanced republic; Estonia and Ukraine seem to have a similar position within the Soviet Union, followed by Latvia and Lithuania, although given reform and conversion of the military-industrial complex Russia's technological capacity and natural resources are formidable. Given the uncertainties we shall say no more about Yugoslavia and the Soviet Union. Albania for all intents and purposes is north African or south-west Asian.

The rest vary greatly. Czechoslovakia was in 1938 a developed country with a GNP per capita above that of France, and industry concentrated in the Czech lands. Half a century later it still had impressive technological strength, as the income per head and scientists/technicians figures suggest, and a relatively small burden of debt. If Slovakia decides to secede, as seems likely, it will have to face the fact that the regional inequalities have by no means disappeared since 1938: the level of Slovak qualifications has been levelled up considerably, but a large proportion of the industry which had been set up there is military, and highly vulnerable. Hungary, with similar 'human capital' to Czechoslovakia, has lower income, a more recent industrial tradition and a much higher burden of debt. On the other hand its ecological situation is rather less disastrous and its reform process rather more advanced. It is reasonable to bracket these two Central European countries together (and add Slovenia).

A clear step down come the more East European countries of Poland, Romania and Bulgaria. According to political history and cultural/religious tradition they should be ranked in this order: Poland, Russia/Prussia/Habsburgs and Catholic; Romania, Ottoman/Habsburg and Orthodox (Catholic/Protestant minorities); Bulgaria, Ottoman and Orthodox (Muslim minority). However, Bulgaria comes top by the income measure, and Romania is (was) uniquely free of debt. Poland, far more advanced politically and institutionally, also has the worst debt burden, and probably also ecological situation, in Eastern Europe. Culture will probably tell in the long run, but for the moment it belongs squarely in the *East* European periphery.

With heroic oversimplification, we have, then:

Core: Germany, Switzerland
Nordic semi-core: Sweden, Norway, Denmark, Finland
Western semi-core: Netherlands, Belgium, France, Austria, Italy
Ex-core: UK
Western semi-periphery: Ireland, Spain
Central semi-periphery: Czechoslovakia, Hungary, Slovenia
Southern periphery: Portugal, Greece
Eastern Periphery: Poland, Romania, Bulgaria

IMPLICATIONS OF INEQUALITY FOR INTEGRATION AND ITS EFFECTS

Types, Causes and Remedies for Current Account Imbalances

Three reasons are possible for major current account deficits or surpluses on the balance of payments:

1. Demand imbalance
2. Cost/price imbalance
3. Other, 'structural' imbalances.

Clearly, to the extent that the cause is (1), monetary and/or fiscal policy is the appropriate remedy. If, however, the problem is not caused by monetary or fiscal action, it can only be controlled by it at the cost of exchanging payments imbalances for imbalances in economic activity. The deficit countries may become permanently depressed. (A foretaste of what may be in store for such countries is provided by the widening gap between 'peripheral' and 'core' unemployment rates shown by Table 11.7; note moreover that in countries like Greece and Portugal the absence of an effective welfare system causes revealed unemployment to be largely replaced by hidden underemployment.) A more optimistic view is only possible if one makes rather strong assumptions about market-clearing mechanisms – i.e. that deflation reduces factor prices which leads to increased employment. If such 'negative feedback' processes are not rather rapid – which they do not seem to be, from the evidence on inflation – they may well be offset by 'positive feedback' processes like Myrdal's (1957) 'backwash' effect; see below.

For malady (2), cost/price imbalance, the obvious remedy is exchange rate policy: a deficit country may devalue, a surplus country revalue. However, devaluation is of course inflationary. The inflationary effects of devaluation have to be taken all the more seriously since the cause of the problem was presumably faster inflation in the first place. Apart from its other drawbacks, inflation will tend to nullify the effects of the devaluation, threatening to lead to a spiral of accelerating inflation and devaluation. Thus devaluation must be combined with effective counter-inflation policy of some kind if it is to be both acceptable and permanently effective. (Alternatively, one might in principle use counter-inflation policy alone to cut costs and prices internally; but see below. And to use 'inflationary' policy instead of revaluation is quite unacceptable politically! It would be wrong, for the reasons already given, to use monetary or fiscal deflation for this purpose; although some such deflation will normally be necessary merely to offset the devaluation's expansionary effects.)

To the extent that there are *other* causes of the deficit, none of the macroeconomic remedies considered seems appropriate. But what other causes might there be? 'Structural' imbalances may be broadly divided into two categories: 'one-off' and 'progressive'. An example of the first is the destruction of an industry by war or obsolescence. Such a problem might be tackled by devaluation, using the resulting cost/price advantages first to compensate for the imbalance, and then to help remove it by encouraging the growth of new export- or import-substituting industries. *Progressive* structural imbalances, on the other hand, tend to produce a continuing increase in payments deficit. One such is a differential rate of product innovation, as argued above. To compensate for such a progressive imbalance would require continuing (real) devaluation, which is bound to be a much more difficult undertaking than a brief period of 'under-valuation' to cope with a 'one-off' structural imbalance. Thus the latter might be backed by a brief period of incomes policy to cope with the inflationary 'side-effects'. The corresponding 'crutch' for the former would be a permanent incomes policy, which no country has yet shown itself capable of sustaining. (Indeed it appears that it is precisely those countries which most need an incomes policy, are least able to operate one effectively over a long period; see below.)

The Effects of a Customs Union on Payments Imbalances and Remedies

The formation of a customs union of (largely) independent states inevitably exacerbates balance of payments problems among them. The smaller are tariff and non-tariff barriers to trade (and transport costs) the larger are the trade imbalances which will arise from given imbalances in price or non-price competitiveness. Such trade imbalances will tend to be matched by differences in rates of economic activity: the countries in surplus will tend to have a high rate of capacity utilization, etc., while those in deficit will tend to be depressed. (If monetary and fiscal policy are used to reduce these differences, the trade imbalances will be further enlarged.) Cutler *et al.* (1989) have shown that Germany has developed a massive trade surplus *vis-à-vis* almost all the other members of the EC, which is equivalent to a large transfer of employment from them to it. Devaluation has a more inflationary effect, as a customs union leads to an increase (1) in the share of import prices in the determination of retail prices, and (2) in the extent to which home producers compete with foreign ones, and thus set prices with an eye to theirs. Similarly, any 'disharmony' in monetary and fiscal policy will have a larger effect on the balance of payments than it would under protection. The effect of this may be qualitative as well as quantitative, if the greater size of the resulting problem makes a particular type of policy response less effective or more unpopular. One example of this is the failure and abandonment of Mitterrand's attempted reflation after 1981, as he found the internal benefits less, and the external side-effects much greater, than expected.

The Impact of Liberalization of Capital Flows

Let us assume that within the customs union there is a free flow of capital, at least for direct investment (as is the case in the European Community). A further problem then arises, for *regional* policy. Previously such policy – policy to even out imbalances among regions in each country – may well have relied, as in the 1950s and 1960s in Britain, on the discouragement or even prohibition of investment in 'overheated' regions, in order to drive it to those which needed it. Such negative measures will no longer be effective: the frustrated industrialist would now be highly likely to take his business abroad, supplying the (ex-) domestic market from there, at the expense of its employment and balance of payments. Only positive measures of encouragement can now be employed. These are expensive, the more so since an 'auction' is likely to develop within the customs union, with the various governments each trying to outbid the others for footloose investments, offering higher and higher subsidies and tax breaks on behalf of their depressed regions.

The Impact of European Monetary Integration

Any moves towards monetary union – that is, towards completely fixed exchange rates and freely convertible currencies – will reduce the number of policy instruments available to deal with the imbalances described. The scope for independent monetary and exchange rate policies declines to zero as monetary union is reached. It might be argued that this matters little in the long run. Fiscal instead of monetary means could be used to regulate demand, and counter-inflation instead of exchange rate policy to improve cost/price competitiveness. The latter substitution, however, has two problems attached. The first is speed. If a deficit has to be corrected by a *large* improvement in cost/price competitiveness, and the 'surplus' partners have low or zero inflation – as is actually the case in the EC – then a large *fall* in prices and wages is required – scarcely conceivable. The second is symmetry. If a surplus partner wishes to take action to correct the imbalance, the only way to reduce its cost and price competiveness, now that revaluation is barred, is to induce faster inflation than in the deficit partners. The very suggestion would be absolutely taboo in Germany.

It follows that no situation must be allowed to arise, after monetary union, where a large improvement in any country's cost/price competitiveness is necessary. Such problems must be resolved beforehand and not allowed to recur. Deficit countries must have sufficient incentive, and sufficient means, to reduce their inflation. These requirements might seem acceptable if one took a neoclassical view of the causes of inflation. Essentially this is that inflation is purely a consequence of (1) macroeconomic mismanagement; (2) expectations; (3) distortion of labour markets by union power and over-generous welfare provisions. If, like the British Conservative government after 1979, one had dealt with (3), only the macroeconomic causes would remain. One need then only choose appropriate initial exchange rate relationships, and harmonize monetary and fiscal policy. As soon as the commitment to fixed exchange rates was unshakeable, and known to be so, the problem of divergent inflationary expectations would be eliminated: for example, unions and employers in a country with a record of high inflation (e.g. Britain) would know that they must remain competitive with a low-inflation country (e.g. Germany) or face the consequences. (There is the small problem that the discipline of the Germans would be correspondingly relaxed.)

This 'mainstream' view of inflation, however, has been strongly challenged in recent years by analyses which place considerable emphasis on structural factors. Tylecote (1981), for example, has argued, in the framework of a bargaining analysis of inflation, that differences among European countries in their long-term trend rates of inflation can be explained by the following four factors. (After each, in parenthesis, I specify the ideal situation, for minimal inflation):

(a) The character and structure of management and its links with the owners of capital. (Management is highly *cohesive* and *solidaristic* within firms and among firms in the same industry, and tends – with the support of shareholders and bankers – to take a long-term view of training, investment and industrial relations.)

(b) The strength and structure of unions. (Unions are weak, moderate and organized on an industry-by-industry basis.)

(c) Linkages within the wage bargaining system. (Linkages are weak, particularly between industries, so that one excessive pay settlement has relatively few repercussions.)

(d) The trend of real devaluation or revaluation of the currency. (There is a trend to revaluation.)

Tylecote (1981) showed that by the end of the 1970s a substantial divergence had taken place on this score within the European Community, with Germany very favourably placed, particularly on (a) and (d), and Britain in a particularly unfavourable position. The problem was the more serious in view of the tendency for a poor showing on one factor to be associated with a poor showing on others (see below). During the 1980s the position for a time appeared to improve. Not only did inflation come down generally in the first half of the decade, but the variance among European countries was reduced (see Table 11.6). In particular, inflation fell sharply in Britain. To a small extent, this narrowing of the gap between Britain and the rest could be ascribed to the weakening of trade unions by legislation; but much more important appears to have been the effect of the North Sea oil and gas 'windfall' which allowed a sharp *revaluation* of the real exchange rate. This, unlike the legislative changes, was temporararily reversed; the effect of a more realistic exchange rate combined with an economic upturn was to allow the inflation rate, both absolutely and relatively, to rebound sharply. The fall in the rate in 1991 was associated with a severe recession and a return to a highly overvalued currency.

Layard (1990) takes a similar view, emphasizing the importance of centralization or co-ordination of wage bargaining as a factor helping to restrain inflation, particularly where it is led by employer cohesion. He assumes that to the extent that it is difficult to restrain inflation otherwise, unemployment will rise, presumably because governments will resort to deflation. Thus he takes unemployment rather than inflation as the dependent variable. Figure 11.5 and Table 11.16 show the relationship of unemployment and collective bargaining structures in twenty OECD countries. This is supported by the results of estimating the equation shown in Table 11.17.

If such an explanation of differences in inflation is broadly correct, what is the prognosis for them under monetary union? The best argument for optimism would revolve around expectations: once, for example, UK unions and management understand that the sterling:Mark rate is absolutely fixed, will they not accept that they *must* remain competitive on prices and wages, and settle accordingly? Is this not what has already happened in Belgium and France? The pessimist will reply that these, as shown in Table 11.16, are moderately well co-ordinated countries, and thus capable, under government pressure, of reaching a collective appreciation of the truth of this proposition, and showing collective restraint. This was achieved even in Ireland, a small enough country to belie Layard's ranking, when the chips were down (see Murdoch, 1991). Where, as in Britain (and to a slightly lesser extent Spain) there really is little co-ordination, the matter must be looked at from the perspective of individual firms and their workers. Most workers are employed in sectors not heavily involved in international trade and they and their employers will therefore not be conscious of the disciplines described. If they win 'excessive' settlements, this will affect the 'internationally competing' (I-C) sectors in two ways: it will raise the prices of those of their inputs which the non-competing sectors supply – a substantial proportion of I-C costs; and it will put upward pressure on I-C sectors' wages, since both workers and employers will wish them to remain competitive within the national labour market. Individual I-C employers may well continue to feel that they have more to lose by insisting on low wage settlements than by paying what it takes to please their workers and attract the skilled labour they need.

Let us suppose, however, for the sake of argument, that the 'high inflation' countries do succeed, after monetary union if not before, in keeping their cost and price inflation in line with the rest. We must then confront the possibility already mentioned, that trade and payments deficits may develop without any cost/price divergence or disharmony of macro-policies, because of *structural* imbalances.

Innovation and Structural Imbalances under Monetary Union

It was argued above that one of the factors making for high inflation was a trend to real devaluation – devaluation which goes beyond that required merely to compensate for a higher rate of inflation – due mainly to relatively poor performance in product innovation. This might well be associated with other inflationary factors. One reason for this could be that countries struggling with high inflation tend to resort to measures like fiscal and monetary deflation which discourage the long-term investment strategies required for successful innovation. Another reason, as the present author has argued (1975, 1977, 1981, 1987) is that short time horizons and an aversion to risk are important causal factors in both high inflation and low innovation. In turn, they can themselves largely be accounted for by factor (a) in the last section: a certain character and structure of management, and its links with the owners of capital. On innovation, Patel and Pavitt take a similar view, distinguishing between 'myopic' and 'dynamic' 'national systems of innovation':

> Myopic systems treat investments in technological activities just like any conventional investment: they are undertaken in response to a well-defined market demand and include a strong discount for risk and time. Dynamic systems, on the other hand, recognise that technological activities are not the same as any other investment. In addition to tangible outcomes in the form of products and profits, they also entail important but intangible by-products in the form of cumulative and irreversible processes of technological, organisational and market learning that enable them to undertake subsequent investments. (Patel and Pavitt, in Freeman *et al.*, 1991, p. 55)

Not surprisingly, they chose Germany as an example of 'dynamism', the UK as typically 'myopic', and pointed to three key institutional differences. The first was financial. The financial system underlying business activity in Germany gave greater weight to longer-term performance, and was able to do so because it provided 'both the information and the competence to enable the value of firm-specific intangible assets to be evaluated by the providers of finance'. The second difference was in methods of management, especially in large firms in R&D-intensive sectors: the UK gave greater power and prestige to financial rather than technical competence, which was associated with incentive and control mechanisms based on short-term financial performance and with decentralized divisional structures 'insensitive to changing technological opportunities'. The third was in education and training: 'the German system of widespread yet rigorous general and vocational education provides a better basis for cumulative learning, especially in the engineering-based industries' (Patel and Pavitt, in Freeman *et al.*, 1991, pp. 55–7).

There is another dimension on which what makes for high inflation also makes for low innovation: *cohesion* and *solidarity* within and among firms. Not only is the time horizon long, but the spatial horizon is broad. This was referred to above *re* inflation. *Re* innovation I have argued (Tylecote, 1991), that innovation and training (and innovation *via* training) were encouraged by *stakeholder rationality* which took account of the interests of others beside the firm's own shareholders – employees, customers, suppliers, banks, even rivals. The result is that structural inferiority in innovation, and in inflation, tend to go together. Worse, the weaker countries structurally tend to be those on the periphery, geographically: Britain, Ireland, Portugal, Spain, Greece, and perhaps Italy. (The disadvantage of the first four increases as Eastern Europe opens up.)

If the customs and monetary union can then expect to develop imbalances among its component states which are analogous to regional imbalances, can we see a similarity in the appropriate solutions? Within the nation state, regional imbalances normally lead to two redistributive responses from the central government. The first is *automatic*: by taxing regions according to income, and spending in them according to need (in some sense), central government redistributes from richer to poorer. The second is *considered*: it takes policy decisions to provide subsidies of one sort or another for poorer regions. The second response at least is already taking place at Community level, but it is on a far smaller scale, proportionately, than similar redistribution within states. It is almost inconceivable that the political will could develop within the next decade or two to achieve the same proportionate redistribution among states of the Community, as within them.

There are also responses below governmental level. The workers of the 'less dynamic' regions are likely to accept lower wages than the rest, and by doing so may well, to some extent, attract investment from industries sensitive to labour costs. Such wage differences already exist, of course, as Table 11.18 shows, and they are having an impact: for example they are clearly affecting investment decisions in the motor industry, such as Nissan and Toyota's new plants in Britain, and Volkswagen's emphasis on small car production in Spain (see Cutler *et al.*, 1989 and JETRO, 1991). However, as has already been seen within states, only a limited proportion of firms and sectors are sensitive enough to wage differences to offset the locational advantages of central regions (see Karlsson and Larsson, 1990). The attraction is even less when the lower wage countries have lower skills (see Table 11.9); there is now serious concern in the UK that its poor standard in this regard may be driving away multinationals, particularly Japanese (see for example Hague, 1991). The limited proportion which give priority to low wages are now finding a much wider range of low-wage countries to choose among, as Eastern Europe moves towards free trade with the West.

Another response, if the industry will not move to the workers, is for the workers to move to the industry: migration from periphery to centre. Again, a great deal of this takes place within states, and it is (just) politically acceptable. Among states, starting from the present position, the migration of a similar proportion seems politically inconceivable. Moreover, as is well known in regional economics, such migration is not at all a satisfactory solution even economically, since it tends to deprive the periphery of its most dynamic inhabitants.

A third response is that a less dynamic region loses ownership and control of its assets. A current account deficit automatically means a worsening of a region's – or state's – net asset position; that in turn tends to worsen the current account deficit. The transfer of ownership is thus not a solution, but part of the problem. The transfer of *control* is a further problem. Firms in a less dynamic region – or state – are likely to be taken over by outside firms expecting to increase the value of existing assets, by an infusion of new capital, technology or managerial expertise. The potential gain for the less dynamic region is the *spread* of advanced technology; but the potential loss, as Myrdal (1957), Hymer (1972) and others have argued, is a *backwash* of technological capacity away from the region, since the individuals and the organizational units capable of innovation, particularly of new *products*, are drawn away to the centres of the multinational ('multiregional') firms. This has been well exemplified by the VW takeover of SEAT of Spain in 1986; see Cutler *et al.* (1989, pp. 37–8). Further, the *networks* of firms which buy from/sell to one another and are close, geographically and culturally, encouraging co-operative innovation, are broken up by MNC takeovers from outside the network (Lundvall, 1988).

CONCLUSIONS AND POLICY IMPLICATIONS

It appears from the preceding arguments that Europe is tending to polarize into a dynamic *core* and less dynamic *periphery*, the core being characterized by a tendency to rapid product innovation and low inflation, and the periphery by the opposite. This structural imbalance will be exacerbated by further economic integration, although the tendency to divergence of inflation will be to some extent suppressed by monetary union. In an effort to keep inflation and payments imbalances in check, 'peripheral' governments will drive down rates of activity and growth which would tend to be relatively low anyway.

The ex-command economies are taking their place, inevitably, as a new periphery. For the time being the processes this implies will be kept in check to some extent by the maintenance of tariff barriers and (limited) exchange controls; however there is at present very little restriction on foreign investment as host governments welcome the infusion of expertise and capital. What is to be done? In Western Europe, to stop the process of economic integration where it is would be both unacceptable politically and ineffective economically: we have gone too far already. I propose three remedies. First, the structural imbalances are not immutable: structures can be reformed. To take only one example, British company law is a serious obstacle to the development of long-term relationships between borrowers and lenders, and between shareholders and managers. It can and should be changed, towards the German model (see Charkham, 1989). Laws and institutions need reform to encourage the development of cohesive local and regional networks of firms and supporting structures. Firms, particularly small and medium sized, should be relieved of the costs of training and of adaptation (e.g. through redundancy). Links should be developed, partly through local banks and 'enterprise boards'' stakes in firms, such as to encourage buying from within the network – *à la* Japonaise *kigyo shudan*. Employee shareholdings and co-determination should be used to similar effect. Such developments would also help protect from outside takeover. (This prescription is largely modelled on Finland, which is the most successful European economy in terms of economic growth since the Second World War and in many ways an excellent model, particularly for the East; see Lantto, 1989.)

Secondly, there are rather more superficial and fast-acting means of improving peripheral performance: training can be improved, both by direct government action, and by the use of various forms of subsidy and penalty on employers, as in France over the last two decades. This will both help 'peripheral' firms to be cost-competitive, and help to attract multinationals – which, if they can be induced to follow the Japanese pattern, will help to nurture a network of local suppliers.

Thirdly, it is now becoming apparent that the social costs of most forms of transport (particularly cars and lorries, followed by aircraft) are far above their current private costs. (The difference, negative externalities, arise partly from accidents and noise, but mainly from congestion and atmospheric pollution, including 'acid rain' and the greenhouse effect.) The technical means now exist to assess and charge for these externalities accurately and cheaply (mainly through electronic road pricing; see Chartered Institute for Transport, 1990). Once this is done, the trend towards the unification of European markets through the elimination of first tariff and then non-tariff barriers would be reversed, but not exactly towards the status quo *ante*: the sharp rise in transport costs would in effect give a measure of protection to regional as well as national economies. Further, one may foresee that the ecological concerns referred to above will lead, largely through 'green taxation', to an economic system giving markedly less emphasis than at present to high-volume manufacture of short-life goods, and more to repair and maintenance, and other services. This implies a shift from activities which are easily centralized, to those which naturally tend to be supplied locally.

The need for such 'green' reforms in taxation is particularly urgent in Central and Eastern Europe. Their ecological problems are appalling already without adding the only one from which they do *not* yet suffer: mass use of cars and lorries. Moreover their roads are quite inadequate to cope with such an onslaught: 'protection' by traffic jams is *not* efficient. Further, the German advantage in transport equipment *vis-à-vis* the rest of Western Europe (Cutler *et al.*, 1989, pp. 40–41) will be even greater *vis-à-vis* Central and Eastern Europe and liable to create an intolerable burden on their balance of payments. In general, one can say that there is a better chance for the Central and Eastern Europeans to compete under a set of rules which are new to everyone, than to do so if the Western European rules are adopted everywhere. Their abundant scientists and engineers could be more easily employed and retained in the new repair/maintenance/service firms than in 'branch plants' of Western European and other, MNCs. There is great scope for these countries, with the help of licensed western technologies and western grants, to build up major locally owned and controlled pollution abatement industries, which may in future win a large export market, particularly in the Third World. (The case of the Greek development of a new filter for diesel engines is an encouraging precedent – see Hope, 1991). Macro economic estimates of the effects of environmental policies are encouraging (Pearce, 1991).

How far is the third proposal in conflict with the second? How can the more peripheral countries be made more attractive relative to the core, in competing for mobile companies and plants, if the costs of moving inputs and outputs between the core and the periphery are increased? We have to distinguish among goods according to their weight (and volume) to value ratios. Where these are relatively low, it is speed and certainty of delivery which are likely to be important to the firms concerned, more than cost. (This is analogous to the requirement for skilled labour: what is vital is that it is available, not that it is cheap.) Assuming that road pricing and higher fuel charges are accompanied by heavy investment in high-speed rail networks (with new methods of road/rail transfer) – and they would be, because they would ensure its profitability – speed and certainty would improve substantially; the roads, after all, would be half empty. Such activities might continue to be centralized to take advantage of scale economies; and the case for centralised supply from a *peripheral* location would even improve. Meanwhile those activities with high weight to value ratios in inputs and outputs would move back towards a more fragmented, locally or regionally based pattern.

It follows that 'green taxation', while requiring no justification beyond environmental considerations, may bring with it a most beneficial side-effect: protection from excessive centralization of economic activity, and from increasing unevenness of economic development between 'core' and 'periphery' in Europe.

Table 11.1   Income levels, Eastern and Western Europe

	GNP per capita[a] 1987		GNP per capita 1987
Eastern Europe		*Western Europe*	
Albania	(953)	Austria	15 440
Bulgaria	(7 229)	Belgium	
Czechoslovakia	(9 709)	Denmark	
East Germany	(11 860)	France	
Hungary	(8 260)	West Germany	18 450
Poland	(6 879)	Greece	4 677
Romania	(6 365)	Ireland	
Soviet Union	(8 662)	Italy	13 010
Yugoslavia	5 434	Netherlands	
Slovenia	12 618	Norway	
Croatia	7 179	Portugal	
Serbia	4 870	Spain	7 282
Vojvodina	6 949	Sweden	
Kosovo	1 302	Switzerland	
Montenegro	3 985	United Kingdom	11 730
Bosnia Hercegovina	3 438		

(a) There are no direct measurements of GNP for COMECON countries. Their statistics use a different measure, Net Material Product. These figures are CIA estimates and are taken from US Arms Control and Disarmament Agency data. They are almost certainly overestimates and the brackets are used to indicate the fact that they are estimates.

Sources: Mary Kaldor, in Freeman *et al.*, 1991, Table 21.1. Yugoslavia: Samuel Brittan, *Financial Times*, Monday, 9 September 1991.

Table 11.2   *Percentage growth rates of national income, Western Europe, 1960–90*

	Real GNP per capita		Real GDP[bc]	
	1960–70	1973–83	1984–87	1988–90
Austria	4.5	2.8	1.8	4.2
Belgium	4.8	1.8	1.7	4.0
Denmark	4.7	1.8	3.0	1.2
Finland	4.6	2.7	3.1	3.5
France	5.7	2.5	2.0	3.6
West Germany	4.4	2.1	2.2	4.0
Greece	6.9	3.0	1.7	2.3
Ireland	4.2	3.2	1.8	4.0
Italy	5.3	2.2	2.8	3.0
Netherlands	5.5	1.5	2.2	3.4
Norway	4.9	3.7	4.3	0.6
Portugal	6.2	2.7[a]	2.6	4.6
Spain	7.1	1.8	3.2	4.5
Sweden	4.4	1.3	2.8	1.6
Switzerland	4.3	0.7	2.6	3.0
United Kingdom	2.9	1.1	3.5	2.2

(a) Real GDP
(b) Real GNP for Germany and Ireland
(c) Crude averages of % changes from previous period for each year.

Source: Williams (1987) p. 27, Table 1, OECD *Economic Outlook*, July 1991, Table R1.

Table 11.3   *Investment income flows of West European countries, 1989*

	$ billion	% of GNP/GDP
Austria	−0.9	−0.5
Belgium	1.3	0.8
Denmark	−4.4	−3.9
Finland	−2.4	−2.1
France	−0.4	−0.0
West Germany	11.6	1.0[a]
Greece	−1.5	−2.7
Ireland	−4.4	−15.0[a]
Italy	−8.3	−0.9
Netherlands	1.2	0.5
Norway	−2.5	−2.4
Portugal	−0.7	−1.8
Spain	−3.0	−0.8
Sweden	−2.2	−1.1
Switzerland	13.1	7.4
United Kingdom	6.2	0.7

(a) Percentage of GNP

Source: OECD *Economic Outlook*, July 1991, Tables 75, 76, R20 and R21.

Table 11.4   Balance of payments on current account, Western Europe, as a percentage of GDP, 1985–90

	1985	1986	1987	1988	1989	1990
Austria	−0.2	0.3	−0.2	−0.3	0.1	0.0
Belgium-Luxembourg	0.8	2.7	1.9	2.3	2.3	2.2
Denmark	−4.6	−5.4	−2.9	−1.1	−0.8	1.2
Finland	−1.3	−1.1	−2.0	−2.6	−4.8	−4.9
France	−0.1	0.3	−0.6	−0.5	−0.5	−0.7
West Germany[a]	2.6	4.4	4.1	4.2	4.8	3.2
Greece	−9.8	−4.3	−2.7	−1.8	−4.7	−5.3
Ireland[a]	−4.1	−3.1	1.4	2.3	1.8	3.0
Italy	−0.8	0.4	−0.1	−0.7	−1.2	−1.3
Netherlands	4.0	2.8	1.4	2.3	3.5	3.8
Norway	5.3	−6.5	−4.9	−4.4	0.2	3.6
Portugal	1.9	3.8	1.8	−1.4	0.4	−0.1
Spain	1.7	1.7	0.0	−1.1	−2.9	−3.3
Sweden	−1.4	0.5	−0.1	−0.4	−1.7	−2.6
Switzerland	5.4	5.1	4.4	4.9	4.2	4.3
United Kingdom	0.8	0.0	−1.0	−3.3	−3.9	−2.4

(a) Percentage of GNP

Source: OECD *Economic Outlook*, July 1991, Table R21.

Table 11.5   Convertible currency debt of Eastern Europe and USSR, 1989

	Net debt $ bn	Net interest payment as % of exports to market economies	Net debt as % exports to market economies
Bulgaria	7.7	24.2	321
Czechoslovakia	3.1	5.1	51
East Germany	11.0	11.2	115
Hungary	19.5	24.6	342
Poland	35.5	41.7	456
Romania	0.1	0.6	−1
E. Europe	77.7	17.7	204
USSR	36.49[a]	4.9	72
E. Europe and USSR	114.1[a]	10.7	136

(a) Includes debt of CMEA banks

Source: Mary Kaldor, p. 357 in Freeman *et al.* (1991).

Table 11.6   Consumer price inflation, Western Europe, 1969–90

| | At average annual rate | | |
	1969–78	1978–87	1988–90
Austria	6.4	4.2	2.6
Belgium	7.4	5.4	2.6
Denmark	9.1	7.7	4.0
Finland	10.6	7.6	5.9
France	8.6	8.6	3.2
West Germany	5.0	3.2	2.3
Greece	11.4	20.7	15.9
Ireland	12.6	11.0	3.2
Italy[a]	12.1	12.8	5.9
Netherlands	7.3	3.4	1.4
Norway	8.8	8.5	5.1
Portugal[c]	16.8	19.6	11.9
Spain	14.1	11.8	6.1
Sweden	8.7	8.2	7.6
Switzerland	5.1	3.5	3.5
United Kingdom	12.4	8.2	7.4
EC[b]	9.9	8.6	4.9

(a) Index for households of wage and salary earners.
(b) The country weights used in the aggregate indices are based on the private consumption and the purchasing power parity for consumer expenditure of the preceding year.
(c) Excluding rent.

Source: OECD *Economic Outlook*, July 1991, Table 45.

Table 11.7   Standardized unemployment rates (% of total labour force)

	1986	1987	1988	1989	1990
Belgium	11.2	11.0	9.7	8.1	7.9
Finland	5.3	5.0	4.5	3.4	3.4
France	10.4	10.5	10.0	9.4	9.0
Germany	6.4	6.2	6.2	5.6	5.1
Greece[a]	7.4	7.4	7.7	7.5	7.7
Italy	10.5	10.9	11.0	10.9	9.9
Ireland	17.1	16.9	16.3	15.0	14.0
Netherlands	9.9	9.6	9.2	8.3	7.5
Norway	2.0	2.1	3.2	4.9	5.2
Portugal	8.5	7.0	5.7	5.0	4.6
Spain	20.8	20.1	19.1	16.9	15.9
Sweden	2.7	1.9	1.6	1.4	1.5
Switzerland[a]	0.7	0.6	0.7	0.6	0.6
United Kingdom	11.2	10.3	8.5	7.1	6.9

(a) Non-standardized definitions.

Source: OECD *Economic Outlook*, July 1991, Table R18.

Table 11.8   Basic indicators

	Population 1987 (m)	Infant mortality rate per thousand (0–1 yrs) 1985	Urban population 1985 (% of total)	Energy consumption per capita (per unit of GNP) 1985 (kgs of oil equivalent)[a]		Scientists and engineers 1985 % of pop.		Technicians 1985 % of pop.	
Albania	3.1	43	34	1 267	(1.31)	–	–	–	–
Bulgaria	9.0	16	68	4 332	(0.61)	48 008	5	13 099	1
Czechoslovakia	15.6	15	66	4 853	(0.51)	61 046	4	47 337	3
East Germany	16.6	10	76	5 670	(0.50)	128 502	8	69 828	4
Hungary	10.6	20	55	2 974	(0.37)	22 479	4	17 869	3
Poland	37.7	19	59	3 438	(0.49)	56 600	2	–	–
Romania	22.9	24	51	3 453	(0.58)	–	–	–	–
Soviet Union	284.0	29	66	4 885	(0.58)	1 491 300	5	–	–
For comparison									
Greece	10.0	16	65	1 341	0.39	2 441[b]	0.3	1 067[b]	0.1
Spain	39.0	10	77	1 932	0.28	15 299[c]	0.4	6 181[c]	0.2
Italy	57.4	12	67	2 606	0.21	63 021[b]	1.0	28 694[b]	0.5
Austria	7.6	11	56	3 217	0.21	6 712[d]	1.0	6 145[d]	1.0
West Germany	61.0	10	86	4 451	0.25	133 115[b]	2.0	119 618[b]	2.0
United Kingdom	56.8	9	92	3 603	0.32	86 500[e]	1.5	76 600[e]	2.0
United States	243.0	11	74	7 278	0.41	728 600	3.0	–	1.3

(a) Estimates of energy consumption per unit of output are of CIA origin – see Table 11.1.
(b) 1983.
(c) 1984.
(d) 1981.
(e) 1978.

Sources: Mary Kaldor, in Freeman *et al.*, 1991, Table 21.1. Yugoslavia: Samuel Brittan, *Financial Times*, Monday, 9 September 1991.

Table 11.9   Proportion of skilled workers in the EC labour force

	Men	Women	Total
Belgium	69	58	67
Denmark	n.a.	n.a.	76
France	80	64	74
West Germany	91	80	87
Ireland	47	55	50
Italy	61	58	61
Netherlands	68	62	67
Portugal	54	43	50
Spain	61	49	57
UK	55	37	48
Greece	61	55	n.a.
EC	70	59	66

Source: Jackman and Rubin, 1991, Table 2.

Table 11.10   Trends in industry-financed R&D as a percentage of GDP in twelve OECD countries, 1967–88 (defence R&D in brackets)

	1967		1985		1988	
United States	1.01	(1.01)	1.35	(0.85)	1.38	(0.83)
Japan	0.83	(0.01)	1.84	(0.02)	1.95	(n.a)
Belgium	0.59	(n.a)	1.06	(n.a)	1.13	(n.a)
Denmark	0.34	(n.a)	0.60	(n.a)	0.68	(n.a)
France	0.61	(0.54)	0.94	(0.46)	0.96	(0.52)
West Germany	0.94	(0.21)	1.58	(0.14)	1.78	(0.13)
Ireland	0.17	(n.a)	0.33	(n.a)	0.49	(n.a)
Italy	0.35	(0.02)	0.58	(0.08)	0.54	(0.08)
Netherlands	1.12	(0.04)	0.96	(0.03)	1.14	(0.03)
Spain	0.08		0.26		0.32	
Sweden	0.72	(0.43)	1.71	(0.30)	1.74	(0.29)
Switzerland	1.78	(0.05)	1.59	(0.03)	2.20	(n.a)
United Kingdom	1.00	(0.60)	0.96	(0.67)	1.06	(0.51)
Western Europe	0.79	(0.28)	1.07	(0.28)	1.17	(0.29)

Notes: Czechoslovakia, Hungary and Poland also have substantial expenditure on R&D. 'Unfortunately, an accurate assessment of their aggregate technological capacity is for the moment impossible ... their sectoral specialisations, as revealed by American patenting, are similar to those of their Western European neighbours, and they clearly do have considerable scientific and technological potential' (Patel and Pavitt, p. 44 in Freeman *et al.*, 1991).

The R&D effort of countries with relatively small firms is understated, since small firms emphasize 'informal' R&D. See Kleinknecht *et al.* (1991, ch. 6). This is particularly relevant to Italy, Denmark and Finland. See Table 11.15.

Source: Patel and Pavitt, Tables 3.1 and 3.3 in Freeman *et al.*, (1991).

Table 11.11   *Trends in investments in science, technology and skills in France, West Germany and the United Kingdom*

Measure	France	West Germany	United Kingdom
Govt. exp. on academic and related research* (UK = 100)			
1987	115	144	100
1980	98	147	100
Output of scientific publications (UK = 100)			
1986	59	71	100
1981	60	75	100
Industry-funded R&D* (UK = 100)			
1988	90	191	100
1981	96	191	100
American patents granted (UK = 100)			
1988	101	268	100
1980	87	239	100
Mechanical and engineering qualifications awarded at craft & technician levels (000s)			
1987	98	134	30
1975	66	103	27
Workforce with vocational or higher qualifications (%)			
1988	47	n.a.	36
1979	38	67 (1978)	31

* Calculated using purchasing power parity

Source: Patel and Pavitt, Table 38 in Freeman *et al.* (1991).

Table 11.12   *Shares of West European patenting in the United States: 1963–88*

	1963–88	1974–88	1984–88	1984–88 % share/ population (millions), 1990
West Germany	33.74	37.16	40.91	0.652
United Kingdom	24.80	18.16	14.67	0.256
France	13.42	14.45	14.60	0.259
Netherlands	4.67	4.32	4.62	0.310
Italy	4.27	4.72	5.83	0.101
Denmark	0.92	1.03	1.03	0.201
Belgium	1.63	1.84	1.55	0.156
Ireland	0.06	0.11	0.20	0.057
Spain	0.42	0.59	0.57	0.014
Greece	0.06	0.07	0.05	0.005
Portugal	0.03	0.03	0.02	0.002
Switzerland	8.66	8.81	7.31	1.128
Sweden	5.24	5.65	4.89	0.587
Austria	1.33	1.76	1.89	0.250
Norway	0.50	0.62	0.60	0.145
Finland	0.25	0.68	1.27	0.262
Total	100.00	100.00	100.00	

Source: First 3 columns: Patel and Pavitt, in Freeman *et al.* (1991), Table 3.4. Last column: own calculations from Column 3 and UN population data.

Table 11.13   Overall patterns of trade

| Country | Trade coverage ratios, 1988[§] | | |
| | High RDI* | Med RDI[†] | Low RDI[‡] |
	(exports/imports)		
United Kingdom	0.93	0.93	0.67
West Germany	1.26	2.30	0.93
France	0.96	1.05	0.85
Italy	0.77	1.18	1.33
Netherlands	0.83	1.04	1.19
Belgium	0.83	1.06	1.18
Spain	0.36	0.73	1.29
Sweden	0.89	1.18	1.41
Austria	0.74	0.82	1.08
Denmark	0.88	0.73	1.19
Finland	0.58	0.68	2.18
Greece	0.13	0.17	0.78
Ireland	1.59	0.78	1.27
Norway	0.28	0.62	0.66
Portugal	0.43	0.28	1.66
Switzerland	1.46	1.10	0.42
Turkey	0.19	0.34	1.96
United States	0.86	0.52	0.35
Japan	5.15	4.23	0.92

* RDI = R&D intensity; high RDI = aerospace, office machinery, computers, electronic components, drugs and medicines, instruments, electrical machinery.
[†] Medium RDI = motor vehicles, chemicals, non-electrical machinery, rubber, plastics, non-ferrous metals, other transport equipment.
[‡] Low RDI = all other industries.
[§] The data for the second group of countries is for 1987.

Note: 'The European patterns of specialisation reflect German strengths in chemicals, mechanical engineering, automobiles and defence, coupled with decline in electronics (with the exception of telecommunications) and continuing weakness in raw materials. This pattern is reproduced – in whole or in part – in some of Germany's neighbours: Austria, Switzerland and even in Czechoslovakia, Hungary and Poland. Italy and Spain share relative strengths in mechanical engineering, automobiles, fine chemicals and (as shown by more detailed data) textiles, while the earlier Swedish model is being reproduced elsewhere in Scandinavia based on the extraction and processing of raw materials. France shows relative strength in fields closely linked to state markets (military and civilian), while the United Kingdom has become increasingly strong in defence and in a sector dependent on a strong base in fundamental science (fine chemicals), while showing particularly rapid decline in electronic capital goods and components. Only the Netherlands in Europe shows consistent specialisation over the whole range of electrical and electronic technologies, related of course to the exceptional position of Philips' (Patel and Pavitt, in Freeman *et al.*, 1991, pp. 46–7).

Source: Saunders *et al.*, Table 2.8 in Freeman *et al.*, 1991; *European Research*, January 1991, p. 15.

Table 11.14   Large and foreign firms in national technological activities, 1981–86

Country	National sources of patenting in USA (3 cols add up to 100%)			Patenting in USA by national firms from outside home country (% of national total)
	Large firms*		*Other*	
	National	Foreign		
Belgium	8.8	39.7	51.5	14.7
France	36.8	10.0	53.2	3.4
West Germany	44.8	10.5	44.2	6.9
Italy	24.1	11.6	64.3	2.2
Netherlands	51.9	8.7	39.4	82.0
Sweden	27.5	3.9	68.6	11.3
Switzerland	40.1	6.0	53.9	28.0
United Kingdom	32.0	19.1	49.0	16.7
Western Europe	44.1	6.2	49.7	8.1
Canada	11.0	16.9	72.1	8.0
Japan	62.5	1.2	36.3	0.6
USA	42.8	3.1	54.1	3.2

* The world's 660 largest, technologically active firms, as measured by their patenting activity in the USA, 1981–86.

Note: All columns as percentage of total national patenting in USA, 1981–86. Shell is assumed to be Dutch and Unilever British. To clarify the meaning of the data, we may take the case of Belgium. The first column shows that large Belgian firms accounted for 8.8% of patenting from Belgium. The second column shows that large foreign multinationals accounted for 39.7% of such patenting. The third column simply points out that the rest was equal to 51.5%. The fourth column is quite different: it shows that Belgian firms patenting from outside Belgium took out a number of patents which amounted to 14.7% of the total taken out from within Belgium.

Source: Patel and Pavitt, in Freeman *et al.* (1991), Table 3.6.

Table 11.15   Scale of industrial production in selected Western European countries

---

Denmark, 1978 (% of firms by number of full-time employees)

1–2	3–5	6–20	21–50	>50	Total
1	56	28	8	7	100

West Germany, 1970 (% of employees by size of firm)

1–9	10–49	50–99	100–499	>500	Total
8	22	30	5	35	100

France, 1980 (% of firms by number of employees)

1–10	10–99	100–499	500–1 999	>2 000	Total
N/A	18	23	19	40	100

Sweden, 1981 (% of firms by number of employees)

1–49	50–200	>200	Total
91	6	3	100

UK, 1976 (% of employees by size of firm)

1–99	100–199	>199	Total
17.1	5.5	77.4	100

Southern Europe (% of firms by number of employees)

	1–9	10–40	50–99	>99	Total
Greece, 1978	93	5	1	1	100
Italy, 1981	85	13	1	1	100
Portugal, 1971	79	16	3	2	100
Spain, 1978	77	18	2	3	100

Netherlands, 1983 (% of firms by number of full-time employees)

1–4	5–9	10–49	50–99	>99	Total
63	14	19	3	1	100

Other Northern European countries (% of firms by number of employees)

	1–99	100–199	>199	Total
Ireland, 1986	33	17	50	100
Belgium, 1970	33	10	57	100
Luxembourg, 1973	19	28	53	100

Source: Williams, (1987), p. 166, Table 26.

Table 11.16   *Unemployment rates and collective bargaining structures in twenty OECD countries*

	Unemployment rate 1983–88 (1)	Union co-ordination (2)	Employer co-ordination (3)
Belgium	11.3	2	2
Denmark	9.0	3	3
France	9.9	2	2
Germany	6.7	2	3
Ireland	16.4	1	1
Italy	7.0	2	1
Netherlands	10.6	2	2
Portugal	7.7	2	2
Spain	19.8	2	1
UK	10.7	1	1
Australia	8.4	2	1
New Zealand	4.6	2	1
Canada	9.9	1	1
US	7.1	1	1
Japan	2.7	2	2
Austria	3.6	3	3
Finland	5.1	3	3
Norway	2.7	3	3
Sweden	2.2	3	3
Switzerland	2.4	1	3

Source: Layard (1990).

Table 11.17   Explaining inflation–unemployment trade-offs in twenty OECD countries

The following equation was estimated by ordinary least squares (t-statistics in brackets):

Average unemployment rate 1983–88 (%)   (t-statistic)

–0.35 Change in inflation 82–88 (% points)	(2.8)
–4.28 Employer co-ordination	(7.0)
–1.42 Union co-ordination	(2.0)
+2.45 Coverage of collective bargaining	(2.4)
+0.17 Replacement ratio	(7.1)
+0.92 Maximum duration of benefits	(2.9)
–0.13 Active labour market spending	(2.3)

$R^2 = 0.91$; s.e. = 1.41

Note: Coverage: greater than 75% = 3; 25–75% = 2; under 25% = 1. Maximum duration of benefits: Over 4 years is set at 4. Active labour market spending. Expenditure per unemployed person relative to output per worker.

Source: Layard (1990).

Table 11.18   Gross wage expenses in 1987 (salaries/wages and various social benefits) in different EC member states (West Germany as base index 100)

West Germany	100.0
Netherlands	84.4
Denmark	83.3
Belgium	80.4
Italy	74.3
France	68.8
Ireland	54.2
UK	54.1
Spain	51.0
Greece	25.0
Portugal	16.3

Source: Jackman and Rubin (1991), Table 1.

Figure 11.1   Regional distribution of GDP per capita, 1977–81

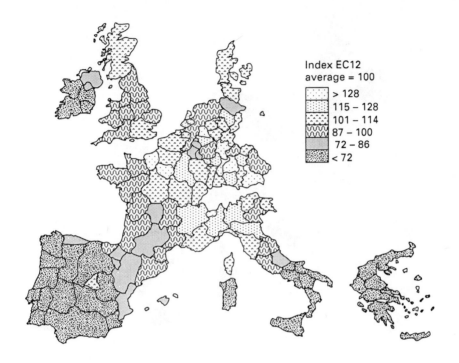

Source: Williams (1987), p. 246.

Figure 11.2   Regional distribution of unemployment rates, April 1985

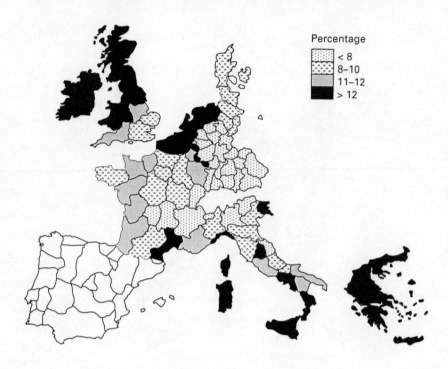

Source: Williams (1987), p. 247.

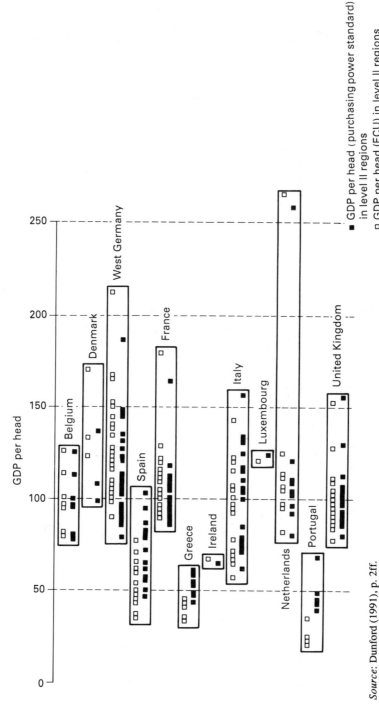

Figure 11.3   European economic development: GDP per capita in Level II regions in ECU and purchasing power standard, 1988 (EC = 100)

GDP per head

■ GDP per head (purchasing power standard) in level II regions
□ GDP per head (ECU) in level II regions

Source: Dunford (1991), p. 2ff.

267

Figure 11.4   National and regional inequalities in the EC, 1960–90

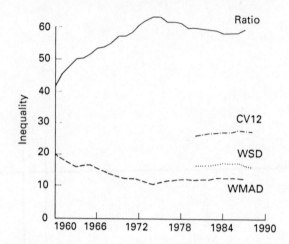

WMAD   – Weighted mean absolute deviation of national GDP per head (PPS)
Ratio   – GDP per head in 4 poorest EC12 countries as ratio of 4 richest (PPS)
WSD   – Weighted standard deviation of regional GDP per head (PPS)
CV12   – Coefficient of variation of regional GDP per head (PPS)

Source: Dunford (1991), p. 2ff.

*Figure 11.5   Average unemployment rate (1983–88) by level of
co-ordination in wage bargaining*

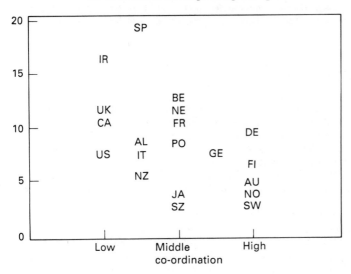

Note: Co-ordination equals average level of employer and union co-ordination.

AL: Australia, AU: Austria, BE: Belgium; CA: Canada, DE: Denmark; FI: Finland; FR: France; GE: Germany; IR: Ireland; IT: Italy; JA: Japan; NE: Netherlands; NO: Norway; NZ: New Zealand; PO: Portugal; SP: Spain; SW: Sweden; SZ: Switzerland; UK: United Kingdom; US: United States.

Source: Layard (1990).

NOTE

* Support from the UK Economic and Social Research Council, the Foundation for European Economic Development, and Sheffield University Management School, is gratefully acknowledged.

REFERENCES

Charkham, Jonathan (1989), *Corporate Governance and the Market for Control of Companies*, (Bank of England Panel Paper **25**) March.

Chartered Institute for Transport (1990), *Paying for Progress*, London: CIT.

Cheese, John (ed.) (1991), *Attitudes to Innovation: Germany and Britain Compared*, London: Centre for the Exploitation of Science and Technology.

Coutts, Ken and Wynne Godley (1990), 'Prosperity and Foreign Trade in the 1990s: Britain's Strategic Problem.' *Oxford Review of Economic Policy*, **6**, (3), pp. 82–92.

Cutler, Tony, Colin Haslem and Karel Williams (1989), *The Struggle for Europe: A Critical Evaluation of the European Community*. Oxford: Berg.

Dunford, M. (1991), 'Socio-economic Trajectories, European Integration and Regional Development in the EC.', in G. Benko and M. Dunford (eds), *Industrial Change and Regional Development: The Transformation of New Industrial Spaces*, London: Frances Pinter.

Edquist, Charles and Bengt-Ake Lundvall (1991), *Comparing the Danish and Swedish Systems of Innovations* (TEMA Working Paper **77**), February.

Fagerberg, J. (1988), 'International Competitiveness', *Economic Journal*, **98**, (391), December, 355–75.

Freeman, C., M. Sharp and W. Walker (eds) (1991), Technology and the Future of *Europe'*, London and New York: Pinter.

Greenhalgh, C. (1990), 'Innovation and Trade Performance in the United Kingdom', *Economic Journal*, **100** (400), supplement, 105–18.

Guerrieri, P. and C. Milana (1990), 'L'Italia e il commercio mondiale'.

Hague, Helen (1991), 'Inward Investment Snagged by Skill Shortages', *Business Quarterly*, Winter 29–36.

Hope, Kerin (1991), 'Greek Bus Stops Smog in its Tracks', *Financial Times*, 25 June, 14.

Hirata, Mitsuhiro (1992), 'The Internationalisation of Japanese Companies and Europe 1992', mimeo.

Hymer, Stephen (1972), 'The Multinational Corporation and the Law of Uneven Development', in J. Bhagwati (ed.), *Economics and World Order from the 1970s to the 1990s,* New York: Collier-Macmillan.

Jackman, Richard and Marcus Rubin (1991), 'Should We Be Afraid Of The Social Charter?', *Employment Institute Economic Report*, **6**, (4), August, 1–4.

Japan External Trade Organisation (JETRO) (1991), Zai Oh Nikkei Kigyo (Seizogyo) no Kelel Jittal, 7th survey, Tokyo: JETRO. (Cited in Hirata, 1992.)

Kaldor, Mary (1991), 'East and West Europe', in Freeman, Sharp and Walker (eds), pp. 348–64.

Karlsson, Charlie and Jan Larsson (1990), 'Product and Price Competition in a Regional Context', *Papers of the Regional Science Association*, **69**, 83–99.

Kleinknecht, A., T. Poot and J. Keijnen (1991), 'Formal and informal R&D and Firm Size: (Survey Results from the Netherlands)', in Z. J. Acs and D.B Audretsch, (eds.), *Innovation and Technical Change*: Harvester Wheatsheaf.

Lantto, Reino (ed.) (1989), *Business Finland, 1990*, Helsinki: Erikoishleidet Oy.

Layard, R. (1990) 'How to End Pay Leapfrogging', *Employment Institute Economic Report*, **5**, (5), July, 1–5.

Lundvall, B-A. (1988), 'Innovations as an Interactive Process: User–Producer Relations', ch. 17 in G. Dosi *et al.* (eds), *Technical Change and Economic Theory*, London: Pinter.

Murdoch, Alan (1991), 'Haughey Collects his Economic Oscar', *Independent*, 16 March, 46.

Myrdal, Gunnar (1957), *Economic Theory and Underdeveloped Regions*, London: Duckworth.

Panic, M. (ed.) (1976), *UK and W. German Manufacturing Industry 1954–72: A Comparison of Structures and Performance*, London: NEDO.

Patel, P. and K. Pavitt (1988), *'Technological Activities in FR Germany and the UK: Differences and Determinants'*, (Science Policy Research Unit DRC Discussion Paper **58**), March.

Patel, P. and K.A.R. Pavitt (1991), 'Europe's Technological Performance', in Freeman *et al.* (1991).

Pearce, David (1991), 'Growth, Employment and Environmental Policy', *Employment Institute Economic Report*, **6**, (1), April, 1–4.

Saunders, C.T., M. Matthews and P. Patel (1991), 'Structural Change and Patterns of Production and Trade', in Freeman, Sharp and Walker (eds), pp. 18–36.

Soete, L. (1981), 'A General Test of Technological Trade Gap Theory', *Weltwirtschaftsliches Archiv*, **117** (4), 639–59.

Stout, D.K. (1977), *International Price Competitiveness, Non-price Factors, and Export Performance*, London: NEDO.

Stout, D.K. (1979), 'Deindustrialisation and Industrial Policy', in F. Blackaby (ed.), *Deindustrialisation*, London: NIESR/Heinemann, ch. 8.

Tylecote, A.B. (1975), 'The Effects of Monetary Policy on Wage Inflation', *Oxford Economic Papers*, July, 204–44.

Tylecote, A.B. (1977), *'Managers, Owners and Bankers in British and German Industry: Causes of German Industrial Superiority'*, (University of Sheffield Division of Economic Studies Discussion Paper **77.10**).

Tylecote, A.B. (1981), *The Causes of the Present Inflation: An Interdisciplinary Explanation of Inflation in Britain, West Germany and United States*, London: Macmillan.

Tylecote, A.B. (1987), 'Time Horizons of Management Decisions: Causes and Effects', *Journal of Economic Studies*, **14**, (4), 51–64.

Tylecote, A.B. (1991), 'Performance Pressures, Short-Termism and Innovation', in Cheese (1991), pp. 66–72.

Williams, A. (1987), *The Western European Economy: a Geography of Post-war Development*, London: Hutchinson.

12. An Evolutionary Approach to Why Growth Rates Differ

Bart Verspagen*

---

1. INTRODUCTION

Like some recent models in the neoclassical tradition (Lucas, 1988; Aghion and Howitt, 1989; Grossman and Helpman, 1991; Romer, 1990)[1] this chapter takes a (renewed) interest in growth theory. Instead of looking at one single economy, it tries to answer the question of *'why growth rates differ'* (Denison, 1967; Fagerberg, 1987). In a heterodox Keynesian tradition, the approach chosen highlights (demand side) interdependencies of economies through trade. Taken from some recent literature with a more evolutionary character (Dosi *et al.*, 1988, 1990) are insights on the character and role of technological change and the way in which selection in the international economy takes place.

The model presented here allows both for the analysis of *structural change* (cf. Pasinetti, 1981), and for the analysis of the 'competitive struggle' for economic growth in an out-of-equilibrium, evolutionary fashion. This does not mean, however, that no equilibrium concepts are used in the model. Most prominently, foreign trade is assumed to balance all the time (balance of payments equilibrium). Moreover, an equilibrium growth path (or balanced growth path) might arise in special cases of the model.

Some of the model's stylized assumptions are in sharp contrast with the richness of the non-formal parts of economic evolutionary theories. However, given the early stage of economic evolutionary modelling, one should not be too hestitant to make simplifying assumptions, if only for the sake of being able to release them in the future. Modelling the way it is done, it is found that convergence of growth rates only arises in some very special cases of complete symmetries between nations, a case not likely to be found in reality. Differences between countries, be it differences in real income, institutions, consumer tastes, technology ('learning rates'), or initial conditions, can all be reasons for diverging growth rates.

The rest of the chapter is organized as follows. Section 2 presents a brief empirical look at the facts of economic growth. In section 3, the basic

272

building blocks of the formal model will be developed. In section 4, the equations will be put together in a simulation model. This model will then be used to test the consequences of some parameter values for growth scenarios. A summary of the main arguments and results is given in section 5.

2. (WHY) DO GROWTH RATES DIFFER?

Before asking the question of why growth rates differ?, it is useful to look at the data on income growth in the world in order to understand to what extent the phenomenon to be explained actually exists. Recent data sets developed by the World Bank (Summers and Heston, 1991) give a good picture of growth performance at the world level.

Figures 12.1–12.3 use these data to illustrate the degree to which growth rates differ in various sub-groups of countries. The figures give the simple mean, and the dispersion (i.e., one standard deviation) around it, of the growth rates of real per capita income for the period 1961–86.[2] One hundred-and-fifteen countries were used in the calculations for the figures.

What emerges first of all from the graphs is the variation of growth rates over time. In all three figures, the recessions of the 1970s obviously leave their trace, as does the recent recovery of the world economy at the begin-

Figure 12.1   Variation around average growth rates of per capita GDP, all countries, 1961–86

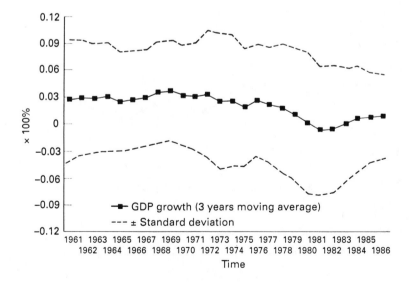

*Figure 12.2   Variation around average growth rates of per capita GDP,
non-African countries, 1961–86*

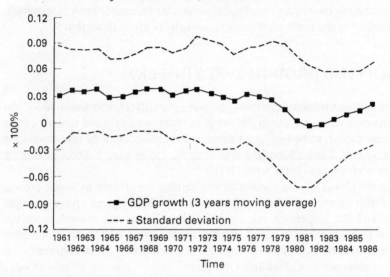

*Figure 12.3   Variation around average growth rates of per capita GDP,
OECD countries, 1961–86*

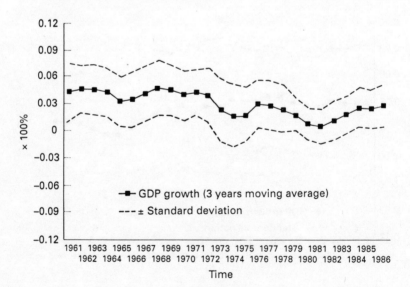

ning of the 1980s. Of course this resemblance is caused by the different economies in the world not being 'islands'. Interacting with each other through trade, monetary flows and factor movements, growth patterns are extorted.

Secondly, it is clear that means of growth rates differ among sub-groups of countries. Successively removing African and non-OECD countries from the sample raises the mean of the growth rate over the whole time period.[3]

Thirdly, regarding the dispersion of growth rates it is clear that there is a considerable degree of this despite the interaction mentioned above. For the first two figures, the difference between being one standard deviation below or above the mean implies the difference between a growth rate well below zero, and one close to 10 per cent. For OECD countries alone, the differences are less drastic, but still considerable. As in the case of the means, the dispersion varies among the sub-groups in the sample. Again, successively removing African and non-OECD countries for the figure leads to smaller dispersion around the mean. Contrary to the mean growth rate, the dispersion around it does not seem to vary systematically with time (except perhaps for the OECD, where some signs of convergence of growth rates over the 1980s is visible).

Having seen that growth rates do not converge or diverge over time, one can ask the question whether per capita income differences will become smaller over time. In other words, must the growth rate differentials from the

Figure 12.4   Convergence in the world economy, 1960–85

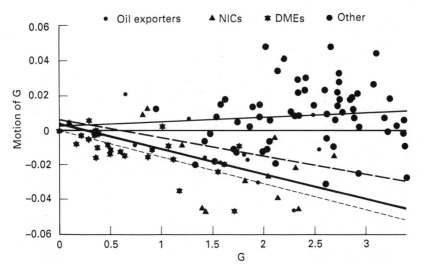

figures be interpreted in the sense that the poorer countries tend to grow faster than the richer ones? This is the question that the literature on catching up has addressed. Looking at the figures for different sub-groups, it has already been concluded that the data rather implies the contrary. However, because the figures give only simple, unweighed means, it is useful to investigate this *convergence hypothesis* further by looking at individual country data.

Figure 12.4 puts the initial (1960) values of countries' per capita income gap (G, defined as the logarithm of per capita income in the USA over per capita income in the country) against its *motion* over the 1960–85 period.[4] The lines drawn in the figure are (linear) regression lines for different sub-samples. Note that a negative change in the income gap implies convergence, or catching up, while a positive change implies falling behind. Hence, negatively sloped regression lines are consistent with convergence.

The figure shows that convergence does take place, but only within limited sub-groups. The poorest (mostly African) developing countries do not succeed in catching up, despite their large 'potential' in the form of a large initial income gap. On the other hand other developing countries (the so-called NICs and oil exporters) and the developed market economies (DMEs) have been able to catch up to the frontier of USA per capita income.

Summarizing, the data presented show that growth rates differ (to a considerable extent) even if movements in time series for average growth for different sub-groups bear great similarity. Per capita income levels converge among some countries, but diverge among others. The degree of both growth and dispersion varies across different groups of countries.

What are the possible explanations for the 'stylized facts'? In order to put forward an explanation, this chapter will concentrate on two different aspects, both inspired by the above observations.

First, the differences in performance across sub-groups of countries suggest that there is a *structural* explanation. Growth rates differ because economies differ with regard to their production, consumption and institutional structure. And because the groups identified in Figures 12.1–12.3 are relatively homogeneous from a structural point of view, the different groups vary in their mean growth rates. One useful way of modelling structural difference stems from the Keynesian tradition, and stresses (sectoral) differences in income elasticities of demand (Pasinetti, 1981). Combined with specialization patterns, these differences will induce growth rate differentials between economies with different production mixes.

The second explanation stresses the interdependence of economies through trade. This way, the process of international economic growth can be seen as an evolutionary selection process, with complex interdependencies between the different actors, influencing each other's performance and competitiveness on world product markets which act as the selection environment.

The concept of competitiveness seems to be explicit in most of the 'heterodox' (i.e., non-equilibrium) economic theorizing on international trade and its relation to growth, but the selection process has not often been modelled formally in an explicit way. There are two main issues that have to be addressed in order for this evolutionary 'selection' view on why growth rates differ to be useful. First, one has to define the concept of competitiveness. Secondly, the way in which the selection process takes place has to be made explicit. Only the latter point will be taken up here in detail, while just a few brief observations will be made on how to measure competitiveness.

Figure 12.5   Growth of production in twenty-eight manufacturing sectors, thirty-five countries, 1963–89

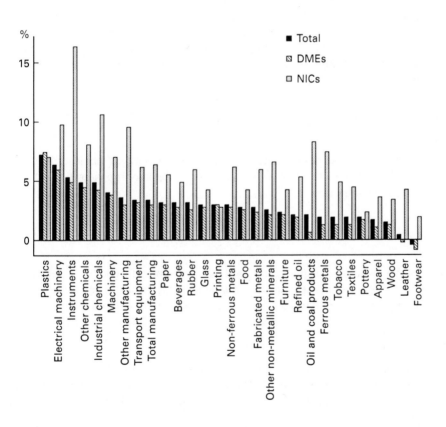

Before developing these two possible explanations for growth rate differentials in a formal model, some additional empirical illustration of the points will be made. First consider Figure 12.5, which gives an (indirect) idea of the differences in income elasticities for twenty-eight manufacturing sectors over the period 1963–89.[5] Obviously, it is the so-called high-tech sectors (new materials, electrical machinery, instruments, chemicals) which are the fast-growing ones. Other, more traditional sectors like basic metals, textiles, leather and food products grow at a much slower rate. Countries specialized in these high-tech sectors are therefore in a more favourable position to grow than countries (like many of the developing countries) specialized in more traditional products.

However, looking at the two different groups of countries shows that some countries are better able to use this potential than others. Production in the NICs has grown faster in almost all sectors (so irrespective of structural differences) than in the traditional developed countries. This illustrates the importance of selection because of differences in competitiveness.

The model developed below tries to explain the phenomenon of differential growth rates in Figures 12.1–12.3. It does so by starting from the differences in income elasticities (Figure 12.5), and sectoral and country-wise differences in competitiveness, the latter consisting of aspects related to technology and cost level (wages).

3. A FORMAL MODEL

The starting point in defining the model are the equations which describe the interaction between different economies. Define the import penetration (z) in sector j in country i by

$$z_{ij} = \frac{M_{ij}}{C_{ij}} \tag{1}$$

C_{ij} is domestic consumption (all goods are consumption goods) of sector j goods, M are imports. Using this equation for the 'rest of the world' (denoted by w), one can write the following expression for exports (X).

$$X_{ij} = C_{wj} z_{wi} \tag{2}$$

The specific evolutionary content of the model comes from the way in which the motion of z is specified. Following Silverberg (1988) an evolutionary selection equation (also called the Fisher equation or replicator equation) is used.[6]

$$z_{ij}^t = z_{ij}^{t-1} + z_{ij}^{t-1} \phi_{ij} \left(\frac{E_{wj}^t}{\bar{E}_{ij}^t} - 1 \right) \tag{3}$$

$$\bar{E}_{ij}^t = E_{ij}^t (1 - z_{ij}^{t-1}) + z_{ij}^{t-1} E_{wj}^t \tag{4}$$

Competitiveness is denoted by E and a bar indicates a market average.[7] Each country's z is determined by an evolutionary market selection process with two groups of producers (domestic and foreign) competing with each other.[8] Consumers tend to buy more of the product with the higher competitiveness. Each one of the producers-groups gains or loses market share according to whether its competitiveness is above or below average market level. The percentage gain in market share is proportional to the percentage deviation from average competitiveness. Whereas *representative agents* are the driving forces of equilibrium growth in neoclassical theory, the replicator equation stresses *differences* between economic agents as the driving force in a disequilibrium growth process.

A crucial feature of equation (3) is of course the definition of E. As a first approximation, let us assume that price competition is the only important mode of competition in international markets. With P denoting price and e denoting the exchange rate (1 unit of foreign currency = e units of domestic currency), it can then be written

$$E_i = \frac{1}{e_i P_i}, 0 < \phi < 1 \tag{5}$$

Note that it does not matter in which currency prices are expressed, since multiplying all prices with one exchange rate leaves the part between brackets on the right-hand side of (3) unaffected. Note also that the restriction that ϕ is positive and smaller than unity rules out the theoretically impossible outcome that z becomes negative.

Having specified the international dimension of growth, some national account identities have to be written. First, real consumption C_{ij} is identified by introducing the variable S_{ij}, which denotes the share of good j in domestic real income R_i. In a later stage, the variable S will be used to model the impact of structural differences related to varying income elasticities in a Pasinetti-like style.

$$C_{ij} = R_i S_{ij} \tag{6}$$

Secondly, real income is defined as being equal to nominal income divided by the price level that is relevant for the consumer, P^c.

$$R_i = \frac{\sum_j Q_{ij} P_{ij}}{P_i^c} \tag{7}$$

Q denotes production. Thirdly, the sectoral and overall consumer price levels are weighted averages of the different producers' prices, with market shares and consumption shares as weights.

Fourthly it is assumed that production Q is equal to demand (domestic plus foreign),

$$P_{ij}^c = (1 - z_{ij})P_{ij} + z_{ij}P_{wj}e_{iw} \tag{8}$$

$$P_i^c = \sum_j S_{ij} P_{ij}^c \tag{9}$$

so that, using (1), one obtains

$$Q_{ij} = (1 - z_{ij})C_{ij} + X_{ij} \tag{10}$$

Fifth, it is assumed that domestic absorption is equal to domestic income, or the S_{ij}s sum to one in each country i. It then follows from (6)–(10) that the current account is in equilibrium. This can be written as follows.

$$\sum_j e_{iw} P_{wj} M_{ij} = \sum_j P_{ij} X_{ij} \tag{11}$$

Substituting (6)–(10) into equation (11), (logarithmically) differentiating and rearranging terms, one arrives at the following equation for differentials between country i's income growth rate and that in the rest of the world. Note that this specific growth rate differential is the one that is consistent with balance of payments equilibrium.

$$\hat{R}_w - \hat{R}_i = \left(\sum_j \hat{P}_{wj} \frac{m_{ij}}{m_i} - \sum_j \hat{P}_{ij} \frac{x_{ij}}{x_i} \right) + \left(\sum_j \hat{z}_{ij} \frac{m_{ij}}{m_i} - \sum_j \hat{z}_{wj} \frac{x_{ij}}{x_i} \right) + \left(\sum_j \hat{S}_{ij} \frac{m_{ij}}{m_i} - \sum_j \hat{S}_{wj} \frac{x_{ij}}{x_i} \right) + \hat{e}_{iw} \tag{12}$$

With initial condition

$$\sum_j P_{ij}^0 X_{ij}^0 = \sum_j e_{wj}^0 P_{wj}^0 M_{ij}^0 \tag{13}$$

A superscript 0 indicates a starting point value, hats denote proportionate growth rates; m and x denote *nominal* imports and exports, respectively.

This equation is the *multi-sector* counterpart of similar expressions in Thirlwall (1979), Fagerberg (1988) and Dosi *et al.* (1990). It assumes that (in the long run) a country can only grow as fast as its balance of payments permits. The intuition behind this is that a country cannot keep on drawing on its foreign reserves, nor keep borrowing money, in order to finance high growth. Also, it does not make sense to keep on accumulating international reserves without spending them on higher growth. Although it might seem that the empirical facts of long-lasting trade surpluses or deficits, and also the debt crisis, seem to contradict the argument, Thirlwall (1979) and Fagerberg (1988) have shown that there is some empirical merit in the balance of payments restriction to economic growth, so that actual growth rates tend to the balance of payments restricted growth rate. Therefore, this chapter uses the trade account to derive the expression for the growth rate differential.

Thus, at the expense of somewhat more complexity, equation (12) explains Thirlwall's exogenous 'import- and export-elasticities' in terms of the different parts on the right-hand side. The first term between brackets reflects the direct effect of a change in the terms of trade over time. If world prices increase at a faster rate than domestic prices, the country can import less given the revenue of its exports. The growth rate consistent with this smaller value of imports will be smaller than the rest of the world's growth rate. This explains the (positive) sign of this term.

The second term between brackets reflects the effect of a change in the import penetration in the country and the rest of the world. With the narrow definition of competitiveness used here, this corresponds to the indirect effect of the terms of trade change (through equation 3). Lower import penetration in the country, and a higher import penetration in the rest of the world (i.e., a better export performance of the country i) leads to a higher growth rate.

The third and last term between brackets is associated with changes in the consumption pattern over time. A positive sign of this term means that consumption patterns in the country and the rest of the world have shifted in such a way that the pattern in the rest of the world is now closer to the strong points in the export position of i, while the patterns in i itself have changed such that they are further away from the strong points of the export position of the rest of the world. This is the argument of the structural influence on the growth rate differential.

Exchange rate movements of course also add to the terms of trade effect. This is reflected by the presence of the growth rate of e_{iw} on the right-hand side. Again, there are direct and indirect effects of a de/revaluation of the domestic currency (a change of e_{iw}). Because the growth rate differential comes out of the balance of payments expression, these effects bear great similarity to the well known Marshall-Lerner condition. In a direct way, changes of the exchange rate have an influence similar to the (direct) terms of trade effect. Indirectly, they have an influence on import penetration and export performance, through the second term. The exact elasticity of the growth rate differential with regard to the rate of change of the exchange rate cannot easily be calculated, since it depends on other variables in the model in a complex nonlinear way.

At this stage, not having specified the motion of some key variables in equation (12), one cannot say much about the long-run values of the growth rate differentials. Therefore, equations for e, P and S will be specified now.

Let us start with P. For simplicity, assume that all goods are produced with labour alone and that profits are equal to zero.[9] One can then write the following identity.

$$P_{ij} = \frac{W_i}{G_{ij}} \tag{13}$$

W stands for the (nominal) wage rate and G is (labour) productivity. This identity shows the two different aspects of competitiveness in the current model: technological change (G)[10] and the cost level (W).

The movement of G is specified using an equation which combines the Verdoorn relation and Kaldor's technical progress function (Kaldor, 1980).

$$\frac{G_{ij}^t - G_{ij}^{t-1}}{G_{ij}^{t-1}} = \lambda_{ij} \left(\frac{Q_{ij}^{t-1} - Q_{ij}^{t-2}}{Q_{ij}^{t-2}} \right)^{\frac{1}{\gamma_{ij}}} \qquad \lambda_{ij} > 0 , \quad \gamma_{ij} > 1 \tag{14}$$

In this equation, γ and λ are country- and sector-specific learning parameters reflecting differences between sectors and countries in the rate of (dynamic) learning. These differences may be related to differences in the sectoral technology opportunities and to institutional differences. Thus, the equation highlights two aspects of technological change that have been put forward in recent literature on the subject (Dosi, 1988), even if it is only in a very stylized way. First, it stresses that different (institutional) circumstances might lead to (persistent) differences in technological performance, in the form of parameter differences in the equation. Secondly, it specifies the innovation process as one with a cumulative character, in which past performance influences present capabilities.

The equation says that the current period growth rate of labour productivity is a nonlinear function (passing through the origin) of the previous period growth rate of output. Thus, there is a one period 'learning lag'. The function is specified such that the marginal increases in productivity growth become smaller and smaller (but stay positive) for larger growth rates of production (decreasing marginal learning rates).

The behaviour of a system in which production growth is equal to productivity growth (i.e. in which there are no influences from the demand side, as in the neoclassical growth model), and productivity growth is described by equation (14) can easily be analysed. Similar to the analysis in Kaldor (1980, pp. 265–70), the equilibrium growth rate of the system is found at the cutting point of the curve describing (14) and the 45 degrees line. For values to the right (left) of this cutting point, the rate of productivity growth is below (above) the rate of output growth, and hence the rate of output growth will fall (increase), leading the system to the cutting point.

Thus, in the long run, the system will, *if no other shocks or tendencies occur*,[11] tend to a rate at which output and productivity will grow at an equal rate. This 'natural rate' is equal to $(1/\lambda)^{\gamma/(1-\gamma)}$. Note that in general, because of technological and institutional differences, one would expect that γ and λ, and hence the *natural* rates of growth, would differ between countries and sectors.

The motion of the wage rate is assumed to be influenced by two sources. The first is the rate of productivity growth. The second is the situation on the labour market. In 'normal' situations, wages grow as fast as productivity. However, if unemployment is above a certain threshold, workers are prepared to work for lower wages, in order to increase their chance of employment. If unemployment is below that same threshold level, workers will demand a growth rate of wages which is higher than productivity growth, because the chances of getting unemployed are relatively low. Thus, only when unemployment is exactly at the threshold level (the 'no inflation rate of unemployment') will wages grow as fast as productivity (see also the model in Goodwin, 1967). This can be specified as follows.

$$W_i^t = W_i^{t-1} + W_i^{t-1}(\hat{G}_i^{t-1} - \delta_i U_i^t + \zeta_i) \tag{15}$$

In this equation, U is the rate of unemployment.[12] The aggregate value of productivity (G_i) is obtained by taking a weighted average of sectoral productivities, with sectoral shares in total employment (at $t-1$) as weights. Equation (15) implies that the 'no-inflation' rate of unemployment is found at δ_i/ζ_i. Note that the parameters in equation (15) are again country specific, thus allowing for institutional differences in national labour markets. L is identified by

$$L_i = \sum_j \frac{Q_{ij}}{G_{ij}} \tag{16}$$

A next step is to define the motion of the exchange rate. Of course there are many determinants of the exchange rate dynamics, among which there are important ones which cannot be taken into account in this model because of its simple nature. In the (empirical) modelling literature, three approaches are used to tackle the problem of endogenizing exchange rates. These are the *purchasing power parity* hypothesis, the *portfolio* approach and the *balance of payments* approach (see Den Butter 1987).

In the purchasing power parity (PPP) approach, it is assumed that the exchange rate moves in such a way as to guarantee (a tendency towards) equality of (consumer) price levels in the two countries. This hypothesis is highly suitable in the present model, since the consumer price level has already been given a prominent role in the selection mechanism. Marking the exchange rate consistent with complete PPP by an asterisk, it can be specified as follows.

$$e_{iw}^* = \frac{P_i^c}{P_w^c} \tag{17}$$

Assume that in each period the exchange rate adjusts partially to a level that would have been consistent with complete equality of PPP in the previous period. This can be put in mathematical terms as follows.

$$\ln e_{iw}^t = \rho(\ln P_i^{ct-1} - \ln P_w^{ct-1}) + (1-\rho)\ln e_{iw}^{t-1} \tag{18}$$

In this equation, ρ is an adjustment parameter. Normally, one would assume $\rho < 1$, in which case the actual exchange rate smoothly adjusts to the PPP warranted rate (which might be a moving target). Assuming $\rho > 1$ would imply *overshooting*. The logarithmic specification is necessary for the equations for e_{ik} and e_{ki} to yield consistent results. This is also the reason why ρ cannot be country specific (or even country-pair specific if there are more than two countries).

To complete the model, one must define the motion of the variable S over time. This is the actual implication of the structural influence on growth rate differentials introduced in the previous section. Following Pasinetti (1981), the following system of differential equations is adopted.[13]

$$\frac{\partial S_{ij}}{\partial R_i} = S_{ij} \sum_{k=1}^{J} \tau_{kj}(S_{ik} - S_{ik}^*) - (S_{ij} - S_{ij}^*) \sum_{k=1}^{J} \tau_{jk} S_{ik} \tag{19}$$

S^* is the share of the sector in total consumption when real income, denoted by R, is infinitely large. The restriction on the parameters τ is that τ_{ij} is equal to zero and all other τs are greater than or equal to zero. It is also convenient, but not necessary, to assume that τs are smaller than one, since then the shares cannot 'overshoot' their 'long run equilibrium' value S^*. The system of differential equations describes the 'real income path' of (real) spending in each sector as a process of adaptation to S^*. The form of the system of equations guarantees that the sum of the changes in S is always zero, so that once 'fed' with initial values of S summing to one, total spending remains equal to total income.

Making the model operationally yields one more specification problem. This problem results from the fact that for n endogenous countries, the model specified so far is underdetermined because there are only $n-1$ independent balance of payment restrictions. Therefore, a country called the rest of the world (denoted by w as before) will be specified. The growth rate in this country is such that full employment (at the 'natural' level) is assured,[14] or

$$\sum_j \frac{Q_{wj}}{G_{wj}} = N_w \frac{\zeta_w}{\delta_w} \tag{20}$$

This equation must be regarded as an extra restriction on the growth rate of country w.

4. SIMULATION RESULTS

Given the complexity of some of the dynamics defined by the equations above, the analysis will be limited to simulation experiments.[15] The case considered is a three-country/two-sector case. There are two countries (called 1 and 2) in which the growth rate is determined by balance of payments equilibrium, and one country ('the rest of the world') where output is always at the full employment level. Initially, the value of all variables is equal in all three countries. Each sector occupies half of the labour resources in the country (and thus accounts for half of the production and income). S is equal to 0.5 in each sector. Trade occurs, although none of the countries has a competitive (or comparative) advantage in either one sector. The import penetration is equal in the two sectors and countries, so that trade between i and the rest of the world is balanced (both in a nominal and real sense) even at the sectoral level. All countries start with a growth rate of production (in both sectors) of a bit above 2 per cent. The initial values of all variables are given in Appendix 2. The time span simulated is 100 periods.

To assess the simulation results, two indicators are used which capture the basic results in a number or sign. First the growth rate differential D is defined as

$$D = \hat{R}_1 - \hat{R}_2. \tag{21}$$

Second, a specialization index, denoted by F, is defined as

$$F = \frac{Q_{11}}{Q_{11} + Q_{12}} - \frac{Q_{21}}{Q_{21} + Q_{22}}. \tag{22}$$

First, some different simulation runs will very briefly be analysed by looking at the signs of D and F that result. After that, the most interesting run will be used to look at some outcomes of the model in a bit more detail. Results of the simulations are summarised in Table 12.1.

Table 12.1   A description of the parameters and the results in some simulation runs*

	1	2	3	4	5	6	7	8	9
γ_{11}	2							2.1	2.1
γ_{12}	2							1.9	1.9
γ_{21}	2							2.05	2.05
γ_{22}	2							1.98	1.98
γ_{w1}	2							2.01	2.01
γ_{w2}	2							2.02	2.02
λ_{11}	0.15			0.1			0.1	0.16	0.16
λ_{12}	0.15			0.2			0.2	0.14	0.14
λ_{21}	0.15			0.2	0.1		0.3	0.12	0.12
λ_{22}	0.15			0.1	0.1		0.1	0.18	0.18
λ_{w1}	0.15							0.14	0.14
λ_{w2}	0.15							0.15	0.15
τ_{112}	0.15					0.05		0.14	0.14
τ_{121}	0.15					0.05		0.12	0.12
τ_{212}	0.15							0.17	0.17
τ_{221}	0.15							0.12	0.12
τ_{w12}	0.15							0.15	0.15
τ_{w21}	0.15							0.11	0.11
ϕ	0.2								
δ	0.5								
ζ	0.025								
ρ	0.25								0
S^{*}_{11}	0.5	0.2	0.2			0.2	0.2	0.31	0.31
S^{*}_{21}	0.5	0.2	0.8			0.2	0.2	0.62	0.62
S^{*}_{w1}	0.5	0.2				0.2	0.2	0.5	0.5
F	0	0	−	−	0	+	−	+	+
D	0	0	0	0	+	+−	−+	+	+

* Empty cells have to be read as containing a value equal to the basic run

First, some experiments which yield zero growth rate differentials are conducted (runs 1–4). After that, experiments which yield uneven growth are explained (run 5–9). Although the first group of simulation runs may not be empirically relevant in this extreme form, they might indicate why it is that, among some groups of countries (OECD, see previous section), growth rate differentials are closer to zero than in others.

Run 1 represents the basic variant of the model. All parameters are equal across countries, and since every country starts from the same situation, each will grow as fast as the others. Market shares will not change and specialization will not occur. Runs 2–4 represent slight variations to this basic variant, all leading to zero growth rate differentials.

Run 2 is the so-called *non-specialization induced scale effects* run. In this experiment, the value of S^*_{il} is decreased for all countries. As expected, this has no result on the growth rate differential or the specialization pattern, since the change affects all countries equally. However, because of increased learning effects at the national level, caused by higher growth rates in the 'larger' sector 2, world income is higher in this case. Thus, we have dynamic increasing returns, like in many of the new neoclassical growth models.

The next two runs are illustrations of cases where scale effects come as a result of specialization. Run 3 illustrates *structure-induced scale effects*. This run shows that in the case of oppositely directed national changes in domestic consumption patterns, there is an incentive for specialization. The changes in S^*_{il} compared to the basic run are of opposite sign for the two countries. Then each country specializes in the good with the largest S^*_{il}. Since the learning rates are equal in the two sectors and S^*_{il} is equal to 0.5 in the rest of the world, this specialization pattern has no influence on the growth rate differential, but again it leads to higher growth, even in the country which does not specialize ('consumer surplus'). Typically, it is differentials in consumption structure which causes dynamic returns to scale.

Next, there is the *technology-induced scale effects* case in run 4. Here, the learning rates are varied in a 'symmetric way'. S^*_{il} is equal to 0.5 again, and each country has a learning advantage in one (different) sector (in the sense that the cutting point of its learning equation with the 45 degrees line lies further to the right). Specialization occurs in the sector where the country has a learning advantage, but because of the symmetry in the consumption structure, no growth rate differential occurs. Thus, in this case, the scale effects are caused by technological differences between countries.

The remaining experiments are cases in which the variations in parameters are less symmetric, such that the different counter-effects no longer cancel out each other. These experiments lead to more interesting conclusions. First, consider the case in which a country has a learning advantage in both sectors, which can be labelled *technology-induced uneven growth*. This is the case in run 5. Since country 1's advantage is proportional between the sectors (i.e., there is no comparative advantage), no specialization occurs. Obviously, the technologically more advanced country keeps on growing faster for a long time (the total simulation period).

Next, there is *structure-induced uneven growth* in run 6. Learning rates are equal among sectors and countries, but in country 1 S^*_{il} adjusts slower (τ) to its (lower) equilibrium value. Thus, S_{ll} becomes higher (compared to the other countries). Initially, this leads to a minor negative growth rate differential, because the country specializes in a sector which is becoming less important internationally. This does, however, lead to *increased* specialization in this sector. Country 2, as the rest of the world, specializes in sector 2, and has to fight a severe competitive struggle in this sector ('the rest of the world' is a large producer). Thus, country 1 finds a 'niche' to specialize in and generates positive growth rate differentials in the long run.

Run 7 is a *mixed structural-technology-induced uneven growth* case. The growth rate differential is first negative, then positive. The negative trend that occurs in first instance is obvious. Country 2 has a learning advantage in sector 1, which is (becoming) less important in terms of total world consumption, because of the S^*_{il}s being less than 0.5. Therefore country 1 specializes in a product which has a smaller market. However, the dynamics are such that the initial advantage that country 2 has places a large burden on the growth rate of its wage rate. At some point (somewhat after half the simulation period), this leads to a declining market share in the rest of the world, and to a declining growth rate of the market share in country 1. Country 1, having a slacker labour market, is therefore able to catch up, and, quite suddenly, generate a positive growth rate differential. In the period for which the simulation was carried out, a fallback was again experienced because of the tension created now on country 1's labour market.

An important role in this process of successful catching up is played by the self-reinforcing learning effects that country 1 captures again when it gains competitiveness. This experiment shows that the nonlinear dynamics of the model can indeed generate results in which different effects offset each other to different degrees over time. Thus, the results are unpredictable in a precise sense by intuition alone. In runs 8 and 9, the parameters have been changed in such a way that almost all symmetries vanish. This is a *mixed uneven growth* case, something that one is most likely to find in actual practice. In run 8, exchange rates are (as before) flexible, while run 9 examines the effect of a fixed exchange rate regime.

These last two runs will be analysed in more detail now. Figures 12.6 and 12.7 give the basic results for this case. In Figure 12.6 it is shown that the growth rate differential shows a pattern which is far from regular. The specialization pattern on the other hand (Figure 12.7) does show a regular

Figure 12.6   The growth rate differential in runs 8 and 9

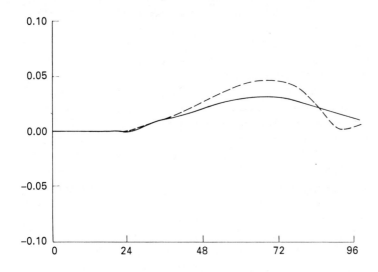

Figure 12.7   The specialization index in runs 8 and 9

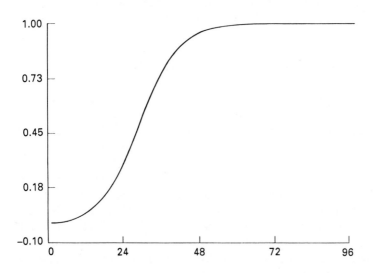

pattern leading to a complete specialization of country 1 in sector 1 and country 2 in sector 2. The different lines in the figures represent the two different cases: one with flexible exchange rates (broken lines, $\rho = 0.25$) and one with fixed exchange rates (solid lines, $\rho = 0$).

The explanation of the specialization pattern that appears is as follows. In country 1, the sectoral consumption share of sector 1 tends to a value smaller than 0.5 (which is the starting value), while in country 2 it tends (although slower for a given increase in income) to a value larger than 0.5. Thus, one would expect that country 1 specializes in sector 2 goods, and country 2 specializes in sector 1 goods (compare run 3 in Table 12.1). This does not happen because the 'comparative technology advantages' are the other way around. Country 1 (2) has a higher (natural) rate of learning in sector 1 (2), so that the selection mechanism in international markets drives country 1 (2) towards specialization in sector 1 (2). Because the learning rates do not change along the simulation period, this specialization tendency drives the two countries towards complete specialization.

The growth rate differential can be explained as follows. First, the case of flexible exchange rates (broken lines) is considered. In the beginning, there is a (very) weak cyclical pattern, which can be explained by wage reactions to unemployment changes which are again caused by the differences in competitiveness. These reactions are largely the same as those one finds in the Goodwin-model (Goodwin, 1967). No large differentials arise, because the markets for both goods are by and large of equal size. Therefore, the real income of the countries 1 and 2 settles by and large on the same level until around period 35. From that period on, the situation on the labour market and sectoral productivity growth rates in the two countries become so different that a substantive growth rate differential arises. The higher level of specialisation of country 1 in sector 1 and the wage dynamics turn out to be such that the growth rate of country 1 is much higher. Immediately, however, a devaluation of country 2's currency (compared to currencies in both 1 and w) sets in. This improves the competitiveness of country 2 bit by bit, and, eventually it leads to a situation in which the growth rate differential drops again.

Thus, run 8 shows the (combined) effects of technological differences, labour market elasticities, consumption patterns and exchange rate movements leading to complex dynamics. Run 9 cancels out one of these effects: exchange rate flexibility. In the picture for the specialization pattern (solid lines), it is seen that exchange rate (in)flexibility does not influence the specialization pattern between 1 and 2. The reason for this is that the comparative advantages are not reversed by flexible exchange rates.

There is a more substantive difference for the growth rate differential. In the beginning, the alternating pattern from the first run is reproduced. Later, the (absolute value of) the differential is much smoother. However, with regard to unemployment (not shown), the pattern is more smooth with flexible exchange rates. The reason for this is that with flexible exchange rates, price differentials (i.e. differences in competitiveness) are to some extent 'polished away' by exchange rate movements. Therefore employment will react more strongly, with wages following in the case of fixed exchange rates. This effect is very strong towards the end of the simulation period. In the case of flexible exchange rates, unemployment in both 1 and 2 boosted to very high levels.

Of course the model overdoes the employment-smoothing effect of flexible exchange rates, both because it does not take into account the effect of exchange rate volatility (i.e. exchange rate risk) on the volume of international transactions, and because it stresses too much the labour market flexibility (leaving too little space for other factors affecting wage rate formation). But still, the model shows clearly that in economies which are heterogenous, fixed exchange rates (or 'one currency') will necessarily invoke other adjustment mechanisms because of the working of international markets. This is a point that is sometimes underestimated in discussions on (for example) a common European currency.

This concludes the analysis of the model. Although many more experiments could be carried out (and indeed have been), the ones presented suffice to indicate the basic characteristics of the model. These will now be summarized briefly.

5. SUMMARY AND CONCLUSION

Empirical data show that growth rate differentials, both between and within relatively homogeneous groups of countries, are a real phenomenon. Contrary to a 'simple' form of the so-called *convergence hypothesis*, it is not unconditionally true that differential growth rates imply faster growth of poor countries.

The model developed in section 3 points to differences in competitiveness and production and consumption structure as possible explanations of uneven growth. The relation between trade, specialization and economic growth is described in an evolutionary way. It starts from the assumption that there are differences between countries with regard to sectoral technological level, learning rates (λ, γ), consumption patterns and adjustment speed of consumption patterns (τ). The model explains growth rates by balance of payments restrictions. Technological progress is seen as a cumulative process, which tends to be mostly favoured in those locations having a high technological level already.

First, the consequences of a model without explicitly specifying the (cumulative) character of technological change, the movement of the wage rate and the changes in the composition of consumption demand were considered. It was found that gains in the terms of trade and changes in its sectoral composition have an influence on (the) growth rate (differentials). In the short run there is an effect that allows the domestic country to grow faster when its export prices increase, but, in the longer run this causes a negative effect through the loss of competitiveness. Changes in the composition of consumption demand in the domestic or world markets can also have a negative or positive effect on the growth rate.

Next, the cumulative character of technological change, along with dynamic equations for the wage rate and the composition of consumption demand, were introduced. Carrying out simulation experiments, it was found that this causes 'Goodwin-like' adjustment paths of national growth rates. It was shown that the cumulativeness of technological change causes specialization patterns. Both differences in learning rates and (adjustment of) consumption patterns can be reasons for such specialization. Non-symmetric consumption structures and non-symmetric differences in learning rates cause differences in growth rates. It was shown that in only a few limitative cases of more or less complete symmetry between countries, are zero growth rate differentials found. Interpreting the evidence in section 2, these symmetries might be a more adequate description of differences between some countries (mostly OECD) than others. In other (more realistic) simulation experiments, non-zero differences in economic growth between countries are found.

APPENDIX 1. COUNTRIES USED IN THE ANALYSIS IN SECTION 2

African Countries

Algeria, Angola, Benin, Botswana, Burundi, Cameroon, Central African Republic, Chad, Congo, Egypt, Ethiopia, Gabon, Gambia, Ghana, Guinea, Ivory Coast, Kenya, Lesotho, Liberia, Madagascar, Malawi, Mali, Mauritania, Mauritius, Morocco, Mozambique, Niger, Nigeria, Rwanda, Senegal, Sierra Leone, Somalia, South Africa, Sudan, Swaziland, Tanzania, Togo, Tunisia, Uganda, Zaire, Zambia, Zimbabwe

OECD Countries

Austria, Belgium, Denmark, Finland, France, West Germany, Greece, Iceland, Ireland, Italy, Luxembourg, Netherlands, Norway, Portugal, Spain,

Sweden, Switzerland, Turkey, United Kingdom, Yugoslavia, Australia, New Zealand, USA, Canada, Japan

Other Countries

Afghanistan, Bangladesh, Burma, People's Republic of China, Hong Kong, India, Indonesia, Iran, Iraq, Israel, Jordan, South Korea, Kuwait, Malaysia, Nepal, Pakistan, Philippines, Saudi Arabia, Singapore, Sri Lanka, Syria, Taiwan, Thailand, Barbados, Costa Rica, Dominican Republic, El Salvador, Guatemala, Haiti, Honduras, Jamaica, Mexico, Nicaragua, Panama, Trinidad and Tobago, Argentina, Bolivia, Brazil, Chile, Colombia, Ecuador, Guyana, Paraguay, Peru, Uruguay, Venezuela

APPENDIX 2. INITIAL VALUES OF THE SIMULATION RUNS FOR THE THREE-COUNTRY TWO-SECTOR CASE

Table 12.A1   Simulation runs: initial values used[*]

Initial values arbitrarily set		Results	
G_{ij}	0.8	P_{ij}	1
W_i	0.8	P^c_{ij}	1
z_{ilj}	0.2	S_{ij}	0.5
C_{ij}	1.1875	Q_{ij}	1.1875
N_i	3.125	R_i	2.375

* Column-indicator 'results' points to values which follow from the values set arbitrarily and the fact that an initial value must be a (static) solution to the model. z_{ilj} indicates the market share of producer l on the market in i in sector j goods.

NOTES

*   I thank Paul Diederen, Gerald Silverberg and Luc Soete for helpful discussions, Adriaan van Zon for helpful discussions and provision of and guidance with his simulation software, and Jan Fagerberg, Pierre Mohnen and participants at the EAEPE conference 1991 in Vienna and research seminars for useful comments and suggestions. The views expressed and any remaining errors are of course entirely my own responsibility.
1.   For an overview of these neoclassical approaches, see Verspagen (forthcoming).
2.   Real GDP Chain Index from the Penn World Table, mark 5 (Summers and Heston 1991). The figures give three-year moving averages of the mean growth rate and the standard deviation. The conclusions drawn here generally also hold for total income (as opposed to per capita).

3. Except for the 1970s, which indicates that the world economic crash coinciding with two oil crises shook the OECD countries harder than others.
4. Data are taken from Verspagen (1991), which also gives a brief summary of the convergence debate and a model explaining the pattern observed from a catching-up perspective. For similar figures, see Baumol (1986) and Grossman and Helpman (1991).
5. Data underlying the calculations are taken from UNIDO, and refer to production, instead of consumption. However, in a country sample this large there are no major differences between *aggregate* production and consumption patterns. Growth rates are estimated by a logarithmic regression.
6. An application of this equation in a microeconomic model can be found in Silverberg *et al.* (1988).
7. From now on, superscripts are omitted in cases where period t is referred to (obviously).
8. Note that for a model with $n>2$ countries, one would have $n-1$ z's: one for each foreign producer. This is indeed the approach used in the simulation experiments below.
9. Alternatively, one could specify some mark-up pricing rule and a fixed capital output ratio, as has been done for example in (respectively) Silverberg *et al.* (1988) and Cantwell (1989). This would not change the conclusions in a qualitative way.
10. Rosenberg (1976) points out that factor substitution due to price changes cannot be seen as independent from technological change.
11. It might be useful to point out that in the present model there are a number of tendencies and shocks which might prevent the system from settling down at the equilibrium growth rate. These are the evolutionary selection equation, exchange rate movements, consumption share movements, foreign demand and wage rate movements.
12. Define U as $(N-L)/N$, where N is labour supply and L is labour demand. N is assumed to be constant, thus outruling a common source of economic growth found in most growth models.
13. Note that while this sytem of differential equations is largely consistent with Pasinetti's view, he does not narrow his model to any specific functional form. It should be realized that the behaviour of this equation, which is specified in continuous time, is different in discrete time as it used in this chapter. If we keep the same form, but writing discrete time changes instead of continuous time changes, the movement of the S's will still be consistent in the sense that they always add up to one, but each prediction of S will only be a linear approximation to the true value according to equation (19). However, this is acceptable for small steps, and non-negative changes in real income.
14. Note that this rules out the unemployment term in the equation of this country's wage rate.
15. The simulation method used is a simultaneous solution of the discrete time model, through a compiler generating a program using the Gauss-Seidel algorithm. The software is developed at MERIT (thanks to Adriaan van Zon), and will be available on the market soon. For reasons of clarity we do not choose to give the results for all variables in each run. These results, as the exact 'EML'-code used for the simulations, are available on request. In order to get some feeling for the basic dynamics of the model, simulations with a one-sector model were also carried out. These revealed that for some parameter values (small ϕ, large δ) the model yields adjustment paths with exploding cyclical behaviour of key variables like z, u and W. The analysis of the two-sector model is limited to parameter values yielding damping cyclical behaviour, however.

REFERENCES

Aghion, P. and P. Howitt (1989), 'A Model of Growth Through Creative Destruction', *Econometrica*, **60**, 323–52.

Baumol, W. J. (1986), 'Productivity Growth, Convergence, and Welfare: What the Long Run Data Show', *American Economic Review*, **76**, 1072–85.

Cantwell, J. (1989), *Technological Innovation and Multinational Corporations*, Oxford: Basil Blackwell.

Den Butter, F.A.G. (1987), *Model en Theorie in de Macro-Economie*, Leiden: Stenfert Kroese.

Denison, E. (1967), *Why Growth Rates Differ*, Washington: Brookings Institution.

Dosi, G. (1988), 'Sources, Procedures and Microeconomic Effects of Innovation,' *Journal of Economic Literature*, **26**, 1120–71.

Dosi, G., C. Freeman, R. Nelson, G. Silverberg and L. Soete (eds) (1988), *Technical Change and Economic Theory*, London: Pinter Publishers.

Dosi, G., K. Pavitt and L. Soete (1990), *The Economics of Technological Change and International Trade*, Brighton: Wheatsheaf.

Fagerberg, J. (1987), 'A Technology Gap Approach to Why Growth Rates Differ', *Research Policy*, **16**, 87–99.

Fagerberg, J. (1988), 'International Competitiveness', *Economic Journal*, **98**, 355–74.

Goodwin, R.M. (1967), 'A Growth Cycle', in: C.H. Feinstein, (ed.), *Socialism, Capitalism and Economic Growth*, London: Macmillan.

Grossman, G. and E. Helpman, (1991), *Innovation and Growth in the Global Economy*, Cambridge MA: MIT Press.

Kaldor, N. (1980), 'A Model of Economic Growth', (*Economic Journal*, 1980), in *Essays on Economic Stability and Growth*, 2nd edn, London: Duckworth.

Lucas, R.E.B. (1988), 'On the Mechanisms of Economic Development', *Journal of Monetary Economics*, **22**, (1), 3–42.

Pasinetti, L.L. (1981), *Structural Change and Economic Growth. A Theoretical Essay on the Dynamics of the Wealth of Nations*, Cambridge: Cambridge University Press.

Romer, P.M. (1990), 'Endogenous Technological Change', *Journal of Political Economy*, **98**, (2), S71–S102.

Rosenberg, N. (1976), *Perspectives on Technology*, Cambridge: Cambridge University Press.

Silverberg, G. (1988), 'Modelling Economic Dynamics and Technical Change: Mathematical Approaches to Self-Organisation and Evolution', in: G. Dosi, C. Freeman, R. Nelson, G. Silverberg, and L. Soete (eds), *Technical Change and Economic Theory*, London: Pinter Publishers, pp. 531–59.

Silverberg, G., G. Dosi and L. Orsenigo (1988), 'Innovation, Diversity and Diffusion: A Self-Organisation Model', *Economic Journal*, **98**, 1032–54.

Summers, R. and A. Heston (1991), The Penn World Table (Mark 5): An Expanded Set of International Comparisons, 1950–1988, *Quarterly Journal of Economics*, May, 1–41.

Thirlwall, A.P. (1979), 'The Balance of Payments Constraint as an Explanation of International Growth Rate Differences', *Banca Nazionale del Lavoro*, **32**, 45–53.

Verspagen, B. (1991), 'A New Statistical Approach to Catching Up or Falling Behind', *Structural Change and Economic Dynamics*, December, 359–80.

Verspagen, B. (forthcoming), 'Endogenous Innovation in Neo-Classical Growth Models: A Survey', *Journal of Macroeconomics*, **14**, (6).

Index